T0300325

Routledge Revivals

Progress in Industrial Geography

This edited collection, first published in 1985, deals with a number of the major themes central to the study of industrial geography. Topics under discussion include new methodologies, the growing service industries, foreign investment and the industrial geography of the developing world. With a detailed introduction from Michael Pacione and comprehensive coverage, the title reflects the extent to which the field of industrial geography changed over the second half of the twentieth century in response to economic change, incorporating the growth of multinational enterprises and the influence of globalisation, alongside traditional discussion of the manufacturing industry. Providing an essential background to developments in industrial geography, this title will be valuable to students with an interest in the economics, characteristics and advancement of industrial change.

Progress in Industrial Geography

Edited by

Michael Pacione

Routledge
Taylor & Francis Group

First published in 1985
by Croom Helm Ltd

This edition first published in 2013 by Routledge
2 Park Square, Milton Park, Abingdon, Oxon, OX14 4RN

Simultaneously published in the USA and Canada
by Routledge
711 Third Avenue, New York, NY 10017

Routledge is an imprint of the Taylor & Francis Group, an informa business

© 1985 Michael Pacione

Publisher's Note
The publisher has gone to great lengths to ensure the quality of this reprint but
points out that some imperfections in the original copies may be apparent.

Disclaimer
The publisher has made every effort to trace copyright holders and welcomes
correspondence from those they have been unable to contact.

A Library of Congress record exists under LC control number: 85014938

ISBN 13: 978-0-415-70761-9 (hbk)
ISBN 13: 978-1-315-88667-1 (ebk)

Progress in Industrial Geography

Edited by Michael Pacione

London and New York

First published in 1985 by Croom Helm Ltd
Reprinted 2001
By Routledge
11 New Fetter Lane
London, EC4P 4EE

Routledge is an imprint of the Taylor & Francis Group

British Library Cataloguing in Publication Data
Progress in industrial geography — (Croom Helm
    progress in geography series)
    1. Industries—Location 2. Geography,
    Economic
    I. Title
    338.09   HC79.D5
    ISBN 0-7099-2072-5

Library of Congress Cataloging in Publication Data
Main entry under title:
Progress in industrial geography.

    (Croom Helm progress in geography series)
    Includes index.
    1. Industry — Location — Addresses, essays,
lectures.   I. Pacione, Michael.   II. Series.
HD58.P76 1985   338.6′042   85-14938
ISBN 0-7099-2072-5

Typeset by Leaper & Gard Ltd, Bristol, England
Printed and bound in Great Britain by
Hobbs The Printers Ltd, Totton, Hants

CONTENTS

To Christine, Michael John and Emma Victoria

FIGURES

TABLES

PREFACE

Since 1970 research in industrial geography has expanded significantly and the subject area now displays considerable diversity.
Traditional approaches to industrial location through descriptive
monitoring have been complemented by applied studies of policy and
planning; by developments in theory in which neo-classical formulations have been challenged by behavioural and structuralist perspectives; and by increasing attention on the Third World and the
operation of multinational corporations as part of a world economy.
Links between national economic change and local trends, and the
spatial influences of multiplant organisations, particularly in the context of regional economic development, have emerged as important
issues within the 'geography of enterprise' approach. Components of
change analyses continue to provide a link between aggregate
analyses and studies of individual firms, with particular attention
focused on plant closures and redundancies. Related themes of
contemporary concern include the phenomena of urban industrial
decline and rural industrialisation, while the broadening perspective
of modern industrial geography also incorporates service industries
in addition to the traditional focus on manufacturing.

This collection of original essays is designed to encapsulate the
major themes and recent developments in a number of areas of
central importance in industrial geography. The volume is a direct
response to the need for a text which reviews the progress and current
state of the subject and which provides a reference point for future
developments in industrial geography.

Michael Pacione
University of Strathclyde
Glasgow

INTRODUCTION

The scope of industrial geography has changed greatly over the present century. The early emphasis on the location of manufacturing industry and on commodity flows has been enlarged, in the post-war period, in response to a number of wider social and economic changes. These include the growing importance of service industries, the growth of multinational and multiplant enterprises, increased direct government involvement in national economies, and the pervasive influence of the global economy on economic change at all scales. In Chapter 1 Bill Lever examines the major theoretical developments underlying modern industrial geography by considering, in turn, neo-classical models, behavioural theories of industrial decision-making, and the more recent structural approach. Attention is also given to methodological questions related to data availability. A discussion of the early theoretical work on industrial location and subsequent extensions of the basic models is followed by a detailed assessment of the interrelationships between, and relative importance of, the different cost factors underlying plant location. Recent geographical interest in the spatial variation of profits is also considered. Over the last two decades, however, the idealised assumptions of neo-classical theory have been superseded by the study of entrepreneurial behaviour. This trend may be explained partly by the declining importance of traditional cost factors for larger enterprises and, particularly in the United Kingdom, the increasing distortion of free-market forces by government policy. Firms operate within an environment of risk and uncertainty, and it is suggested that the notion of corporate behaviour as an adaptive response to different environments can be employed to explain both the growth of larger firms and the continued survival of the small-scale sector. For geographers the spatial expression of entrepreneurial decisions remains a focal concern and within this framework the question of the appropriate scale of investigation is of fundamental importance. The difficulty of inferring the organisational behaviour of companies from aggregate-level data is partly overcome by the use of establishment-based data sets and 'components of change' analyses which seek to relate employment

1

change to the type and location of establishment. Study of ownership characteristics (e.g. whether locally owned or foreign controlled) can also provide further understanding of regional
industrial structure, while studies of individual firms or of cohort
groups offer valuable insight into entrepreneurial decisions. In
contrast to the 'geography of enterprise' perspective underlying
behavioural theories the more recent structuralist approach
emphasises the links between enterprises and the wider society in
which decisions are the outcome of conflict between different
power groups (e.g. capital and labour). In essence the structuralist
approach does not employ abstract models of the firm, recognises
spatial change as a product of non-spatial (structural) forces in the
macro-economy, and focuses on particular product markets to
explain the behaviour of different types of company. Application
of this perspective is illustrated by considering the locational
consequences of three types of production reorganisation (intensification, investment and technical change, and rationalisation).
Particular attention is given to economic structures within local
labour markets dominated by a single industrial employer. It is
concluded that while the three major paradigms do represent a
chronological development in industrial geography they are not
mutually exclusive and elements of each can be usefully employed
in the basic task of understanding the location and activity of
industry.

In Chapter 2 Tony Hoare examines the state of the art in
industrial linkage studies, from its basis in Marshallian economics
to more recent analyses of large scale extra-local linkages. He first
identifies the character of backward and forward linkages using a
model of a manufacturing plant and its relationship with flows of
materials, information and personnel. The importance of the
spatial scale over which such linkages occur is emphasised. The
practical importance of industrial linkages is demonstrated by
considering their economic significance for plant location and
relocation; the way they operate in the diffusion of economic
trends across space, formally operationalised in growth pole
strategies; and the ways in which they serve as a mechanism
whereby firms acquire knowledge of wider operating environments. Attention is then given to the factors which influence the
geographical patterning of linkages. First, the relative importance
of distance-constraining forces is assessed. These include economic
factors (such as transport costs and time), psychological factors

(awareness of possible contacts, local loyalties, risk minimisation), political (e.g. regional policy) and technological factors (such as process requirements). This is complemented by discussion of the influence of dispersal-inducing forces, such as improved communications technology, standardisation of production processes, and the growth of large industrial corporations. In the second part of the chapter, the geographical nature of industrial linkages is examined at both the aggregate industry and individual plant levels. At the macro scale, the related concepts of industrial linkage and spatial linkage are introduced and evidence presented to suggest that a significant relationship exists between the two, even in advanced economies in which dispersal-inducing forces are operating. At the micro level, analysis of research into the geographical scale of, and controls on industrial linkages emphasises the validity of a 'simple firm — local linkage' paradigm. Micro scale investigations of the relationship between actual and potential linkages, of linkage changes over time, and of the perceived importance of linkages in locational evaluations are also discussed. It is clear that the focus of attention in industrial linkage studies has moved away from the Marshallian agglomeration-through-linkage model towards a more spatially diffuse form of association in which the importance of physical distance is diminished. It is suggested that economic geographers must adopt a broader viewpoint, including, for example, analysis of the structure of manufacturing firms, if they are to fully understand the nature of the industrial linkages which form an integral part of the modern manufacturing process.

In Chapter 3 Paul Bull discusses the dynamics of industrial location at the intra-urban scale. Particular attention is given to recent theoretical developments which offer a framework to explain the changing geography of urban industrial activity. A review of the components of change approach is followed by consideration of the relationship between factor costs and establishment type as embodied in the dual economy model. An alternative paradigm illustrates the ways in which the interaction of labour costs and fixed and circulating capital costs can produce a three-fold typology of central city, suburban and non-metropolitan occupiers. The significance of technological change in stimulating urban locational change is of key importance, and the need to understand the locational demands of different production processes is stressed. Technological changes in best-practice production methods can lead to changes in the type of industrial property demanded with, in some inner-city areas, older 'constrained locations' being vacated and left to filter down through increasingly marginal and transitory establishments until redevelopment. It follows, therefore, that knowledge of a city's stock of industrial premises and how they may constrain the adoption of the most profitable forms of production underlies fuller understanding of the industrial geography and economic stability of a city. While the majority of urban firms will be single-plant enterprises, in some cities multiplant corporations assume great significance in terms of output and employment. In such circumstances, information on the strategies and plans pursued by the controlling firms is of critical importance. In practice, however, international, corporate, technological, sectoral and local factors may act simultaneously to influence plant behaviour and so compound the difficulties of explaining the process of industrial change within cities. It is suggested that the complexity of the situation may be reduced by focusing research attention on the prime-mover firms in a study area. It is concluded that the relatively minor role of intra-urban plant transfers in the suburbanisation process may best be understood by classifying businesses not by products but in terms of their level of economic power, with different types attracted to particular premises and locations. Accordingly, for a small firm to move successfully from a traditional central location to a suburban site would necessitate a fundamental change in its organisation and behaviour. As recent empirical evidence indicates, few firms have made this transition successfully. Finally, several areas into which further research might profitably be directed are indicated including the impact of corporate decisions at the intra-urban scale, the consequences of the recession, and the role of small firms in generating new employment opportunities.

The increasing importance of service industries in national economies and the implications of this trend for urban structure and for the nature and distribution of urban and regional employment opportunities are key issues in contemporary industrial geography. In Chapter 4 Peter Daniels outlines the growth of the service sector and illustrates its importance in the employment structure of advanced economies. He then identifies two basic types of service industry, consumer services (such as retailing) which exist primarily to serve final demand, and producer services (e.g. research and development) which provide specialist inputs to other industries producing a final good or service. Discussion is then focused on the latter type, with two prominent themes in recent research being the locational behaviour and growth of office-based activities, and, more recently, exploration of the locational and related behaviour of specific producer functions. It is suggested that the empirical orientation of most work in the field has created a lacuna in the development of theory and, until recently, a consequent dependence for explanation upon the established tenets of classical urban economic and industrial location theories. Detailed consideration is then given to efforts to model office location including evaluation of frameworks which incorporate behavioural approaches to decision-making, employ economic equilibrium techniques, or which use more descriptive approaches based on cost-benefit analysis of different locations. Attention then turns to examine sector-specific studies. Office-based business services, research and development, and distribution and warehousing are identified as significant growth services and areas of particular interest. The effects of new technology on service employment and its location and, at the larger scale, the international configuration of service industries are also examined. Other potentially fruitful areas for further investigation include (a) comparative studies of the location of producer services and the consequences for cities and regions; (b) systematic analysis of the function, establishment size, organisational status, client and input linkages, and other facets of suburban office development; (c) examination of the transactional bases of metropolitan areas, including the relationship between central cities and suburbs; and (d) assessment of the impact of new commercial developments, such as office and science parks, on transportation and on the demand for consumer services. Finally, it is suggested that although the service sector does not operate in isolation from other parts of the economy, its particular locational, physical and transactional attributes underline the importance of analysing service industries as a separate and distinctive part of the whole.

Multinational enterprises have assumed an increasingly important role in the process of national and regional economic change. Even those seeking explanations for industrial change at an intranational scale cannot fail to consider the operations of such firms within the world economy. Foreign direct investment is the major route for the development of multinational corporations. In Chapter 5 Ian Smith examines foreign direct investment and divestment trends in industrial countries since the mid 1960s — a period which marked the beginning of a major phase of internationalisation. He first outlines the chief data and definitional difficulties facing researchers and considers how these may be overcome. Analyses of aggregate trends reveal the substantial increase in importance of foreign direct investment in all OECD countries as a result of a reduction in trade barriers to international capital flows, protectionist policies which make foreign direct investment more profitable than exporting, and increased government assistance. Examination of the geographical distribution of these trends identifies (a) a reduction in the share of developed countries' assets located in developing countries, (with the exception of tax havens), owing to increased foreign direct investment among the developed countries; (b) a major redirection of foreign direct investment flows towards high income markets such as the USA and West Germany; and (c) greater diversification of sources of foreign direct investment as enterprises from the majority of OECD countries increasingly internationalise their operations. Each of these major trends is subjected to detailed analysis. Consideration of sectoral trends is impeded by a dearth of satisfactory data and it is suggested that it is this deficiency that is responsible for the continued absence of a unified theory of foreign direct investment. Attention then turns to international disinvestment trends and the rationalisation strategies employed by multinationals. The situation in Britain forms the basis for a detailed investigation of the extent to which the trends that emerged during the late 1970s have continued during the current recession, and secondly, how the internationalisation process contributed to deindustrialisation in a relatively slow-growing industrialised country. Finally, the international evidence is synthesised to isolate the part played by foreign direct investment in growth differences between the major industrialised nations.

Although plant closures and compulsory redundancies have long been an integral component of industrial change, the scale and widespread occurrence of these phenomena in the 1980s have been unprecedented. Mass redundancy, often leading to long-term unemployment, is a characteristic of the process of industrial contraction currently affecting Western capitalist economies, and large-scale redundancy programmes play a key role in the economic policy of many governments. In their discussion of mass redundancy Alan Townsend and Frank Peck underline the crucial causal role of major corporations in generating regional and sub-regional employment change. Following a general review of international trends, detailed attention is focused on the situation in the UK, which has experienced significant levels of job loss across a wide range of modern corporations and industries. An empirical analysis covering the period 1977-81 is based on a unique data set compiled from the financial press and the nature and validity of this information source are discussed. Consideration is then given to the spatial pattern of decline within UK corporations. Particular attention is given to the type of area and settlement most affected by job losses, and to the impact of corporate job loss on government assisted areas. The evidence suggests that, up to 1979, the collective effect of large corporations upon settlements of different types was to concentrate employment decline in industrial towns and coalfield areas; during 1980-1 a greater impact was felt by coastal, overspill and rural locations. The study period was characterised by a weakening of the traditional north-south division in terms of relative job loss, prior to a general manufacturing decline in 1980-1. The advent of mass redundancy in 1980 represented a breakpoint before which government assisted areas were worst affected by job loss, but after which there was a relative decrease in job losses in these areas and an increase in non-assisted areas. The value of making connections between the meso-economy and aggregate trends is emphasised, and a strong recommendation is made for further work on the role of corporations in the meso-economy, as a means of relating overall trends to events in local geographic areas.

Regional development policies are defined as those operated by the state or state agencies in order to influence economic development between major areas of a country. Since the Second World War such policies have been employed extensively by governments. In Chapter 7 Chris Law provides an overview of this important policy area. He first discusses the rationale for and objectives of regional development policies. While regional inequality in socio-economic well-being is the most commonly cited reason, other stimuli include strategic considerations (e.g. to populate a disputed territory or to disperse vulnerable economic activities), aesthetic and environmental factors (such as avoidance of urban sprawl) and cultural reasons (e.g. to placate minority groups). The economic justification for regional development policy has been related to the debates over optimum city size and, in particular, to the underutilisation of social capital, labour and physical resources in the poorer regions. A fundamental guiding principle, however, is a state's political and governmental structure, with regional development policy more likely to be adopted in democratic rather than totalitarian regimes. The basic strategy behind the instruments of regional policy is to affect the operating costs in different parts of a country so as to influence the locational decisions of firms. The second section of the paper therefore examines the nature and operation of both positive instruments (e.g. provision of infrastructure, financial incentives, planning agreements between governments and firms, and government investment in the equity of firms) and negative disincentives (such as development permits and taxation). Questions related to the delimitation of problem regions, including the selection of criteria and scale of definition, are then discussed. In the final section, the impact of regional development policies is assessed. The key question of whether the policies have created self-sustained growth is examined with reference to studies of industrial movement and, in particular, the branch plant economy and multiplier effect of new plants. While there is no doubt that regional development policy can cause significant shifts in the spatial distribution of economic activity its ability to produce self-sustained growth in problem regions is less certain. It is concluded that whereas regional development policy formed a central element of government economic strategy in the 1960s and early 1970s the emergence of general problems related to the world recession has made the strategy less effective and consequently its future as a policy instrument less assured.

The growth of world systems of production, marketing and corporate ownership has created a complex mesh of economic inter-relationships. Of particular significance in the contemporary world are the links between the Developed and Developing realms. In Chapter 8 Glen Norcliffe examines the industrial geography of the Third World. The discussion is based on a three-fold categorisation of production systems which range from the international activities of multinational enterprises, through formal domestic production, to the small-scale informal sector. Transnational corporations are relatively few in number and employ comparatively few workers but the fact that the capital assets of the largest companies often exceed the GNP of many Third World states assigns them a crucial importance in Third World industrialisation.

Four main types of multinationals are recognised, each characterised by different operating objectives. These may include a desire to control resource inputs, avoid tariff barriers, take advantage of cheap labour, or engage in portfolio investment strategies. Both the old and new international division of labour are then examined, and it is argued that the south-north flow of resources which underlay the mercantilist empires of past centuries is still evident, albeit with different products involved. The new international division of labour operates in such a way as to enable some Third World countries to become major exporters of labour-intensive manufactured goods. The existence of large labour surpluses can also give rise to the authoritarian corporations common in most newly industrialised countries. Discussion on the nature of such states is followed by consideration of the moves towards liberalising world trade via export processing, free trade and maritime industrial areas. The role of foreign capital in Third World industrial development is then analysed. At the national level, the structure and location of domestically owned formal enterprises are first analysed before particular attention is devoted to small-scale informal production. Examination of the relationship between the informal sector and the modernisation and dependency paradigms of development is followed by detailed analysis of the types and operational characteristics of small-scale enterprises. Finally the link between small-scale industry and development is explored and the potential value of small-scale production underlined. It is concluded that since the nature and level of development realised in a country are related to the prevalent industrial structure, definition of the most appropriate form of development is the most important task facing industrial planners in the Third World.

1 THEORY AND METHODOLOGY IN INDUSTRIAL GEOGRAPHY

W.F. Lever

Introduction

Industrial geography has been a major component of economic geography since the turn of the century. Much of the early work concerned the location of industries, particularly in the developed world, and the flows of raw materials and finished goods from and to the developing world. Its focus was largely on manufacturing industry operated within a capitalist economy. For its theories and concepts it tended, not unnaturally, to borrow from the discipline of economics: the output, if it was applied at all, tended to feed into physical and regional economic planning and to explain some social problems. During the post-war period a number of changes have occurred which in turn have forced industrial geographers to re-evaluate what they do. First, the role of government has expanded dramatically, as an industrialist itself operating whole sectors (coal, steel) or very substantial parts of sectors (motor vehicles, shipbuilding, aerospace), as an influence on investment and locational decisions of the private sector, and as a major customer of the private sector. Secondly, in the developed world there has been a steady transition from manufacturing to service industries, when measured in terms of employment. Thirdly, the perspective with which geographers have looked at manufacturing has had to become increasingly global. Explanations of industrial change in Britain will remain at best only partial unless they recognise the changing nature of the world economy in the post-colonial age. Lastly, industrial organisational structures have changed dramatically. Whereas the most common form of enterprise 30 years ago would have been the single indigenously owned and managed plant, the growth of multinational multiplant companies has recently become a major feature of industrial geography. At the same time, in the current recession, less formal industrial enterprises based upon worker co-operatives or community initiatives have also grown in number.

These changes have forced geographers to alter how they think about industry. In this chapter we trace recent developments in three ways of thinking about industry. We begin with neoclassical theories, founded on assumptions of locational adjustment for profit maximisation. This is followed by a section on behavioural theories of industrial decision-making, covered in the literature by what is often termed 'the geography of enterprise'. Thirdly, we consider the more recent structuralist approach, which uses the dialectic between labour and capital as the conceptual approach to decision-making.

A conceptual approach to any subject, including industrial geography, requires an effective methodology to support it. Industrial geography has always been a data-prodigal area of research where official statistics, especially on employment but also on output, production functions, trade flows, capital and land are produced in large quantities. The industrial geographer's most difficult task has been, and remains, to take this aggregate data and from it derive a realistic model of how individual industrial enterprises behave and, in particular, take decisions. In many cases the industrial geographer has been forced to collect his own data at establishment level, and this in its turn raises other methodological problems of representativeness, reflexivity and conceptual transference. In this respect research into industrial geography can be seen to be no different from the vast body of research in the social sciences generally.

Neoclassical Location Theory

Neoclassical location theory in industrial geography is based upon assumptions of economic rationality amongst entrepreneurs who seek an optimal location defined in terms of a single criterion, or on the basis of trade-offs between several criteria. In this sense it derives from neoclassical theory in economics in which the utilisation of productive resources (land, labour and capital) and the allocation through market mechanisms yielded an optimal result measured in terms of gross utility. Thus just as in neoclassical economic theory any change in production functions or allocative processes would move production away from optimality with a consequent net loss of utility, so in neoclassical location theory a locational shift would, unless a direct response to spatial shifts in the prices of production factors such as labour or land or to a spatial shift in revenue, generate a suboptimal location.

Neoclassical location theory in geography has evolved from the work of Weber (1909). Weber was concerned with the simple geometric identification of a least-transportation-cost point within a geographical triangle with a single raw material source at one apex and two separate markets at the other two. The identification of such a point is a simple function of the volumes of material shipped and unit transport costs. Weber recognised the conceptual simplicity of this approach to the calculation of the optimal location and sought to extend the comprehensivity of the theory in order to take into account operating costs attaching to production rather than merely those of transport. This he did by utilising the concept of the 'critical isodapane'. If labour costs vary in space, it is conceivable that a labour cost saving at some point may more than offset the fact that aggregate transport costs at that point exceed the minimum. Isodapanes represented lines or contours of equal total transport cost: if a labour cost saving of £10.00 per unit of output could be achieved at some point then the £10.00 isodapane becomes critical. If that point lies within the critical isodapane, then the optimising firm will move its location from the minimum transport cost point to the point where the labour cost savings can be realised.

The strictly neoclassical model of industrial location was then subsequently developed by Palander (1935) and Hoover (1937, 1948). Palander extended the analysis by relating choice of location and production costs to market areas. Although his treatment of the problem of defining market areas for competing plants or firms in different locations was largely graphical, he did accept the concept of different production costs and extended the Weberian argument that these could offset transport costs. The nature of these differing production costs is not clarified by Palander but they could be attributable either to scale economies or greater managerial efficiency (variables which do not vary systematically in space), or to differing factor costs which might vary systematically in space. Hoover further extended these arguments by dealing explicitly with some scale economies, particularly those available in bulk transport over long distances where the marginal transport cost falls regularly.

Unlike transport costs which are regularly if not linearly related to distance, the costs of other factors of production may not vary systematically in space. Capital for investment does not appear to vary in cost at different locations to any significant extent. Interest rates on borrowed capital are generally determined nationally and therefore do not act as a significant locational variable. *Availability* of capital may vary between establishments but this is likely to reflect establishment characteristics such as size, ownership and product market rather than location. Labour costs may vary significantly in space but they have rarely proved attractive to geographers as the basis of a significant locational theory. In a country such as the United Kingdom, the existence of nationally negotiated wage settlements through national trade unions covering a particular industry or occupational skill has been a sufficient argument to downgrade labour cost as a systematic element in classical location theory. Other aspects of the local labour force — skill, good industrial relations, willingness to accept and adopt new technologies or methods of production — have been adduced to explain particular industrial locational decisions, but price alone is rarely cited. Indeed, this may reflect a recognition on the part of geographers that the true index of labour costs which might inform a cost-minimising, classical locational model is not wage rate but the efficiency wage, which defines labour costs per unit of output, rather than hourly wage rate, and therefore captures the effect of productivity differentials. Such efficiency wages are notoriously difficult to estimate reliably. In larger national systems, and in countries where national wage agreements are less common, such as the United States, labour costs may be an element in industrial locational decision-making. The recent success of the southern United States in attracting industrial development has in part been attributed to such money wage differentials (Foster 1972).

The price of land has entered industrial and indeed general locational modelling to a much greater extent than either labour or capital. As land prices or rents vary sharply over relatively short distances, land prices tend to be used in intra-urban theories of industrial location rather than in inter-regional theories. Alonso (1967), for example, has shown that one can establish an equilibrium firm location site with respect to distance from the city centre. Given the assumptions of the existence of a centralised city, with all customers located at its centre, profit-maximising firms, and a land price structure which varies inversely with distance from the city centre, firms opt to move away from the city centre to locations at which their revenues are lower, operating costs are higher (because of poorer accessibility) but land costs are lower. If the land price savings are sufficient to offset lower revenues and higher operating costs, then firms will find optimal locations away from the city centre. If the rent gradient is not such as to offer adequate savings, then firms will remain at the city centre.

Locational theories based upon cost minimisation have found it simpler to assume that the combination of inputs is fixed and one cannot be substituted for another. This is rarely the case in reality, where as the relative prices of inputs change, producers substitute cheaper inputs for more expensive ones. In terms of the three major factors of production — land, labour and capital — the post-war period has seen a very rapid rise in the price of labour, measured in hourly wage terms, relative to the prices of the other two. This has in general meant that manufacturing firms have tended to use more capital (i.e. in the form of machinery) and less labour per unit of output, the extreme version of this process being the entirely automated assembly plants which are currently being developed. As more capital equipment has been employed, the need to arrange it in the most flexible and convenient manner has led to the choice of single-storey premises, and thus the quantity of land utilised by industry per unit of output has been increased also. The most simple locational theory based upon substitution effects is that which explains the suburbanisation of manufacturing in terms of using more capital for which the price is spatially invariant, more land which is cheapest at the city edge, and less labour which is more expensive at the city edge.

The theoretical treatment of substitution between factor inputs with different prices at different locations begins with the work of Moses (1958) in which lines of equal outlay on two substitutable inputs are graphically superimposed upon an equal product curve. Where the latter touches but does not intersect that equal outlay line which lies closest to the origin of the graph (i.e. touches the lowest equal outlay line) there lies the optimal ratio between the two inputs. All other points on the equal product curve mark points which require more input but which by definition generate no additional output.

The concept of firms making locational choices on the basis of different locations having different factor endowments and consequently different factor prices derives from work done on international comparisons of comparative advantage and then subsequently applied at the regional level. Early international work on this Heckscher-Ohlin theory was undertaken by Leontief (1953, 1956) who found that the United States' exports tended to reflect more capital than labour as a consequence of the relatively high labour costs of that country. Moroney and Walker (1966) applied the same argument at the regional level, hypothesising that industries with relatively low capital-labour ratios would tend to concentrate in the southern states. It was not assumed that such industries would necessarily have a location quotient greater than unity but that they should be highest ranked in the region's industrial structure. However, correlating capital intensity to rank in industrial structure yielded results insignificantly different from zero and with the wrong sign. Moroney and Walker's conclusion was that initial factor endowments would dictate the initial comparative advantage of a region's economy but that relative availability and price of labour and capital would subsequently lead to an adjustment in the regional economy.

At the intra-urban scale the recent study by Scott (1982) summarises the comparative advantage argument for shifts within the location of manufacturing industry. However, Scott chooses to define capital in an explicitly spatial form, namely interindustrial linkages. The justification for this is that goods and services in transit absorb investment finance: the longer those linkages, the greater the amount of finance thus unproductively absorbed. The argument is thus developed that major cities, and particularly their inner areas, are characterised by nodal complexes of industrial activities deriving financial (capital) benefit from their close proximity and short linkages (e.g. Czamanski and Czamanski, 1977). Scott points out that many of the studies of intra-urban linkages have been ambiguous, failing to reveal a clear relationship between intersectoral linkage and spatial proximity (e.g. Hoare, 1975; Streit, 1969): this he attributes both to the declining unit costs of transport over time, some of it due to technological innovations, and to the increasing use of preferential tariffs on freight negotiated by large industrial concerns. He concludes that at the intra-urban scale the real costs of moving goods over distances have declined to a point where they are no longer the most important factor in the locational decision, but that negotiation and communication costs on unstandardised flows may have declined much less markedly and therefore have a more significant role in the growth of industrial complexes.

Scott comments that geographers have been less willing to

examine the shape of local labour markets within cities in order to throw light upon the labour cost element of the locational choice. Drawing on the early studies of Moses (1962) and Muth (1969) we assume generally that workers require to be compensated for both the pecuniary cost and the time expended in the journey to work. Thus employers who locate at some distance from the residential locations of their workforces are likely to have to pay higher wages than those who are close to them. In the neoclassical urban location model with most of the employment located at the city centre, city centre employers are likely to have to pay higher wages than those in the residential suburbs (Rees and Schultz, 1970). The post-war suburbanisation of industrial and commercial employment has altered the balance of the urban wage gradient. As a higher proportion of jobs are found on the urban periphery, and given the lower population densities and the greater difficulty of travelling by public transport in the suburbs, wage rates now tend to be positively correlated with distance from the city centre (e.g. O'Cleireacain, 1974). It can be argued that, if there are significant differences in the capital and labour costs at different locations in the city, then the land price will reflect these. If labour and capital costs are low at the city centre then many establishments will seek to locate there and the price of land and floorspace rents will be forced up. In a perfectly competitive market the rise in space costs will just offset the savings achieved in capital and labour costs. However, all bidders for space in the urban land market do not have the same factor mix, as we have already seen, and thus a single rent gradient serves to allocate different activities to different locations within the city. As factor prices change relative to one another, establishments both substitute one for another and change location in order to reduce production costs.

The ultimate rationale of neoclassical industrial location theory is that establishments will locate where profits are higher: theories based upon maximising revenue or minimising some or all production costs (e.g. transport) are only partial theories at best. Geographers have only recently begun to mount empirical studies of the spatial variation of profits and most have been concerned with the urban-rural shift in manufacturing industry. The study by Moore, Rhodes and Tyler (1980) uses Census of Production data for the 1960s. This study shows (Table 1.1) that there was a generally lower level of profit generated by establishments in the standard conurbations than by those in their respective hinter-

Table 1.1: Profit per Employee: Conurbations and Regions

	1963	1968		1963	1968
Tyneside	£450	£645	Rest of North	£492	£668
W. Yorks. con.	£380	£534	Yorks., Humberside	£457	£714
S.E. Lancs. con.	£405	£684	Rest of N.W.	£439	£706
Merseyside	£511	£600			
London	£526	£799	Rest of S.E.	£567	£780
W. Midlands con.	£412	£556	Rest of W. Midlands	£412	£652
Clydeside	£419	£542	Rest of Scotland	£551	£741

Source: Moore, Rhodes and Tyler, 1980.

lands. The only exceptions were Merseyside in 1963 and London in 1968. At the same time, the Moore, Rhodes and Tyler study shows that the rate of profit was generally rising more rapidly in the hinterlands than it was in the conurbations. It is not clear from the study to what extent the differences in profitability per employee are attributable to differences in industrial structure — it is quite possible, for example, that the difference in profitability between Clydeside and the rest of Scotland reflects the fact that the former's industrial structure is dominated by shipbuilding, steel, metal goods production and heavy engineering sectors whereas the high profit-making sectors (whisky distilling, light engineering and electrical engineering) are relatively absent from the Clydeside conurbation (Toothill, 1961). The more recent studies by Fothergill, Kitson and Monk (1982, 1984) using data provided by the Centre for Interfirm Comparison, and an earlier study by Fothergill and Gudgin (NEDO, 1975, 1976) using National Economic Development Office data, do, however, standardise for industrial sector. The NEDO covered two industrial sectors, mechanical engineering and clothing. Some 420 firms were included in the analysis, and the measure of profitability was the four- or five-year average of pre-tax, pre-interest profits as a percentage of capital employed. The results, as Table 1.2 shows, indicate a marked tendency for profitability to be lowest in the large cities and for the profitability to rise as urban size decreases. Only mechanical engineering in London significantly contradicts this relationship. Overall, the differential in profitability between conurbations and rural areas is approximately 25 per cent in mechanical engineering and 45 per cent in clothing. The subsequent study using CIFC data confirms these findings, showing

Table 1.2: Average Profitability by Type of Area

	Mechanical engineering 1970/71 — 1974/75		Clothing 1968/69 — 1973/74	
	Profitability	UK = 100	Profitability	UK = 100
London	14.0	105	11.2	87
Conurbations	11.1	86	11.4	88
Freestanding cities	12.7	96	14.1	106
Industrial towns	13.7	103	14.7	110
Rural areas	16.4	122	18.5	134

Source: Fothergill, Kitson and Monk, 1982.

lower levels of profitability in the conurbations, using profit as a ratio of operating assets as the overall measure of profitability. The Fothergill, Kitson and Monk studies go somewhat further, seeking to explain the reasons for this higher profitability in smaller centres. They find that conurbation firms have higher levels of both current and fixed assets per volume of sales, and thus they diagnose higher levels of plant, land and buildings (in value terms) in relation to sales as poor asset utilisation. In addition overheads are higher in the conurbations, and labour productivity is significantly lower, as measured by value added per production employee.

These findings are supported by a study by Lever (1982) which used Census of Production data at establishment level to compare firms in Clydeside with their national average business performance for seven industrial sectors (MLHs or grouped MLHs). Although this study does not include measures of profitability, it seeks to explain the poor performance of businesses in Clydeside in terms of the use they make of capital and labour. Gross output per head in the seven sectors ranges between a low of 52 per cent of the national average in paper products to 92 per cent in metal goods (Table 1.3). This pattern is largely replicated when net output per head (i.e. once the purchase of raw materials and components is taken into account) is used as the measure of labour efficiency. The wage bill, when expressed as a percentage of gross value added, shows that the Clydeside firms in the study did have to pay more for labour than the national average. When it is realised that hourly wage *rates* are lower in Clydeside than nationally, it becomes clear that larger *amounts* of labour, expressed as man-hours per unit of output, must be employed in the conurbation. Certainly low levels of capital investment seem to

Table 1.3: Clydeside: U.K. Production Ratios 1978

	Bread	Paper	Clothing	Mech. eng.	Ind. plant	Heavy eng.	Metal
			Clydeside/U.K. × 100				
Gross output/head	74	52	66	81	53	82	92
Net output/head	81	67	81	88	56	56	102
Gross value added/ head	85	78	87	93	59	60	105
Wages as % GVA	102	107	107	97	125	150	136
Capital as % GVA	111	90	63	71	137	45	30

Source: Lever, 1982.

be the most common pattern in the study's industries when the capital : gross value added ratios are examined. It would thus appear that conurbation firms are less profitable and this is because wage costs are higher whilst capital investment is lower.

A neoclassical theory of industrial location at the intra-urban level can thus be based on an assumption that in order to increase or maximise profits establishments are likely to avoid the largest urban centres. Land costs are lower away from the largest centres and if wage costs (in hourly rates) are higher then this is more than offset by the more efficient use of labour, both directly and as a result of greater capital intensity. This raises two further theoretical questions. First, how is it possible for labour price differentials and significant differences in labour productivity to be sustained over considerable lengths of time? And, secondly, is there a linkage between location and stage of the product life cycle which explains differences in factor mix and profitability? We turn to these questions in subsequent sections.

Behavioural Location Theory

The behavioural approach to decision-making within enterprises on issues relating not only to location but also to pricing, product development, markets and production processes developed initially in the United States in the 1960s. There were a number of developments which led to the study of entrepreneurial behaviour. First, there was growing dissatisfaction with the rather idealised assumptions which underpinned much of the classical approach to locational analysis. Restrictive assumptions about the entrepreneurial desire to minimise transport cost had, it was argued, produced a set of theories which were of little help in confronting real issues facing urban and regional planners (Krumme, 1969; Wood, 1969). At the same time, empirical studies of entrepreneurial decision-making were stressing how little information formed the basis of many locational choices, and how imperfect such information often was, thus undermining the fundamental assumption of economic rationality as a basis of classical location theory. Thirdly, the increasing concentration of manufacturing into larger and larger concerns meant that large companies were often in a position to control the local price of labour, inputs or land, in a manner which ensured that they did not have to make locational choices on the basis of selecting a site which minimised such costs: they were large enough to select a location on other criteria and distort local cost surfaces. Fourthly, evidence was appearing to show that profit and cost surfaces were so gently sloping that there was ample scope for businesses to choose locations on non-pecuniary criteria including environmental preference, and not be too disadvantaged by the resultant shortfall in profits. Fifthly, in the British context there was increasing concern about the need to incorporate within locational theory the effects of regional and urban economic and physical planning policies which were totally excluded by the neoclassical approach. Lastly, in the United States the growth of management science as an academic discipline was opening up a new body of literature on the nature of decision-making within corporate structures, of which locational choice was just one element, and a rather minor one at that.

Behavioural theories of location drew attention to two respects in which underlying assumptions of neoclassical theory were not reflected in reality. Firstly, decision-makers did not have perfect information upon which to base their locational choice, nor, even in the largest enterprises, did they have the perfect ability to use their information. Pred (1967) developed the behavioural matrix in a probabilistic sense to show that the better the information and the greater the ability to use it, the more likely it was that the location chosen would lie at, or close to, the point which maximised profit. With less information and less ability, there was less probability that the location chosen would be optimal. Within this probabilistic model, however, there was always a chance that any enterprise, however ill-informed, would make the optimal choice. Pred's model, as a methodological tool, has only limited utility, as

Claus and Claus (1971) pointed out, but it did enable geographers to appreciate the behavioural models of industrial decision-making being developed by Simon (1959) and others.

The second respect in which behavioural theories went beyond neoclassical assumptions was to show that it was perfectly possible for entrepreneurs to make a conscious choice of location well away from the optimal one, in the full knowledge that profits were not being maximised. There were two types of reason for this sort of locational choice. First, the locational choice might be regarded as a utility-maximising choice in which profit is only one element. The entrepreneur might therefore choose a location in which social or environmental attributes outweighed, to a certain extent, profit. Such a set of preferences might weigh heavily with the small firm, single plant, indigenously owned enterprise, where the entrepreneur's place of birth and knowledge of local educational, residential and leisure facilities would play an important part in framing his utility function. However, in the rapid growth of multiplant firms there has also been ample scope for non-profit considerations to shape the locational pattern. Multiplant firms, of course, create their spatial pattern not only by opening new branches *de novo*, but by the choice of mergers and take-overs. Recent studies (Pounce, 1981; Killick, 1983) have shown that new branch plant openings have occurred at a declining rate since the early 1970s, whilst the merger and acquisition process has continued, thereby gaining a greater proportionate importance (Leigh and North, 1978). Secondly, as Simon (1959) and others pointed out, entrepreneurs may have business objectives other than profit maximisation. Cyert and March (1963) drew attention to the possibility of multiple business goals in organisations with large numbers of individuals. These multiple goals might include growth, security, the minimisation of risk, entrepreneurial satisfaction or merely self-preservation (Hamilton, 1974).

Perhaps the most influential study of organisations such as large industrial companies, as decision-makers, is that by Burns and Stalker (1961). They described the need for organisations to develop mechanisms for the resolution of conflicts and to co-ordinate decision-making. They found that different types of organisational structures are best adapted for different environments. An organisation with well-defined tasks and a rigidly hierarchical system of decision-making and implementation was, they argued, most suitable for stable environments. In contrast, an organic form of organisation structure is better suited to a dynamic environment in which tasks are flexibly defined and the various decision-makers co-operate on the basis of their respective skills — not merely according to roles defined within a hierarchy (Marshall, 1982).

The work of Burns and Stalker has focused the attention of industrial geographers on the concept of *environment*. The most commonly cited classification of environments was developed by Emery and Trist (1965). They used a wide range of characteristics including the degree of competition, risk and uncertainty strategy and the strength and complexity of networks. Four ideal types were defined, although combinations of these types in the real world produced a much wider range of settings for industrial decision-making. The simplest category was placid and randomised, where change was slow and there was very little instability. In this environment, the best decisions approximated to neoclassical solutions to utility-maximising criteria in a very local context (Harrison, 1978). More complicated was the second type of environment — the placid, clustered environment, in which environmental benefits and disbenefits were not randomly allocated but clustered, thereby making it more important that decision-makers secured more data, with strategy replacing tactics. This has been equated with the economist's concept of imperfect competition (McDermott and Taylor, 1982). The third type of environment, termed disturbed-reactive, comprises a number of similar organisations linked in an oligopolistic set of relationships. In this system both uncertainty and complexity are extremely high, and organisations require to be very flexible to meet the inherent competitive challenges in a wide range of strategies including acquisition of other organisations. The fourth type, which Emery and Trist term turbulent, comprises a situation of such unpredictability and uncertainty that organisations are unable to respond with any estimate of the consequences: it therefore remains a concept, required for comprehensivity, but one which is difficult to use as an analytic tool.

In the context provided by a typology of environments, geographers have been able to study the behaviour of organisations such as industrial enterprises. Some of the decisions, on pricing, product development, production process and corporate rationalisation, are totally or largely aspatial, although they may have spatial impacts such as their effect on local labour markets or the patterns of backward and forward linkages. Some of the decisions, however, do have spatial effects through openings, closures, expansions, contractions and acquisition behaviour. The typology of Emery and Trist and others such as Duncan (1972) have as their basis a scale of increasing uncertainty and risk. Uncertainty about future outcomes means that the process of entrepreneurial decision-making needs to weight the relative returns to, on the one hand, seizing commercial opportunities (with a high risk factor) and on the other, minimising the risk of failure. The more that firms can control elements in the external environment, the more they can reduce the element of risk and make more predictable the outcome of decisions. The external environment in this context includes a wide range of elements including the price of inputs, the market price of (and demand for) products in different markets, the flow and price of capital, labour and land. There are several responses to these uncertainties: these include enhanced information gathering (hence the increasing emphasis upon research and development), professional business services such as labour recruitment and marketing, locational choice and the reduction of competition through acquisition and merger and by location to 'capture' a monopolistic or quasi-monopolistic position in a local or regional market.

This pattern of adaptive response explains two of the predominant trends of industrial geography in the recent past. In the first of these, the growth of successively larger and larger firms represents three aspects of the move to reduce uncertainty: firstly, the process of merger and acquisition reduces competition and permits oligopolistic price-fixing in, for example, the chemical and vehicle-manufacturing industry, and also serves to reduce the possibility of an unanticipated product-market innovation from outside the oligopoly; secondly, as uncertainty and risk are reduced by enhanced information, the economies of scale in information acquisition and processing enhance the competitiveness of larger enterprises; thirdly, with increasing government intervention in industry, both for economic and social reasons, the larger the enterprise becomes the more power it is able to bring to its negotiations with the public sector. For example, in the United Kingdom the largest hundred enterprises in 1948 accounted for about 21 per cent of all output; by 1970 the figure was 45 per cent (Watts, 1980). The second trend is the continued survival of the small firm sector. Whilst on the basis of the above argument the small firm sector would appear to be vulnerable, insufficient in scale to afford to gather information which would reduce uncertainty, and insufficiently powerful to exert some control on the external environment, this sector has retained its share of the national industrial workforce at about 22 per cent (Binks and Coyne, 1983). The reason for this survival is that small firms are able to reduce risk by restricting themselves to known local markets and a limited product range. They therefore reduce the risks associated with potentially high yield investments directed at new product developments and remote markets. This is almost a formula which guarantees a fixed stock of small enterprises, or indeed, when recession has a serious impact on the larger firms, a growth in the rate of new small firm creations, even if this is paralleled by a corresponding rise in their closure rate (Storey, 1982). The closure or contraction of larger enterprises creates market niches in which small firms can both satisfy the unmet market demands and utilise the freed resources (premises, labour and entrepreneurial skill).

In this way, the external environment influences the behaviour and the decision-making processes of different types of enterprise. Geographers have stressed that large enterprises in different product markets have more in common with one another than they have with small enterprises in the same product market because their sheer size offers them similar amounts of power to influence their external environment and means that they are likely to have similar organisation structures. From a methodological point of view, it has proved easier for geographers to examine decisions on locational patterns than on any other aspect of corporate management. This is because decisions on output, pricing, product change or process technology are recorded in data which are less easily available to geographers, whereas data on the location of employment, whilst not easy to collect at the enterprise or establishment level, are often readily available at sector level at fine levels of spatial disaggregation (Healey, 1983).

Aggregate locational patterns based on employment data since the mid-1960s show a number of broad trends from which geographers have inferred behavioural choices on the part of industrialists. The most common technique has been to link employment changes to area characteristics. For example, Keeble (1976) was able to show, with aggregate data for the period 1959-71, that the division between a prosperous core and a depressed periphery within Britain was substantially narrowed. The emphasis moved away from a 'regional' perspective in which successful regions such as the South East and the West Midlands could be clearly distinguished from the depressed regions such as the North and Scotland, to an urban perspective in which the economies of the large conurbations, particularly London, performed far worse than did those of smaller urban centres. In consequence, regions such as the four named above, with a large proportion of their workforce located in large cities, performed poorly, whereas regions such as East Anglia and the South West, which lacked conurbations, performed well (Keeble 1980). This trend, in a behavioural sense, represents a rejection of the hitherto assumed advantages of location in large urban centres (access to labour, large local markets and the benefits of proximity to information and innovation) and an acceptance of new advantages to be found in small urban centres. Whilst some geographers (e.g. Fothergill and Gudgin, 1982) have stressed the important part played by space constraints in the growth of manufacturing industries in the largest cities, compared with both the availability and lower prices of industrial floorspace in smaller centres, others (e.g. Lever, 1984) have stressed that small local labour markets offer many enterprises the opportunity of greater control over labour, and even local government, which in turn reduces the element of risk and enhances competitiveness for firms in smaller urban centres. (We return to this point later.) Aggregate data, not only on employment, but also on redundancies, have recently been used to infer behavioural processes in the changing shift from large city to small urban locations (e.g. Townsend, 1981, 1982).

Inferring the organisational behavioural aspects of companies from aggregate data, usually by using multivariate statistical techniques to relate employment change to areal characteristics, presents several conceptual and methodological difficulties. The enterprise, or the establishment, which is the focus of study, is missing from the equation. In order to rectify this omission geographers have turned to the construction of establishment-based data banks. At their simplest level these have permitted 'components-of-change' analyses which resolve aggregate employment change into its several parts — new establishment creations (either new companies or new branches of existing companies), establishment closures, *in situ* growth and decline, and employment change due to movement into or out of the area under study. By relating employment change to type and location of establishment, a fuller understanding of the decisions involved is achieved. Many of these studies have focused on the problems of the economies of the largest cities, referred to above (e.g. Dennis, 1978; Lloyd, 1979; Lloyd and Mason, 1978), and especially their inner areas. The most important elements in the job loss profile of these areas have been plant closures, both in the large and small firm sectors, and the *in situ* contraction of surviving firms, whilst actual outward movement from the cities has been a relatively small component. The behavioural implication of this pattern is that firms have responded to the macro-economic forces of the recession by cutting back or closing, rather than by evaluating whether survival would be possible in a different location. At the same time, these studies have shown that, even during a period of deepening recession (at least prior to 1981), considerable numbers of new firms were being founded, thereby provoking further research into the nature of entrepreneurship.

The extension of the data set into ownership characteristics has permitted further analysis. For example, Lloyd and Reeve (1982) were able to identify 54 'prime movers' in the economy of North West England by ownership type, defined as foreign multi-national owned, UK multiplant company owned and managed from outside the region, locally controlled, and public sector enterprise. Comparing employment change by enterprise type showed that locally controlled plants had experienced a much lower rate of employment decline (−11.8 per cent) between 1975 and 1981 than had those which were either foreign owned (−26.1 per cent) or those which were externally controlled from elsewhere in Britain (−25.4 per cent) (Thompson, 1983). These findings compare with those in an earlier study (Lever, McPhail and Norris, 1978) in which not overall decline but the extent of employment fluctuation in large plants in different ownership types was measured. Once again locally owned and controlled plants were found to have a much more stable employment pattern than foreign multinationals or non-locally controlled plants of British multi-plant companies. In both these studies there is evidence that employers, faced with similar external conditions, respond in different ways so that locally owned plants appear more benign, taking actions which attempt to insulate their workforces from some of the adverse conditions which non-locally controlled plants pass directly on to their employees.

At this point the study of economic change in regions, with the use of establishment-based data banks, passes into the more selective use of individual firm studies or the use of cohort studies (see Hayter and Watts, 1983; Keeble, 1977-79; Wood, 1980-2). Wood (1982) has suggested that establishment-based studies of this type address three major questions in a behavioural context: first, locational choice; secondly, what is the relationship between ownership and economic change; and thirdly, what are the critical external relationships. Whilst locational choice had always been of interest to geographers, renewed interest was sparked by the discussions on the existence of 'mobile' industry which was amenable to relocation when offered government inducements in the form of regional policy, especially in the 1960s (Sant, 1975). Others (e.g. Hamilton, 1974; North, 1974) stressed, however, that mobility and relocation were only one strategy pursued by companies faced with external pressures (including those created by a government which had an explicit spatial policy for the distribution of industry) and that relocation was often regarded as a last resort when other cheaper alternatives had been rejected. As the recession has deepened, relocational decisions have increasingly been taken in the context of closures and contractions rather than as a process of allocating growth. Hamilton (1978) provides a comprehensive survey of 1,500 medium-sized firms who were asked to describe how they had changed their spatial pattern of production. Almost two-thirds of the firms had opened at least one new plant in a 12-year period, but over 600 had also closed at least one plant, with a high level of overlap, so that many firms had both opened and closed plants. Forty-three per cent of the firms had adjusted their spatial patterns by merger and acquisition. Less dramatic (and less costly) adjustments were more common, with over 1,000 of the firms having expanded floorspace at one or more sites in order to avoid setting up a new branch and a substantial number had changed production processes within existing sites.

On ownership, it has become increasingly clear that regional or local economies which are reliant for a large proportion of their employment upon plants which are externally controlled may experience difficulties. Although initially thought to confer benefits upon the recipient regions not only in the form of employment and associated multiplier effects due to plant and wage expenditure but also through the transfer of improved technology, doubts now attach to the wisdom of basing regional economies, typically the regions of the depressed northern and western periphery of the British economy, on inward investment. Functional specialisation within multi-plant and multinational companies appears to ensure that the marginal branch plants are left with routine, low wage activities in the latter stage of the production cycle which leaves the plant vulnerable both to product market changes and production technology change. Even where local autonomy is fairly high, this does not guarantee employment stability. Whilst ownership is undoubtedly an important conceptual variable, methodologically it presents problems of definition. Patterns of investment by shareholders do not accurately define the locus of decision-making any more than do the locations of the directors. Detailed analyses of the corporate decision-making hierarchy may offer some indication of the extent of 'external' control. Even then, what is being defined is control *within* the company and it is possible that external forces imposed by government, major suppliers or major customers via monopsony effects, may be so strong as to remove effective control from within the company altogether.

This brings us to the third of Wood's questions, namely that of external linkages and their relative importance. Studies by Marshall (1979, 1982) have sought to relate linkages to company ownership, and have concluded that, at least for material linkages, volume of output and production technology type were more important explanations. The demand for services, however, is likely to be dictated by the locus of corporate ownership: where a plant is externally controlled there is a much greater probability that services will be supplied from outside the region. There has recently been a good deal of interest in the linkages between the small firm sector and large industrial plants, and work by Storey (1982, 1983) has indicated that regional employment growth policies which lay great stress upon fostering the small firm sector disregard the dependence of this sector for its continued survival upon its links with the large industrial plants, and with the public sector.

Structuralist Theories

As a response to the behavioural theories of industrial decision-making which stress the geography of enterprise, structuralist or radical theories have more recently emerged which stress that the enterprises are part of the wider structure of society in which the interplay of capital and labour is based upon power coalitions whose interests are usually in conflict. Much of industrial geography is concerned with production in the capitalist mode in which capital and labour combine to generate wages for labour and profit for capital, but a growth in one is likely, *ceteris paribus*, to be achieved at the expense of the other. The major elements in the structuralist approach have been the role of very large enterprises in using their economic and political power to achieve authority over their workforces, the role of organised labour in responding to this control, and the overall patterns of change in the world economy. Massey (1979) argued that an alternative, radical approach to neoclassical industrial location theory was required. What was distinctive about this approach, she argued, was firstly that it applied no abstract model of the firm or enterprise. The form of abstraction used was that of isolating the determining structure of the actual situation under study. Only within the context of a severe national economic crisis, and its implications for the production process and consequently for locational requirements, could the spatial behaviour of the individual firms be understood. Secondly, the spatial dimension was introduced only as a last step in the causal sequence: spatial change is viewed only as an effect of the response to non-spatial changes in the macro-economy. Thirdly, by dealing with particular product markets the macro-economic effects are held constant, thus permitting an analysis of different responses by different types of company.

Massey and Meegan (1982) point out that employment change is the net result of two factors, output and productivity *per capita*. They identify on this basis three types of production reorganisation. First, there is intensification, which is defined as changes designed to increase labour productivity without major new investment or changes in production technology. Secondly, there is investment and technical change, where job loss occurs in the context of substantial investment often related to changes in production technology. Lastly there is rationalisation which is defined as a simple reduction in total capacity. Table 1.4 lists 31 industrial sectors by the type of reorganisation which they were undergoing in the period of the late 1960s and early 1970s. Massey and Meegan then go on to examine the spatial implications of the three types of reorganisation. Intensification reduces the level of labour employed in plants but does not involve plant

Table 1.4: Important Forms of Production Reorganisation in the Industries Studied, 1968-73

Rationalisation	Intensification	Investment and technical change
Grain milling	Cycles	Biscuits
Iron castings	Textile finishing	Sugar
Metal-working machine tools	Leather	Brewing and malting
Electrical machinery	Men's and boys' tailored outerwear	Coke ovens
Insulated wires and cables	Footwear	General chemicals
Locomotives and railway track equipment/ railway carriages	Other printing and publishing	Synthetic resins, etc.
		Fertilisers
Weaving of cotton, linen and man-made fibres		Iron and steel/steel tubes
		Aluminium
Woollen and worsted		Miscellaneous base metals
Paper and board		Textile machinery
		Scientific and Industrial instruments and systems
		Cutlery
		Jute
		Carpets
		Bricks and refractory goods

Source: Massey and Meegan, 1982.

closure. It does not have major spatial effects as there are no job transfers between regions and no new job creations at new locations. Rationalisation is different. It involves no new locations, and changes of productive capacity take place within the stock of existing locations. However, job mobility may occur as production is rationalised between sites. The reorganisation of the electrical engineering industry provides good examples of both inter- and intraregional shifts. However, the overall pattern was for recipient areas to gain fewer jobs than those lost in the donor areas, thus creating the concept of the 'transfer loss' of jobs. Technical change, however, does create mobile employment.

In using examples of industries undergoing specific forms of restructuring, Massey and Meegan are able to demonstrate the locational consequences of the three types of change. In the case of rationalisation, the iron-castings industry lost 16,000 jobs between 1968 and 1973. Output *grew* significantly in regions such as Wales and the West Midlands where the buoyant markets for automobile castings and ingot moulds expanded, whereas output in the Northern region was stagnant as sales were dependent upon the declining sectors such as steel manufacture, heavy engineering and shipbuilding. However, changes in output did not correlate with changes in employment, as productivity per worker showed significant differences. Thus in Wales, a 50 per cent rise in output was accompanied by a 35 per cent decline in employment, as continuous casting, mass production methods were introduced, radically improving output per worker. In the North, however, the pattern was different with job loss attributable to complete plant closures (especially amongst smaller plants) rather than to changes in markets and production techniques. Massey and Meegan stressed that in the Northern region the preponderance of small, jobbing foundries made it difficult to increase productivity in the way that the Welsh foundries had, thereby rendering them more vulnerable to closure. As an example of intensification, the tailored outerwear industry is cited. In this sector the range of employment rate changes at the regional level is much narrower than in iron castings. Three regions show small net gains over the study period 1968-73 (Scotland, West Midlands and East Anglia). In this sector some expansion did occur with new branch plants being opened by the medium-sized or larger enterprises. They seem selectively to have picked regions where there was little history of the industry (avoiding the East Midlands and the South East) and where wages were low for garment workers.

In seeking a sector which exhibits the characteristics of investment and technical change, Massey and Meegan selected the fletton brick industry. Whilst some expansion into low wage areas might have been expected when de-skilling took place as a consequence of increased technology, the locational constraints of access to raw material and the patterns of land ownership by the market leading company forced expansions to occur in the same locations as earlier developments.

Using examples of sectors undergoing different types of restructuring, Massey and Meegan introduce a number of factors which contribute to an explanation of regional shifts in employment: these include labour costs, access to local markets, corporate form and size of enterprise, and capital vintage. In an earlier study showing how industrial restructuring had operated to the disadvantage of the inner areas of the largest cities, Massey and Meegan (1978) suggested that capital vintage played an important role. As companies sought to reduce capacity or to improve productivity by technologically upgrading production, it was the oldest plant which was removed and this typically was to be found in the inner areas of the largest cities. Where new plant was installed it was not likely to be installed in the largest cities but at new locations either on the urban periphery or, more probably, in small to medium-sized urban centres. The reasons for this choice lie largely in the different natures of the two types of labour market.

The ability of an employer to control the operation of the local labour market through recruitment, lay-offs and wages, is a function of the relative size of the employer and the labour market. No employer in large cities is likely to be large enough, in relative terms, to be able to influence the performance of the overall local labour market. A single large plant, however, can influence, and in extreme cases control, the local labour force in smaller urban centres. Such control can minimise the risks of high rates of wage inflation, industrial disruption and problems of high labour turnover rates. Lever (1978, 1981) has identified those British local labour markets which could be considered to be dominated by a single non-tertiary employer. He hypothesises that this degree of control is likely to be reflected in lower wages, lower turnover rates and better industrial relations than those experienced by plants of a similar size in similar sectors in larger cities where it would not be possible for a single employer to dominate or control the workforce. It can be argued that where a single employer employs *all* the labour in a local labour market he can depress wages to a point where labour will be prepared to migrate to another town, incurring considerable costs in so doing. In reality such extreme cases are rare and are absent in a closely knit urban structure such as that of Britain. A comparison by McPhail (1982), however, does show (Table 1.5) that hourly wage rates paid by large plants in small towns were lower than those paid by similar plants in non-dominated labour markets. For three different types of labour, skilled male manual, other male manual and female manual, hourly wage rates were 4 per cent to 12 per cent lower in the former type of location. Weekly wages (including overtime, bonuses, etc.) confirmed the existence of these differentials, as Table 1.6 shows. The differential in both cases is greatest for female workers, reflecting the fact that they are less mobile and therefore more likely to be controlled by a major employer in a small labour market.

If wages are lower in these small towns, then it might be expected that despite 'controlling' the local labour market, firms might find difficulty in recruiting some forms of labour. The McPhail study, however, demonstrated that, for all three types of labour covered by the survey, large plants in small labour markets were *less* likely to experience labour shortages than comparable plants in larger towns (Table 1.7). When queried on the reason for this, the former pointed to links with local colleges and schools, the effectiveness of word of mouth recruitment methods and the firm's generally high visibility within the town. Large plants in large towns did not have such a close relationship with the local pool of available labour and claimed to suffer from labour poaching.

Proneness to industrial stoppages is a third area in which dominant plants may be able to exert some control over the labour

Table 1.5: Average Hourly Wages

Skill group	Average hourly wages (pence), 1981		% difference
	Dominant	Control group	
Skilled male manual	160	172	7.3
Other male manual	139	145	4.4
Female manual	126	141	12.5

Source: McPhail, 1982.

Table 1.6: Average Weekly Earnings

Skill group	Average weekly earnings (£), 1981		% difference
	Dominant	Control group	
Skilled male manual	84.9	88.8	4.0
Other male manual	71.9	76.9	6.9
Female manual	58.1	65.3	12.4

Source: Based on McPhail, 1982.

Table 1.7: Labour Shortages

	Dominant			Control group		
	Skilled male	Other male	Female	Skilled male	Other male	Female
Difficulty in recruiting	79%	27%	11%	83%	40%	20%
No difficulty in recruiting	21%	73%	89%	17%	60%	80%

Source: Based on McPhail, 1982.

force. Massey and Meegan (1982) suggest that one reason why, when multi-plant companies reduce capacity by plant closures, they do so by shutting inner city plants, is that levels of unionisation are known to be higher in large cities. Thus by increasingly concentrating production in smaller urban centres, companies are able to reduce levels of union penetration. Fothergill, Kitson and Monk (1982) further emphasise this point by saying that higher levels of union militancy in large cities lower company profitability there. A study comparing firms in Glasgow with a similar group in the smaller manufacturing towns of Lanarkshire (Lever, Danson and Malcolm, 1981) cited industrial relations as a problem in about one-fifth of the plants surveyed, and as a greater problem in the inner city than in the small towns. The same study also found that high rates of labour turnover were a greater problem to inner-city firms than to those in the smaller towns where the range of alternative employment was restricted.

The second area of risk-minimisation is in the field of 'unfortunate effects' of local authority policy. Where a small town is dependent upon a large plant or upon a small number of medium-sized plants, the local authority is likely both to take care that policies such as urban renewal do not adventitiously harm the employers, and to ensure that local authority services can be directed positively to benefit the employers. Large local authorities, however, have such complicated urban strategies that not all the unfortunate effects of some policies can be anticipated. No one employer is likely to be so relatively large as to warrant special treatment by the local authority. Evidence to support this hypothesis, although piecemeal and at times anecdotal, does exist.

The most obvious area of urban policy which may have a prejudicial effect on local industry — urban renewal — is often associated with urban road construction. In the context of Glasgow, early urban renewal was largely restricted to residential areas; the effect on local industry was indirect through dislocation of the local labour market, especially for female workers. As renewal was expanded through the 1960s, more industrial premises were affected, although at first acceptable alternative premises were often not too far away. With the further renewal programmes, however, the stock of old, cheap inner-city premises for industry was significantly eroded and firms displaced later were either forced toward peripheral locations with considerable disruption, accepted new inner-city premises at greatly increased rents, or, increasingly, went out of business (Bull, 1981). The impact of urban renewal on inner-city business, however, greatly exceeds the effect on those firms whose premises lie on the route of new urban roads or are scheduled for treatment within comprehensive development areas. The uncertainty which attaches to the lengthy process of designation, public participation, and consultation before actual implementation, may make it extremely difficult to make rational decisions on such matters as capital investment. A number of firms leaving the eastern part of Glasgow's inner city in favour of locations in New Towns made their choice in the knowledge that the new premises, usually on industrial estates, are unlikely to be affected by uncertainties in the foreseeable future, and that the local labour supply is virtually guaranteed through housing-allocation policies of local authorities. In contrast, inner-city labour markets are often disrupted by urban renewal.

The relationship between the local authority and its large employers, in the case of relatively small towns, may be even closer when employees became elected to the town council. Phelan and Pozen (1973) in a study of the influence of the du Pont company on Wilmington, Delaware, state that the company has the right to nominate members to the State legislature, presumably to safe-guard the company's interests. The political power of large employers in small towns in Britain does not extend as far as that into the democratic process, but Lane and Roberts (1971, pp. 30-1) in a study of the influence of Pilkington's the glass manufac-turing company, at that time employing 32 per cent of the work-force of St. Helens, suggested that:

> No doubt, Pilkington's have given the council the odd nudge from time to time but generally speaking the councillors and aldermen will not have needed reminding that anything affect-ing their (Pilkington's) interests required the most sympathetic and careful consideration. We would be very surprised if any of Pilkington's planning proposals had been rejected.

Conclusion

We have identified three paradigms within which industrial geography has been viewed. In one sense they may be regarded as a chronological sequence with behaviouralism representing a response to the perceived inadequacies of the neoclassical approach, and structuralism being a response to what might be regarded as the failure of behaviouralists to take a sufficiently wide view of macro-economic and social forces such as the interaction of labour and capital. However, most industrial geographers would appear to approach their field of enquiry with at least an element of all three in their theoretical armoury: it is merely the balance between the three which differs. In relating theory to methodology, all three theoretical approaches address the same research problem, namely the acquisition of a better understanding of decisions on location, product, and production, by industry. As in much of the social sciences, rigorous experimentation — the mainstay of the natural sciences — is not available as a research technique. *Post hoc* inference, from macrodata, remains one of the two major methods of approaching the discipline: it has the merit that data are fairly readily available, although their quality is increasingly being called into account, but the demerit that the 'enterprise' dimension is lacking. The establishment-based data banks carry us nearer to an understanding of why businessmen take certain decisions, but very often, in the so-called components-of-change approach, inference again is the main approach. Lastly, the detailed questioning of the actual decision-makers remains the preferred approach despite the fact that it is so much more prodigal of resources.

References

Alonso, W. (1967) 'A reformulation of classical location theory and its relation to rent theory,' *Papers, Regional Science Association 19*, 23-44

Binks, M. and Coyne, J. (1983) 'The birth of enterprise: an analysis and empirical study of the growth of small firms,' Hobart Paper No. 98, Institute of Economic Affairs, London

Bull, P. (1981) 'Redevelopment schemes and manufacturing activity in Glasgow,' *Environment and Planning, 13*, 991-1000

Burns, T. and Stalker, G.M. (1961) *The Management of Innovation*, Tavistock, London

Claus, R.J. and Claus, K.E. (1971) 'Behavioural location theory: a review,' *Australian Geographer, 11*, 522-30

Cyert, R.M. and March, J.G. (1963) *A Behavioural Theory of the Firm*, Prentice-Hall, Englewood Cliffs, N.J.

Czamanski, D.Z. and Czamanski, S. (1977) 'Industrial complexes: their typology, structure and relation to economic development,' *Papers, Regional Science Association, 38*, 93-111

Dennis, R. (1978) 'The decline of manufacturing employment in Greater London,

1966-74,' *Urban Studies, 15,* 63-74

Duncan, R.B. (1972) 'Characteristics of organisational environments and perceived environmental uncertainty,' *Administrative Science Quarterly, 17,* 312-27

Emery, F.E. and Trist, E.L. (1965) 'The causal texture of organisational environment,' *Human Relations, 18,* 21-31

Foster, M.I. (1972) 'Is the south still a backward region, and why?' *American Economic Review, Papers and Proceedings, 62,* 195-203

Fothergill, S. and Gudgin, G. (1982) *Unequal Growth: Urban and Regional Employment Change in the UK,* Heinemann, London

Fothergill, S., Kitson, M. and Monk, S. (1982) 'The profitability of manufacturing industry in the UK conurbations,' Industrial Location Research Project, Working Paper No. 2, Department of Land Economy, University of Cambridge, Cambridge

Fothergill, S., Kitson, M. and Monk, S. (1984) *Urban Industrial Decline: The Causes of Urban/Rural Contrasts in Manufacturing Employment Change,* HMSO, London

Hamilton, F.E.I. (1974) (ed.) *Spatial Perspectives on Industrial Organisation and Decision Making,* Wiley, Chichester

Hamilton, F.E.I. (1978) 'Aspects of industrial mobility in the British economy,' *Regional Studies, 12,* 153-66

Harrison, E.F. (1978) *Management and Organisations,* Houghton-Mifflin, Boston, Mass.

Hayter, R. and Watts, H.D. (1983) 'The geography of enterprise: a reappraisal,' *Progress in Human Geography, 7,* 157-81

Healey, M.J. (1983) 'The changing data base: an overview,' in M.J. Healey (ed.) *Urban and Regional Industrial Research: The Changing UK Data Base,* Geo Books, Norwich

Hoare, A.G. (1975) 'Linkage flows, locational evaluation and industrial geography: a case study of Greater London,' *Environment and Planning, 7,* 41-58

Hoover, E.M. (1937) *Location Theory and the Shoe and Leather Industries,* Harvard University Press, Cambridge, Mass.

Hoover, E.M. (1948) *The Location of Economic Activity,* McGraw-Hill, New York

Keeble, D.E. (1976) *Industrial Location and Planning in the United Kingdom,* Methuen, London

Keeble, D.E. (1977-79) 'Industrial geography,' *Progress in Human Geography, 1,* 304-12; *2,* 318-23; *3,* 425-33

Keeble, D.E. (1980) 'Industrial decline, regional policy and the urban-rural manufacturing shift in the UK,' *Environment and Planning A, 12,* 945-62

Killick, T. (1983) 'Manufacturing plant openings 1976-80: analysis of transfer and branches,' *British Business, 17,* 466-8

Krumme, G. (1969) 'Towards a geography of enterprise,' *Economic Geography, 45,* 30-40

Lane, T. and Roberts, K. (1971) *Strike at Pilkington's,* Collins, London

Leigh, R. and North, D. (1978) 'Regional aspects of acquisition activity in British manufacturing activity,' *Regional Studies, 12,* 227-45

Leontief, W. (1953) 'Domestic production and foreign trade: the American capital position re-examined,' *Proceedings, American Philosophical Society, 97,* 332-49

Leontief, W. (1956) 'Factor proportions and the structure of American trade,' *Review of Economics and Statistics, 38,* 386-407

Lever, W.F. (1978) Company dominated labour markets: the British case. *Tijdshrift voor Economische en Sociale Geografie, 69,* 306-12

Lever, W.F. (1981) 'The measurement and implications of employment concentration ratios in British local labour markets,' *Papers and Proceedings of the Regional Science Association, 47,* 139-54

Lever, W.F. (1982) 'Urban scale as a determinant of employment growth or decline '
in L. Collins (ed.), *Industrial Decline and Regeneration*, Department of
Geography, University of Edinburgh, Edinburgh

Lever, W.F. (1984) 'Industrial change and urban size: a risk theory approach' in
B.M. Barr and N.M. Waters (eds.), *Regional Diversification and Structural
Change*, Tantalus Research, Vancouver

Lever, W.F., Danson, M.W. and Malcolm, J.F. (1981) *Manufacturing and Service
Industries in the Inner City* (Report prepared for the Dept. of the Environment),
Dept. of Social and Economic Research, University of Glasgow

Lever, W.F., McPhail, C. and Norris, G. (1978) *The Dominant Industrial Plant and
Economic Development* (Final Report, Social Sciences Research Council
Project), Dept. of Social and Economic Research, Glasgow

Lloyd, P.E. (1979) 'The components of industrial change for the Merseyside inner
area: 1966-75,' *Urban Studies, 16*, 45-60

Lloyd, P.E. and Mason, C.M. (1978) 'Manufacturing industry in the inner city: a
case study of Greater Manchester,' *Transactions, Institute British Geographers,*
NS, *3*, 66-90

Lloyd, P.E. and Reeve, D.E. (1982) 'North West England 1971-77: a case study in
industrial decline and economic restructuring,' *Regional Studies, 16*, 345-60

McDermott, P. and Taylor, M. (1982) *Industrial Organisation and Location*,
Cambridge University Press, Cambridge

McPhail, C.M. (1982) 'The impact of plant dominance on employer personnel
policy and local labour market behaviour,' Unpublished PhD thesis, University of
Glasgow, Glasgow

Marshall, J.N. (1979) 'Ownership, organisation and industrial linkage: a case study
in the Northern region of England,' *Regional Studies, 13*, 531-58

Marshall, J.N. (1982) 'Organisational theory and industrial location,' *Environment
and Planning A, 14*, 1667-83

Massey, D. (1979) 'A critical evaluation of industrial location theory' in F.E.I.
Hamilton and G.J.R. Linge (eds.), *Spatial Analysis, Industry and the Industrial
Environment, Vol. 1: Industrial Systems*, Wiley, Chichester

Massey, D. and Meegan, R. (1978) 'Industrial restructuring versus the cities,' *Urban
Studies, 15*, 273-88

Massey, D. and Meegan, R. (1982) *The Anatomy of Job Loss*, Methuen, London

Moore, B., Rhodes, J. and Tyler, P. (1980) 'New developments in the evaluation of
regional policy,' Paper presented to the SSRC Urban and Regional Economics
Study Group, University of Birmingham

Moroney, J.R. and Walker, J.M. (1966) 'A regional test of the Heckscher-Ohlin
hypothesis,' *Journal of Political Economy, 74*, 573-86

Moses, L.N. (1958) 'Location and the theory of production', *Quarterly Journal of
Economics, 73*, 259-72

Moses, L.N. (1962) 'Towards a theory of intraurban wage differentials and their
influence on travel patterns,' *Papers and Proceedings of the Regional Science
Association, 9*, 53-63

Muth, R.F. (1969) *Cities and Housing*, University of Chicago Press, Chicago

NEDO (1975) *Financial Tables for the Clothing Industry 1973-74*, NEDO, London

NEDO (1976) *Company Financial Results 1970-71 — 1974-75: Mechanical
Engineering EDC*, NEDO, London

North, D.J. (1974) 'The process of locational change in different manufacturing
organisations in F.E.I. Hamilton (ed.), *Spatial Perspectives on Industrial
Organisation and Decision Making*, Wiley, Chichester

O'Cleireacain, C.C. (1974) 'Labour market trends in London and the rest of the
South East,' *Urban Studies, 11*, 329-39

Palander, T. (1935) *Beitrage zur Standortstheorie*, Almqvist & Wiksells Boktryckeri,
Uppsala

Phelan, J. and Pozen, R. (1973) *The Nader Report, the Company State*, Grossman, New York

Pounce, R.J. (1981) *Industrial Movement in the United Kingdom, 1966-75*, HMSO, London

Pred, A. (1967) 'Behavior and location: foundations for a geographic and dynamic location theory, Part I,' *Lund Studies in Geography*, Series B, 27

Rees, A. and Schultz, G.P. (1970) *Workers and Wages in an Urban Labour Market*, University of Chicago Press, Chicago

Sant, M. (1975) *Industrial Movement and Regional Development: The British Case*, Pergamon, Oxford

Scott, A.J. (1982) 'Locational patterns and dynamics of industrial activity in the modern metropolis,' *Urban Studies, 19*, 111-42

Simon, H.A. (1959) 'Theories of decision-making in economics and behavioral science,' *American Economic Revue, 49*, 253-83

Storey, D.J. (1982) *Entrepreneurship and the New Firm*, Croom Helm, London

Storey, D.J. (1983) 'Job accounts and firm size,' *Area, 15*, 231-7

Streit, M.E. (1969) 'Spatial associations and economic linkages between industries,' *Journal of Regional Science, 9*, 177-88

Thompson, A. (1983) 'The prospects for establishment-level data-banks' in M.E. Healey (ed.), *Urban and Regional Industrial Research: The Changing UK Data Base*, Geo Books, Norwich

Toothill Report (1961) Report of the Committee of Enquiry into the Scottish Economy, Scottish Council for Development and Industry, Edinburgh

Townsend, A.R. (1981) 'Geographical perspectives on major job losses in the United Kingdom 1977-1980,' *Area, 13*, 31-8

Townsend, A.R. (1982) 'Recession and the regions in Great Britain, 1976-1980: analyses of redundancy data,' *Environment and Planning A, 14*, 1389-404

Watts, H.D. (1980) *The Large Industrial Enterprise*, Croom Helm, Beckenham

Weber, A. (1909) *Uber der Standort der Industrien*, translated by C.J. Friedrich as *Weber's Theory of Industrial Location* (1929), University of Chicago Press, Chicago

Wood, P.A. (1969) 'Industrial location and linkage,' *Area, 2*, 32-9

Wood, P.A. (1980-82) Industrial geography, *Progress in Human Geography, 4*, 406-16; *5*, 414-9; *6*, 576-83

Wood, P.A. (1985) 'Behavioural approaches to industrial location studies' in W.F. Lever (ed.), *Industrial Change in the United Kingdom*, Longman, London

2 INDUSTRIAL LINKAGE STUDIES

A.G. Hoare

Linkages past and present

Industrial linkages are often on the front page. December 28th, 1983 saw the collapse of the multi-million pound deal to sell cold slab steel from the British Steel Corporation's loss-making Ravenscraig plant, outside Motherwell, to the United States Steel Corporation's equally loss-making Fairless works in Pennsylvania for further processing. Then in early January 1984, the riots following Peugeot's decision to close its Talbot plant outside Paris threatened supply lines to the company's Ruyton (Coventry) works of French-made body panels, gearboxes and other parts for assembly of the Horizon, Alpine and Solara models in Britain. About a week later the focus switched to Ford's car plant at Dagenham where the management decided to close the foundry that supplied engine blocks for the plant, preferring to import engine blocks from the European mainland. Union officials argued Fords were making Dagenham little more than an assembly factory for Ford parts made elsewhere. Finally, and again from the car industry, on February 1st, MPs were told of the much-leaked agreement by Nissan with the Department of Industry to build a Datsun manufacturing plant somewhere in Britain. Initially the cars would be built from kits imported from the Japanese parent company but the hope is to build up the 'local' (i.e. British and EEC) content of the finished product to 80 per cent of ex works price in 1991.

What these examples have in common is their focus upon one sort of industrial linkage — the movement of manufactured material goods from one factory site to another. In two of the cases the origin and destination factories belong to the same parent company, in the steel case the linkage would have been between two giant but independent producers, while the Nissan case is a hybrid of these two, promising both inter-plant, intra-firm flows and also inter-firm links from a host of European suppliers to the motor trade.

What they also have in common is their international scale,

40

involving interaction between British factories and four other countries, separated by as much as 5,000 miles. This sort of industrial linkage has become a central feature of modern manufacturing economy, but it could scarcely be further removed from the first exposure that most geographical students have to this branch of economic geography.

Consider, for example, the view espoused by Alfred Marshall writing as the sun set on his country's pre-eminence as a world industrial power:

> When an industry has once thus chosen a locality for itself, it is likely to stay there long; so great are the advantages which people following the same skilled trade get from near neighbourhood to one another. The mysteries of the trade become no mysteries; but are as it were in the air, and children learn many of them unconsciously. Good work is rightly appreciated; inventions and improvements in machinery, in processes and the general organization of the business have their merits promptly discussed; if one man starts a new idea it is taken up by others and combined with suggestions of their own, and thus becomes the source of further new ideas. And presently subsidiary trades grow up in the neighbourhood, supplying it with implements and materials, organizing its traffic, and in many ways conducing to the economy of its material.
>
> Again, the economic use of expensive machinery can sometimes be attained in a very high degree in a district in which there is a large aggregate production of the same kind, even though no individual capital employed in the trade be very large. For subsidiary industries devoting themselves each to one small branch of the process of production, and working it for a great many of their neighbours, are able to keep in constant use machinery of the most highly specialized character; and to make it pay its expenses, though its original cost may have been high, and its rate of depreciation very rapid. (Marshall, 1898, pp. 178-9)

Those geographers who examined the detailed industrial structures of the agglomerations of Marshall's age placed a similar emphasis upon the spatial binding forces exercised by these industrial linkages (Keeble (1969) provides a summary of this work relating to Britain). But working from an historical perspective they inevitably lacked access to detailed information on actual flows among the member firms of these agglomerations: instead, they were forced to a methodology of detailed mapping of industrial producers in similar lines of manufacture, supplemented with fragmentary documentation throwing light on some bits and pieces of the industrial world of the last century. The present intention is not to decry this scholarship, which had many admirable properties, nor to suggest that its 'agglomeration through linkage' message was wrong (the reasons why mutual proximity would bring mutual economic benefit are far more convincing in the industrial environment of the last century than this). Rather it is to suggest that this Marshallian view of linkage may have survived beyond its time.

Thus we find that some of the authorities on the industrial geography of the last century bring forward these self-same ideas to apply them to the modern spatial patterning of manufacturing in the same cities. London is a prime example, as Keeble (1969) demonstrates with the views of Hall and Martin on the (presumed) importance of local industrial linkage attractions in the growth of modern engineering and vehicle trades in west London. And more generally, it seems almost obligatory for modern textbooks to treat the question of industrial linkages under some broad heading relating to 'agglomeration', 'external economies' and the like. The seed of the idea thus is sown that industrial linkages are *still* a powerful sustainer of industrial agglomerations.

So just as the geography of industry may have been slow to cast off the patterns inherited from an earlier age so industrial geographers may have been hesitant in discarding some of the thinking associated with these earlier geographies. But attitudes are changing rapidly. The second half of this chapter reviews what can only be a selection of recent work in industrial linkage geography to illustrate these changes, but before that we review some of the reasons why geographers are interested in such linkages, and what, indeed, they think industrial linkages are.

Geography and Linkages

Definitions and sub-divisions

Look up 'industrial linkages' in the index of most modern industrial geography texts and you will look in vain. Most just provide an entry for 'linkages' instead, and under this heading you are likely to find a very wide spectrum of the inter-relationships between manufacturing firms and each other, between them and other sectors of the economy, and between them and the wider environment. But you will find too industrial linkages in the sense used in this chapter, a sense probably best understood by means of Figure 2.1.

Here we depict a manufacturing plant as being locked into a wider web of flows of material items and/or what for want of a better shorthand is usually termed 'information', associated with both of which there is always a monetary transaction and sometimes too, a movement of personnel of the linked partners. Thus the plant P in Figure 2.1 receives raw materials from producers in the primary sector (R) or, from fellow manufacturing plants, materials processed beyond the 'raw material' state to a greater or lesser degree (M_p) (confusingly, some writers refer to these also as 'raw materials'). Other manufacturers (M_e) will supply equipment and machinery for the processes undertaken at P, while others still will provide subcontracting services (M_s) by undertaking some manufacturing process at the specific behest of, and to the particular requirements of, client firm P (Friedman, 1977). Sometimes the subcontractor may receive the relevant material for treatment from P and return it there duly processed, but sometimes it comes directly from M_p- or R-type suppliers at P's instructions. Sometimes, too, the subcontractor may undertake the full range of the work normally undertaken at P as when demand temporarily exceeds P's capacity to supply the market. Further inputs to P come in the form of information from service sector firms (S) such as its legal advisers, accountants, advertising agents, computer data processors, marketing consultants and transport hauliers. Taken together, these inputs are dubbed '*backward* linkages' in the geographical literature. The other side of the coin, '*forward* linkages', represents flows to P's customers. Here material linkages are all important, although P can sometimes make money through forward information flows, as when it provides technical information for a brother producer, perhaps leading to an agreement to manufacture under licence. Again, these forward links can be to all sectors of the economy. Some of these want P's output as it stands, and not for any further processing ('final consumption'). So if P makes typing paper he can sell to householders (H) either directly or, more commonly, through the retail

Figure 2.1: A Schematic Representation of a Manufacturing Plant's Linkages

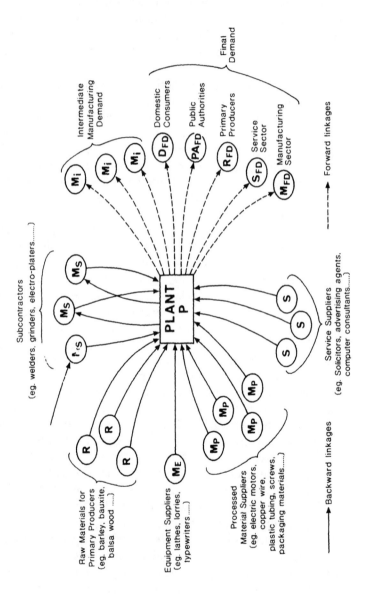

sector (R_{fd}). Equally, he could sell to offices in the service sector (S_{fd}) to public authorities (PA_{fd}) as well as to the stationery-consuming sections of manufacturing firms (M_{fd}) or of primary producers (R_{fd}). But output from P can also be the inputs for further links in a chain of manufacturing, so the forward link to other manufacturers of such 'intermediate' sales (M_i) become the backward (M_p-type) links for another set of manufacturers further down the line.

Figure 2.1 does not embrace all the flows of goods and information with which a firm may be involved — sample goods may have to be inspected by the public health authority periodically, staff may visit trade meetings, government departments, trade union offices, and information may be disbursed to the local and national press or be received from the consumers association of the local chamber of commerce. Even so, such flows are not as essential to the commercial being of the firm as those in Figure 2.1, nor do they usually involve a monetary exchange between affected parties, hence their exclusion from further discussion here, although they can form an important ingredient in the 'office linkage' literature as reviewed by Goddard (1975).

This, then, represents the broadest framework within which the great majority of industrial linkage studies are to be found and hence forms the outer limits of the way the term will be interpreted here. The relative importance of the different material and information flows shown will obviously vary from firm to firm, and plant to plant within a firm. Thus a yoghurt maker will buy in materials from the primary sector, from other manufacturers (sugar, containers etc.) as well as necessary business input services, while his output will be entirely confined to the 'final demand' sector. A producer of sheet steel, though, might buy in relatively more from primary producers than other manufacturers (depending on whether or not his plant is an integrated steel mill) and sell exclusively within the intermediate output sector to other manufacturers. In these and other cases, too, a proportion of the links of Figure 2.1 may be between locations owned by the same parent firm, rather than between different firms. As we shall see, the way these inter-site, intra-firm links are organised can be very different geographically from inter-firm ones, and they have become relatively more important through time.

It must not be thought that those links encapsulated in Figure 2.1 represent a universal consensus view among geographers as to what 'industrial linkages' are. Far from it. Many geographical writers are surprisingly reluctant to nail their colours to the mast in this respect so one has to judge their definition more by inference from what they write. Keeble is one exception, and for him industrial linkages occur 'when one manufacturing firm purchases inputs of goods or services from, or sells outputs to, another manufacturing firm' (Keeble, 1976 p. 61). Presumably we could write 'plant' for 'firm' since later he presents interesting maps of interplant linkages among the various United Kingdom units of Chrysler. One wonders, too, why service (information) inputs from other manufacturers are included, but not those from the tertiary (services) sector, inherently a more likely source of such inputs. While some writers take a similarly tight 'manufacturer-to-manufacturer' view of linkages (e.g. Huggett & Meyer, 1981; Jarrett, 1977), many others take a wider perspective, so the *Dictionary of Human Geography* (Johnston, 1981) considers that 'as far as industrial geography is concerned "backward linkages" involve *all* other firms which provide it [the manufacturing company], its goods and services' and 'forward linkages' as 'involving *all* of its customers'. With the same proviso as before about 'plants' and 'firms' this otherwise seems identical to the widest bounds of Figure 2.1. Of course, some writers deliberately limit their attention to certain sorts of linkages within these broad limits to make their studies manageable and/or to plug some perceived gap in the academic literature, while for others who embrace what we shall label the 'macro' research approach, pre-existing data structures may prescribe how 'linkage' has to be interpreted.

All this might seem to be hair-splitting, but is not really. There is no reason to believe that all the types of links depicted in Figure 2.1 behave in the same way geographically. As just one example, in their survey of linkages among Swedish manufacturers Fredriksson and Lindmark (1979) claim that their surveyed firms obtain only about 10 per cent of their inputs from other local industrial firms, but if wholesalers and retailers are included the local input rises substantially to nearly one-third. Our views on the geography of industrial linkages may well thus depend heavily upon how we choose to interpret this term.

Although other classifications of linkages are to be found in text books (e.g. Hurst, 1972, pp. 128-9; Jarrett, 1977, p. 72; Riley, 1973, pp. 5-6), that between 'forward' and 'backward' is a particularly useful one when explaining the 'applied' relevance of industrial linkings. Another important practical question, and one we have ignored so far, is that of the spatial scale(s) over which these flows can and do take place. Are any of plant P's linkages likely to be short distance? If so, which, why, and has this changed over time? In the answers to these sorts of questions lies much of the interest and importance of the geographical examination of industrial linkages.

The Practical Importance of Industrial Linkages

Linkages as a Factor in Location and Relocation. Later evidence will show how widely linkage considerations are quoted as an important consideration when industrial firms come to make location choices. Assuming that some economic logic underlies such survey responses it follows that manufacturing plants which locate away from their optimal locations in terms of access to backward and forward linkages will, *ceteris paribus*, suffer financial penalties through higher costs than otherwise necessary or through reduced revenues (or both). Hence profits will be lower, growth potential less and long term economic viability more uncertain. If so, the national economy too has at least some of its industry operating at less than full throttle in the competitive world economy. Hence the break-up of industrial agglomerations, however desirable on a host of other economic, social and environmental issues as Barlow (1940) was among the first to demonstrate, may have its debit side too. On the same theme, we might go on to argue that certain plants in an agglomeration may be less intimately locked into it than others and, again other things being equal, might be the best candidates for decentralisation. As far as destination locations are concerned, too, there are advantages in attracting new investment that will lock itself into the existing network of linkage partners in the new region rather than retaining its old links (Livesey, 1972). Some destination regions may be more suitable for certain types of in-migrant firms — for example, a region with a strong metal-working base to migrant engineering plants. Similarly Hewlett Packard stated that its decision to establish disc drive production in north Bristol in 1981 was partly influenced by the established complex of potential suppliers in the same part of the city, serving its existing aerospace complex.

Diffusion of Economic Growth and Decline through Space

Industrial linkages provide an important channel whereby what happens economically at one location influences what happens at others. Thus, referring again to Figure 2.1, if plant P increases output following a rise in demand this should stimulate increased monetary flows along its backward linkage paths to the localities of its various suppliers, which in turn, may stimulate further expansion of them and their backward linkage suppliers, and so on. Forward linkages are unlikely to react in the same way (there seems no reason why others of P's customers will buy more from it merely because it is raising its output for one of them) and so backward linkages are seen as being the more important channel in this transmission of economic impulses (see Campbell, 1974). If P's business declines a similar, though negative, set of impulses will pass down the same linkage paths, while if it is hit by strike action the impacts will be felt by suppliers, (whose outlet for work is disrupted), by its customers (whose production schedules may be thrown to the winds), and by the communities dependent on them both. These interactions among linkage partners, whether positive or negative, represent one of the routes by which the economic multiplier operates, to enhance further some initial change in activity in part of the economy through its interdependencies with others.

The apparently logical extension of this argument is the formal planning of 'growth centres' or 'growth poles' to establish, in a confined geographical area, a nexus of linked economic processes to the mutual convenience and economic benefit of all concerned. This spatial extension of Perroux's original aspatial concept gained much currency in the spatial planning of developed and underdeveloped countries alike (Kuklinski, 1981; Moseley, 1974). The archetypal example of this is seen in the Soviet Union's policy of planning 'territorial production complexes' a concept first explored in 1947 by Kolosovski (see Linge *et al.*, 1978; Pallot and Shaw, 1981; Smith, 1981). Here, productive activities could be assigned to 'linked' groups of activities and planned spatially to maximise the proximity of linked sectors and in regions endowed with the physical resources suitable for the *raison d'etre* of the complexes (ferrous metals, petrochemicals, lumbering, or whatever).

In practice, linkage flows outside the USSR (and within it?) have not always followed the planners' intentions, leading to far less ancillary development than hoped for (Moseley's (1974) study of two Expanded Towns in East Anglia and Rodgers' (1979) study of the Alfa Sud plant's impact in the Naples region are but two examples). More recently, in-depth studies of the variety of controls upon whether new industrial implantations do stimulate local growth have led to more sophisticated policy proposals to maximise this benefit, such as those of O'Farrell and O'Loughlin (1981), from their study of grant-aided manufacturing investment in Ireland.

Linkages Broaden the Mind. A third and more contentious argument over the practical significance of linkage flows is that they serve as a sort of 'Indian scout' mechanism whereby manufacturers can build up experience of, and confidence in, ever wider segments of space as operating environments. Taylor (1975) suggests that material linkages, followed by information ones, serve to widen a firm's knowledge of space through time from its existing base, and that this in turn encourages a wider casting around for possible operating locations when such are needed. If so, this represents an important way in which geographical behaviour and geographical location of manufacturers interact (Hoare, 1983), with the leading role being assumed by the firm's linkage requirements and associated procedures. Such a view has not passed unchallenged (Harrison *et al.*, 1979) but Taylor's interesting model demonstrates how linkages might be viewed as precursors of major changes in the geographical growth of particular firms, and not merely as camp-followers.

Linkages: Short-distance or Long-distance?

Given the practical importance of linkages, what factors will influence their geographical patterning?

As we have seen, the nineteenth century view of linkages placed strong emphasis on the 'short distance' nature of such flows. From the standpoint of the 1980s we might identify one set of forces that could still encourage locally constrained linkage flows and another set that could encourage their wider dispersal.

Distance Constraining

(a) Economic. (i) <u>Transport costs</u>: Transport *costs* might seem the most important factor here. The shorter the distance, the lower the cost of shipment of materials, whether to customers or from suppliers: so argued the PEP report on industrial location in

Britain, at the eve of the last war: 'the usual reason for juxta-position of linked industries is to minimise transport costs ...' (PEP, 1939, p. 82)

Writing nearly four decades later Lloyd and Dicken are more cautious, prefacing their discussion of 'distance minimisation' among linked activities thus, 'apart from the *apparently* obvious transfer-cost benefits of close spatial juxtaposition ...' (1977, p. 290). The fact is that since the last war transport costs have been shown to represent only a small percentage of total production costs in manufacturing in advanced economies (around 5 per cent as a rough British average, perhaps, though measurement problems and industry-to-industry variance have to be entered as caveats (Edwards, 1970)), and of this the 'terminal' element, invariant with distance, represents well over half of the transport costs for the average industrial haul in Britain (Chisholm and O'Sullivan, 1973). Many goods also now are charged on a 'delivered price' basis independent of the distance between supplier and customer, so, all in all, we have ample reason not to place too much stress on this particular 'rationale' for distance restraint among linked companies.

(ii) <u>Transport time</u>: Not so with time. Thus, quoting from a then-contemporary survey, Dennison (1939) noted the importance for manufacturers to have contact with the London market where 'the question is often one of being able to supply orders in the least possible time' (p. 70). Close proximity to suppliers means that any shortages or breakdowns can be rectified quickly. Disruption can be kept to a minimum. Dennison noted that the clothing trade was a good example 'where retailers (and even wholesalers) may order one day for delivery the next, in which case even an hour's difference in the time taken by transport may be an important matter' (p. 70). A reliable contact with one's suppliers also reduces the need to maintain extensive stocks, which can be space-consuming, and also lock up capital, both in the stocks and storage space, that can be better employed elsewhere. Thus printing firms in New York city devote only half the proportion of their assets to stocks that those outside the city do (Lloyd and Dicken, 1977), while Soderman (1975) cites a leather goods firm which had to increase its stock holding by 20 per cent on moving some 180 miles from the east end of London to Barnstaple. And on an international scale Delta Airlines reportedly granted its aero-engine contract in December 1980 to the American Pratt and Whitney company rather than Britain's Rolls Royce over the questionable reliability of trans-Atlantic supply links.

(iii) <u>Staff travel</u>: Many material and information flows will also involve travel of staff of linked companies, in any or all of which the value of minimal inconvenience to staff, and minimal disruption in their work schedules, may be far more important than the monetary cost of the petrol or rail fare involved. Such considerations are likely to be most marked in industries where business conditions fluctuate widely in a short time placing a premium on person-to-person connections, as with printing companies specialising in 'one off' jobs and fashion firms manufacturing for a highly volatile and unpredictable *haute couture* clientele.

(b) *Psychological.* (i) <u>Spatial perception of possible contacts</u>: To the extent that these links depend upon personal knowledge and recommendation, potential suppliers close at hand are more likely to be known about and thus considered for supply work than those 50 miles away. Limited awareness of market outlets may have a similar restraining effect on forward linkages.

(ii) <u>Local loyalty</u>: Here, Estall and Buchanan (1980, p. 149) present the interesting argument that local linkages may be based on subtle social reasons, which translate into preferential linkage treatment for those close at hand.

(iii) <u>Risk minimisation</u>: Once local links are forged, manufacturers may subsequently assume an attitude towards them better described by the 'behavioural' approach to decision-making than the 'economic man' model. The continued localisation of industrial linkages thus becomes bound up 'not with pecuniary benefits but simply reduced perceived risk and uncertainty of their operations' (Taylor, 1980, p. 266), an attitude of mind and explanation of localised linkages the same author has dubbed 'parochialism'.

Any or all of these psychological and economic arguments can help bind together geographically an individual pair of linked activities. Bear in mind, though, that most manufacturers draw on a large number of input suppliers and serve several different markets so their location in a substantial manufacturing centre, close to a multitude of existing and potential linkage contacts, increases cumulatively in importance with the complexity of their linkage structures. And the large industrial agglomeration also enhances the *choice* of contact partners available within a given distance, making it more likely that the manufacturer will find suppliers able to meet his demanding supply needs or providing the types of market outlets he is seeking.

(c) *Political.* Though operating on a wider spatial scale than the others above, this too can constrain the length of linkage contacts as when a particular company comes under political pressure to keep its lucrative linkages within the confines of a particular nation. The Nissan example quoted earlier is a case in point. In political systems with strong sub-national tiers of government the same might operate at more localised scales.

(d) *Technological.* The natures of some industrial processes themselves may predispose linked activities to locate close together. Avoidance of heat loss in the further moulding of iron or steel is a popular example, while in petrochemical complexes the dangers in handling refinery gases for use in 'downstream' chemical processes under extremes of temperature and pressure, places a premium on minimising the distance over which they are moved to plants which transform them into more solid, and transportable, products. (Chapman, 1970)

Dispersal-inducing Forces

(a) *Economic.* (i) <u>Improved communications</u>: Any improvement in information communications from the penny post to the most sophisticated modern confravision and electronic data transmission system erodes the need for linkage proximity. The significance of such improvements now lies more in improving reliability, convenience and speed, although transport cost savings can still be significant as in the 'freeing' effect of pipeline technology upon petrochemical and refinery-based industrial complexes (Chapman, 1970).

(ii) <u>Standardisation of production</u>: As particular products move through the stages of the so-called product cycle (see Vernon, 1979, for example) to mass production in standardised form so the scheduling of production becomes easier and unexpected interruptions to production fewer. Strikes and plant failures still occur, but there should be none of the teething-trouble disruptions of the early, prototype stages of manufacture. It comes as no surprise to find manufacturers prepared to locate plants producing large runs of standardised products with less concern for industrial agglomerations (though there are other factors stimulating this same trend).

(iii) <u>The growth of the big company</u>: Advanced economies display abundant evidence of the growing share of industrial output controlled by a small number of industrial corporations (Prais, 1976). Accompanying this, too, has been a growth in the numbers of plants so controlled. The larger the company the more it is able to undertake internally more and more processes and services for which it otherwise would seek outside linkage partners. Its multi-plant, multi-locational form also offers the modern industrial company the potential to specialise in particular functions as geographically appropriate (a cheap labour region for a labour-intensive produce, a major university town for its R. and D. site). The consequent need for inter-plant transfers may be of minor significance when set against the ability to programme production to a central timetable without dependence on the whims of outside suppliers, and the ability to transport materials inter-plant in 'own fleet' vehicles or those hired at very favourable rates from outside suppliers on the strength of the large firm's bargaining muscle.

(b) *Political.* (i) The planned location of industrial plants by local or central authorities can help break up linked industrial agglomerations. In Britain withholding planning permission, compulsory purchase orders on decrepit industrial premises and establishing corporation-run industrial estates can all lead to a local scale re-sorting of industrial quarters, while nationally spatial selectivity in the granting of Industrial Development Certificates and of Assisted Area incentives do the same.
(ii) For their own 'political' reasons companies may not wish to maintain dependence on one single supplier for a critical input, so the geographical proximity of 'single sourcing' may be sacrificed in a deliberate widening both of the companies with whom contracts are placed and of the areas drawn upon for inputs.
(iii) Third, close international integration as among the production economies of the countries of Eastern Europe partly reflects the desire of the dominant partner in Comecon, the Soviet Union, to maintain the dependence of its satellite states upon its own economy (Bora, 1979; Kortus and Kaczorowski, 1979).

(c) *Technological/Strategic.* In some sensitive industrial activities a list of approved suppliers for particular tasks, from which relevant manufacturers have to select, may be drawn up by government departments. Given the demanding and specialist nature of such work 'distance minimisation' criteria are not likely to play a major part in this filtering process. Thus subcontractors used by British Aerospace have to rely on that company's approved list of tried and tested suppliers, compiled by the company's Quality Assurance department on behalf of the Civil Aviation Authority (Daniell, 1982).

From this inventory of possible controls on the geography of linkages we can see that, not only is this subject to a range of conflicting pulls, but also that the dispersal-inducing forces are likely to have become more powerful through time (economic growth going hand in hand with communications advances, corporate growth and greater government involvement in industrial location, for example). How have these conflicting influences impressed themselves in practice upon the evolution of manufacturing linkages in advanced economies?

The Geography of Linkages

In the next two sections we review progress made by researchers into the geographical nature of industrial linkages. This neatly falls into two categories: first, 'macro' research work has analysed industrial data in fairly aggregated form and, second, 'micro' work concentrates on the collection and analysis of field data on linkages, at the level of the individual firm or plant.

Macro Studies

Given the cost of such original 'micro' data there is an obvious appeal in the use of second-best but readily available data, especially as this usually relates to a far larger trawl of manufacturing firms than can be covered by even the most enthusiastic field team. In turn this sheds light on linkage issues in three main ways.

(a) *The Aggregate Geography of Industrial Employment.* The first, bearing in mind the previous argument that linkage bonds acting upon manufacturing plants may be less geographically restraining than of yore, is the question of the degree to which the manufacturing sector does agglomerate, and how this has changed through time.

National censuses of employment disaggregated by economic sector and by spatial sub-division supply the obvious input data for this. The United States and Great Britain have been the most intensively studied in this respect. In the first, geographers have claimed to identify a decentralisation of manufacturing jobs at a number of scales — the regional, intra-regional and from inner cities to outer suburbs (Cohen and Berry, 1975). Between 1969 and 1978, for example, once we standardise definitional boundaries, the share of manufacturing jobs in the 50 largest Standard Metropolitan Labour Areas fell from 51.8 per cent to 47.8 per cent with a corresponding rise in non-metropolitan areas from 26.1 per cent to 29.9 per cent (Estall, 1983), although many of the latter areas were 'urban fringe' rather than 'deep rural' localities. At the grander, regional, level the same period saw the relative and absolute decline of similar jobs in the traditional industrial heartland regions of the north east and a rise in the 'Sun Belt' south and west (Estall, 1983). The same goes for Britain. Taking a rather longer time period and examining manufacturing job distributions at the scale of the counties (or groups thereof) shows how, while consistently more clustered at this scale than jobs in the economy as a whole, manufacturing jobs have again become less concentrated over time, and especially so since about 1951 (Hoare, 1983). We cannot conclude what part, if any, the loosening of spatial linkage constraints has played here, but we can at least see that, overall, the forces of agglomeration are not as powerful as they once were.

(b) *The Agglomeration of Particular Industrial Sectors.* Little attention has been paid by linkage studies to the pattern of concentration of particular industries taken in isolation, surprisingly so given the amount of linkage interaction occurring within the confines of individual industrial slices of the manufacturing economy. In the British national input-output table of 1974, for example, 17 per cent by value of all manufacturing-to-manufacturing flows recorded were within the same 'industry', some 14 times the amount one would expect on a 'fair share' basis given that the manufacturing sector was disaggregated into 82 individual industries. We cannot use this same fine-grained disaggregation to examine the changing geography of industrial concentration, rather a much coarser 17-industry basis for which directly comparable data are available over time (Lee, 1979).

Clearly, the coarser the industrial classification used the higher the percentage of input-output flows that will qualify as 'intra-industry' and the stronger should be linkage bonds operating within these industrial categories rather than between them. Examining industrial employment change in this way at the regional scale in Britain shows how almost every industry's jobs have become more widely spread over the nation's ten regions in the half century since 1921 when set against the regional distribution of manufacturing jobs as a whole (Hoare, 1983). Chemicals, a capital-intensive industry with some peculiar linkage ties of its own is the main exception. Although the data do not tell us *why* this is happening, this aspect of Britain's industrial geography is again trending in the same way as a weakening of the spatial constraints of industrial linkage would imply.

(c) Inter-sectoral Linkages and Geographies. By far the largest part of the 'macro' work has focused on links between different industries rather than within them, and the basic logic behind such work can perhaps best be understood by means of Figure 2.2. Here certain sectors of the economy (shown here by pairs of industries, though the logic is extendable to multi-industry groupings) are 'spatially linked' (SL) through displaying similar geographical distributions. Similarly, some others (IL in Figure 2.2) are 'linked' through industrial linkages as defined earlier, and as measured through input-output tables. A third group of industrial pairs is associated in both these ways (IL & SL in Figure 2.2) and a final set (NOL) in neither of them. The basic intention of a by-now extensive literature is to unravel all or part of Figure 2.2 in terms of the types of industrial groupings falling into these four categories. For some researchers the emphasis is on one or other of these groups rather than the full suite of them. Roepke *et al.*, (1974) concentrate upon the IL subset, while for others the SL subset is the focus, as with Bergsman *et al.*, (1972, 1975), although in both these cases comments are usually made about the possible tie-ins with the 'other' subset. Thus Roepke *et al.*'s examination of industrial links among Ontario manufacturers suggests incorporating the spatial dimension as the next obvious line of research. At times, though, workers claim more for their results than is justified here, as when Campbell (1972) draws inferences from his IL-type analysis of the Washington state economy about the suitability of industrial groups so identified for growth pole planning, despite his

not showing whether these groups display any corresponding associations in the state's economic *geography*. For others more attention is given to the overlap group (IL & SL), where spatial and functional linkage is combined (Czamanski and Czamanski, 1977). This type of research as a whole tends to be characterised by detailed accounts, illustrations and tables of the minutiae of composition of the particular group under the microscope.

Another body of macro work looks more closely at the *relative sizes* of the four groups in Figure 2.2 and asks whether inter-industry groups characterised by one type of linkage also display the other, and whether absence of one goes with absence of the other. If so, we should expect to find the IL + SL and NOL segments of Figure 2.2 appreciably larger than those of IL and of SL. As this involves more explicit emphasis on the *spatial* significance of industrial linkage flows we shall concentrate more on the results of this work, but before so doing it is important to back-

Figure 2.2: Types of Linkage among Different Industries

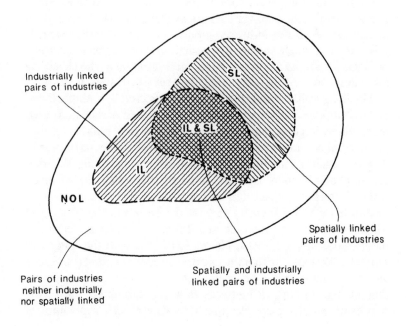

track a little to appreciate the variety of ways in which both spatial and industrial linkage can be measured in this sort of study.

(d) Industrial Linkage. Where the spotlight is on *pair-wise* relationships two industries are considered as linked if their monetary input-output transaction exceeds some threshold value. Figure 2.3 shows the principle at issue and the variations upon it. To identify *groups* of more than two industries so linked three alternative approaches are popular. The first makes use of factor analysis (e.g. Roepke *et al.*, 1974) on input data derived from some aspect of the flow matrix among industries (and here yet further modifications are current — compare Czamanski, 1971 and Roepke *et al.*, 1974, for example) to identify common groupings of industries. These may represent groups based on similar profiles of inputs alone, or just of outputs, or of the two in aggregate. Industries may not be allocated unambiguously to one and only one grouping, nor need there be strong direct flows between each and every member of any one group — indeed, it is quite possible for a group to consist of members with no intra-group flows whatsoever, brought together through sharing similar patterns of interaction with the other 'non group' industries in the economy.

Cluster analysis, in its various forms, forms the second route. Here again a number of variants are available, some of which lead to mutually-exclusive industrial groups, in contrast to factor analysis. Like it, though, the input transactions data can be in a variety of forms leading to a corresponding multiplication in the clustering procedures that can be run on any data set (see Harrigan, 1982).

Finally, graph theoretical measures, pioneered by Campbell and Slater, employ indices of industry-to-industry association used more widely in geographical studies of networks to build up groups of inter-linked industries. The direction as well as the magnitude of flow (set against some threshold constraint) is important. Whether the emphasis is upon backward linkages (Campbell, 1974) or on forward flows as well, a set of *ad hoc* house rules is often necessary to decide on which industry to base the groups in the first place, which to allocate to them subsequently, and when to terminate them (see Campbell, 1974; Slater, 1977). As with the other two grouping versions, no guarantees are offered that strong (or indeed any) transactions exist between each intra-group pair, a feature that Latham (1976) at least sees as a strong selling point of the outwardly simpler pair-wise approach. Given such a plethora of

Figure 2.3: The Measurement of Pair-wise Relationships between Industries

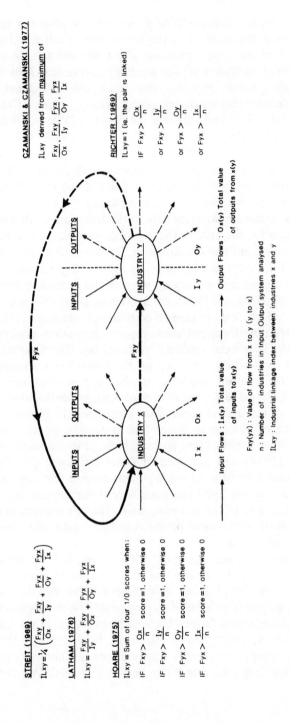

STREIT (1969)

$$ILxy = \tfrac{1}{4}\left(\frac{Fxy}{Ox} + \frac{Fxy}{Iy} + \frac{Fyx}{Oy} + \frac{Fyx}{Ix}\right)$$

LATHAM (1976)

$$ILxy = \frac{Fxy}{Iy} + \frac{Fxy}{Ox} + \frac{Fyx}{Oy} + \frac{Fyx}{Ix}$$

HOARE (1975)

ILxy = Sum of four 1/0 scores when:

IF $Fxy > \frac{Ox}{n}$ score =1, otherwise 0

or $Fxy > \frac{Iy}{n}$ score =1, otherwise 0

IF $Fyx > \frac{Oy}{n}$ score =1, otherwise 0

IF $Fyx > \frac{Ix}{n}$ score =1, otherwise 0

CZAMANSKI & CZAMANSKI (1977)

ILxy derived from <u>maximum</u> of

$$\frac{Fxy}{Ox}, \frac{Fxy}{Iy}, \frac{Fyx}{Oy}, \frac{Fyx}{Ix}$$

RICHTER (1969)

ILxy =1 (ie. the pair is linked)

IF $Fxy > \frac{Ox}{n}$

or $Fxy > \frac{Iy}{n}$

or $Fyx > \frac{Oy}{n}$

or $Fyx > \frac{Ix}{n}$

Input Flows : Ix(y) Total value of inputs to x(y)

Output Flows : Ox(y) Total value of outputs from x(y)

Fxy(yx) : Value of flow from x to y (y to x)

n : Number of industries in Input Output system analysed

ILxy : Industrial linkage index between industries x and y

measuring techniques it might be asked whether any results will be more a consequence of the use of one or other technique rather than of anything significant about the industrial and/or spatial linkage structures of the economy concerned. Two independent studies tackle precisely this point, but unfortunately, as one concludes that results are pretty 'technique-free' (Czamanski and Ablas, 1979) and the other the opposite (Taylor, 1980), this must remain as disputatious a question as it is a vital one!

(e) Spatial Linkage. This, conventionally, is tackled through the correlation coefficient between pairs of industries over the appropriate set of geographical observation units. Most writers argue that crude employment data, by industry, are inadequate in themselves for the task, without further modification. One such is to correlate not raw employments, but the percentage contribution of each industry to a given area's overall employment, thus filtering out the effects of varying sizes of the recording areas (Richter, 1969; Harrigan, 1982). An alternative is to attempt to 'correct' for the effects of more general non-linkage urbanisation economies by correlating industrial employments once other conurbation influences have been removed in some way. The Czamanskis (1977) are the trail-blazers here, but their method of standardising only one of a pair of correlated variables against conurbation size is not well argued and a question mark hangs over the logic of the exercise if the sizes of some urban centres are the part consequence of linkage-inducing agglomeration in the first place. Finally, neither of these modifications deals with the problem, cited by Roepke *et al.* (1974) and discussed in detail by Hoare (1975), that such correlations of areal employments assume that any spatial attraction between industrial pairs is conveniently captured within the boundaries of the recording units. Hoare's solution is to correlate pairs of employment potential surfaces rather than area job totals as such.

So much for methods, what of results? In particular, have geographers found any tendency for pairs of groups of industries that are linked in an input-output sense also to adopt similar geographical patterns of employment? The short answer is 'yes', by and large, they have. This is so from studies in the United States (Richter, 1969), Britain (Harrigan, 1982; Lever, 1975) and West Germany (Streit, 1969). The implication is *not* that each and every industrially linked industry pair is also spatially linked and *vice versa*, merely that, statistically, there is more than a fair share chance of this happening, so that, in terms of Figure 2.2, IL + SL and NOC are proportionately large compared to IL and SL. Although similar studies in France (Streit, 1969) and, at the intra-urban scale, within London (Hoare, 1975) are less convincing on this point, we have, on balance, an *a priori* case for industrial linkages having at least some geographical expression within advanced economies where we might expect those liberating forces as discussed above to be most developed. The same is true of studies taking a rather different approach of seeing how far the geography of individual industries corresponds to the idea of their being linked to their backward and forward linkage partners considered *in aggregate* rather than on a pair-by-pair basis. Comparing the actual distribution of jobs in manufacturing industries by county in Southern Ontario with that predicted by the potential surfaces of linkage partners, Kenyon finds 'a reasonably high correlation between the two patterns' (1975, p. 241), while in their finer scale multivariate analysis of intra-metropolitan Detroit, Tybout and Mattila (1977) find that one or other of two linkage explanatory variables (relating to supply and market potential) adds significantly to the statistical 'explanation' of employment distribution in six out of seven industries studied.

Does not the trend of these 'IL/SL' studies run against previous 'macro' findings reviewed, which suggested a *loosening* of the linkage ties on location? Not necessarily: perhaps IL/SL studies from earlier dates would have shown stronger linkage-location ties than those of the late 1960s and beyond. And as manufacturers are still more clustered than other types of employment, may there not be still room for some agglomeration through linkage even in this era of decentralisation?

But other criticisms have also been levelled at the IL/SL approach, making us unsure of the interpretations we should place on its findings. It assumes that national input-output tables provide a sound basis for identifying the IL associations of particular industries in each and every part of that nation, ignoring that sub-national input-output relationships can be markedly different from those of their parent nation (Harrigan *et al.*, 1980; Kipnis, 1976). It also assumes that any transactions between a pair of linked industries will be ordered on a 'distance minimisation' basis. Finally, there is often the implied presumption that any IL/SL relationship at the aggregated industry level holds too for its constituent firms and plants (raising the so-called 'ecological correlation' problem), and that no other explanations for linkage-location ties need to be entertained (cf. Hoare, 1975).

Perhaps most serious of all is the possibility that macro work is measuring the wrong sorts of linkage flows from the viewpoint of their geographical impact on firms' locations. The bigger the flows the more macro studies place significance on them. But bigger flows should also be easier to timetable into a firm's production schedule. The flows that cause trouble, the flows that still require proximity, need not be picked up in this way at all (Fredriksson and Lindmark, 1979; Hoare, 1975; Scott, 1983a). This could underlie Hoare's finding that macro-linkage measures are neither successful in 'explaining' industrial location within Greater London, nor in predicting those industries that are decentralising from the capital. But a roughly contemporary field survey of London manufacturers showed that the perception of linkage ties with the capital was very important in dissuading firms from thinking about decentralisation and also strongly *inversely* corre-lated with those industries that were decentralising (i.e. the more an industry stressed the value of London's linkage advantages, the *less* it decentralised). Here is at least a strong hint that the influ-ence that a linkage bond has upon a manufacturer may have little to do with the volume or value of the materials involved.

Micro Studies

Field work directed at individual plants or firms provides informa-tion tailor-made for the job in hand, both about linkages them-selves, their development through time, and the possible controls and constraints that act upon them. But this is at a considerably greater cost in time and effort in data collection than applies to macro studies, with the inevitable consequence that such work is limited in scope in terms of types of industries and/or linkages covered, and the geographical area investigated. It runs into the further problems of the non-co-operation of some of the firms approached for data — sometimes a large portion (Taylor (1978a) reports a 70 per cent non-response rate to a survey of Auckland manufacturers, for example), and one that may be biased in some way in terms of the very things we want to measure: perhaps big firms will be more co-operative, but big firms have different link-age properties to small ones. Further problems arise through the multitude of ways in which workers have measured linkage ties in the field and, sometimes, the imprecise questions they have put to manufacturers. Yet despite these difficulties the micro approach has both revealed some important and unsuspected facets of linkage geography, and a fair measure of agreement.

(a) *The Geographical Scale of Industrial Linkages.* Michael Wise's examination of the Birmingham gun and jewellery quarters (Wise, 1949) is often seen as the forerunner of modern micro investigations into linkages. Yet for all his diligence in pinpointing the spatial juxtaposition of a myriad of small, minutely-specialised processing firms in these same industries, linkage flows among these same plants were not measured with equivalent detail, and hence the evidence of an association between the two remains circumstantial (even if highly probable!) It was 20 years later that Keeble (1969), in a study of a modern industrial 'quarter' (in north west London) first really quantified these in any sense at all via a composite index of forward and backward links. Much against the then conventional wisdom he showed how half of his 124 north west London manufacturers had no 'local' links of any sort whatsoever.

A number of other British studies have underlined this finding. Thus three years after Keeble's field work, the London Employment Survey (SEJPT, 1971a) identified both how manufacturing firms in the capital were heavily oriented towards 'outside' markets and also how their forward linkages were also much less locally constrained than other sectors of the capital's economy, as indeed befits a 'basic' sector of the economy (Hoare, 1983). In the London region too, the South East Joint Planning Team's consultants showed how only 28 per cent of manufacturing sales by value and 21 per cent of purchases took place within a 30 mile radius (SEJPT, 1971b), a finding doubtless 'helped' by their concentrating on large plants of over 100 workers which tend to be more wide ranging in their linkage geographies, while Bale's (1973) study of trading estates in South Wales demonstrated how the claimed advantages of close linkage proximity for their tenants were more apparent than real:

> the type of linkage between estate firms usually seemed to account for less than 1 per cent of turnover and frequently casual loans of equipment and servicing, undertaken more as a

favour than anything else, formed the basis of inter-firm linkages. (p. 322)

In North America the same seems to hold. Thus Karaska's (1969) survey of 282 Philadelphia manufacturers showed the average respondent purchased his major material input from outside the city and how, on average, only about 37 per cent of all inputs came from Philadelphia sources. Similarly, firms in sub-urban Toronto sold only about 35 per cent of their output within that metropolis, (Field and Kerr, 1968) while Gilmour (1974) estimated that the dependence of his 198 manufacturers upon their 'home' metropolis of Montreal amounted to only 27 per cent and 31 per cent for forward and backward linkages respectively.

Thus a new literature emerged which played down the local dependence of manufacturers upon their local suppliers, even in major industrial centres of advanced countries. In this new light the disappointing track record of growth centres and the like, wedded to the distance-constrained spatial diffusion of growth, becomes less surprising.

(b) *Controls on Linkage Geography.* Within this emerging picture of modest local linkages can we identify any characteristics of manufacturers or of their linkages that predispose them to being 'local' rather than spatially widespread? Here we will look at three not wholly unrelated themes that have attracted attention.

Industrial types: Many authors have deliberately confined their linkage attention to a small number of sectors (usually in the engineering/metal working trades) but those taking a broader industrial view find patterns of linkage concentration as in Table 2.1. All show marked variations in 'local' linkage dependence from one industry to the other but there is not much agreement over the finer details. Clothing would appear to generate low local input linkages (though the reverse with forward ones, in London at least), while the food industry serves local markets in two of the surveys. However, the results for vehicles and mechanical engin-eering are very different in the South East study from those of Keeble's, while the wide variance between food and tobacco (in Greater London) and between printing and paper making (in Philadelphia) places a question mark against those studies which lump these two apparently different performers in the same industrial heading.

Table 2.1: Variations of Local Linkage Orientation by Industrial Type

Keeble (1969): North West London in 1963 (BLs and FLs combined)

Low	High
Vehicles	Clothing, Leather and
Electrical Engineering	Textiles
Metals and Mechanical	Chemicals and Allies
Engineering	Paper, Printing and
	Publishing

Karaska (1969): Philadelphia in 1960 (BLs)

Low	High
Clothing	Petroleum
Rubber	Printing
Paper	Instruments
Stone, Clay, Glass	Lumber
Miscellaneous	Furniture

SEJPT (1971a): Greater London in 1966 (London Employment Survey; FLs)

Low	High
Tobacco	Footwear
Coke, Oil	Timber and Furniture
Radio goods	Clothing
Pharmaceuticals	Leather and Fur
Shipbuilding	Food

SEJPT (1971b): South East England in 1968

BLs		FLs	
Low	High	Low	High
Textiles, Leather,	Food, Drink,	Mechanical	Food, Drink,
Clothing	Tobacco	Engineering	Tobacco
Other	Bricks, Pottery and	Vehicles	Paper, Printing and
manufacturing	Glass	Other	Publishing
Vehicles	Paper, Printing and	manufacturing	Bricks
	Publishing		

Note: FLs — Forward linkages. BLs — Backward linkages.
     Low (high) — low (high) percentage of inputs/outputs linked to local area.

In part, this lack of consistency may also reflect differences in industrial environment from one locality to another (perhaps there are more locally available linkage contacts for a given industry in one city than another), in which case some inclusion of the population of plants 'at risk' of having linkage contact with particular industries in particular areas becomes a necessary addition (see Hoare, 1978b). Perhaps too, though, other controls are at least as important which run across the grain of an end-product, 'industry'-based, classification. We shall take these possibilities in reverse order.

Plant size: Here we find more consensus. Most workers who examine the significance of plant size on linkage geography hypothesise that small firms will be more locally linked than big ones and, by and large, that is what they find. Among Keeble's (1969) north west London firms, for example, the 10-24 employee group was the only one with a 'no local linkage' score below 50 per cent. Lever (1974) found the same in the Glasgow region, where local backward and forward linkages were stronger among small firms (averaging about 50 workers in this case) while McDermott's (1979) research, also in Scotland but confined to the electronics industry, showed a negative association between turnover (a function of plant size) and sales to the Scottish economy. Similarly, Taylor and Wood's (1973) West Midlands iron foundry study revealed that smaller plants, again, were more locally linked both through inputs and sales. Some of these results are obtained from relatively small samples, but evidence from North America corroborates these British findings, whether in Hamilton (Bater and Walker, 1974) or two separate studies in Montreal (Brooks *et al.*, 1973; Gilmour, 1974).

Even so, O'Farrell and O'Loughlin (1981) find no relationship between either each plant or firm size and the local backward linkages forged between new industrial enterprises investing in the Republic of Ireland, a finding they admit is 'surprising' in the light of evidence such as that just summarised. Their respondents may be a somewhat peculiar subset of manufacturing as a whole, in their newness and presumed 'growthfulness'. But perhaps, too, 'size' may not be so important in itself as for its relationships with other aspects of the organisation of manufacturing companies, and it may be more useful to view it in this somewhat broader context.

Types of Organisation: This represents one of the major thrusts of current research in industrial geography. Measured in various ways by different authors, the overall message is that plants belonging to simple organisations, frequently being small, single-plant, privately-owned, technically unsophisticated companies, have a more localised input and output linkage orientation than plants of larger size and greater organisational complexity — such as publicly-owned, multi-plant and multi-national companies. Multivariate analysis of the West Midlands ironfounders has shown how closely intertwined these issues of size, organisational complexity and ownership type are, and how collectively they discriminate between locally and non-locally linked plants (Taylor and Wood, 1973).

Why should the small/simple/private end of the industrial spectrum be more localised in its linkage geography? An earlier section made suggestions here — perhaps 'parochialism', perhaps the concern with the early non-standardised stages of the product cycle (Vernon, 1979) where close contact with suppliers and clients is especially crucial, perhaps their simple inability to 'internalise' input origins and output destinations within the linkage networks of a large firm, networks that seem relatively unconstrained by space. Taylor and Thrift (1982) have recently suggested a more fundamental force may lie in the uneven access of firms to resources and consequentially asymmetrical power

Table 2.2: Organisational Controls and Linkage Geography

Source	
Britton (1976) Britton and Gilmour (1978)	BLs among US plants in S. Ontario oriented to long-distance, intra-company sources despite high local linkage potential in Toronto area.
Hoare (1978a)	Outside-controlled plants in N. Ireland and plants with low decision-making autonomy weakly linked into NI economy through BLs and FLs.
Lever (1974)	Externally-controlled firms in Glasgow region had lower level of Scottish BLs and FLs than indigenous ones.
McDermott (1979)	Externally-controlled electronics firms in Scotland heavily dependent on non-Scottish and non-UK sources for BLs and less orientation to Scottish markets than equivalent Scottish controlled firms.
Marshall (1979)	Externally-owned plants in N. England tended to use non-regional sources for service inputs than indigenous ones (but no such differences for material BLs).
O'Farrell and O'Laughlin (1981)	Irish-owned and 'high autonomy' plants in Republic of Ireland had stronger BLs to Irish sources (though the same did not hold for 'local' (< 20 ml) sources).
Taylor (1978a)	More complex organisational types among Auckland manufacturers have less localised FLs.
Taylor (1978b)	Increase in organisational complexity over time associated with reduction of local linkage ties among W. Midlands manufacturers.
Taylor and Wood (1973)	More complex organisational types among W. Midlands iron foundry firms less locally linked for range of FLs and BLs.

relationships that exist within the industrial environment. Certainly, small firms depend on large customers more than probably applies in reverse (Crompton *et al.*, 1976; Fredriksson and Lindmark, 1979), although we then have to ask why some firms are more 'powerful' than others. The complexities of what is really causing what can rapidly assume a Byzantine complexity. Whatever its real causes are, this 'simple firm–local linkage' phenomenon may become relatively less important with time. With the growth of large firms' share of industrial activity so some of the parochial minnows will become swallowed up and more activities brought within the umbrella of a single firm, including the invention and innovation of new products and processes stressed by the 'product cycle' interpretation above (Malecki, 1983).

On the question of the internalisation of material and service linkages within large organisations comparatively little has been written to date. What there is consists mostly of the mapping and description of inter-plant material flows within the car industry (e.g. Goodwin, 1965; Keeble, 1976; Law, 1964), but Healey's work among clothing and textile firms (quoted in Watts, 1980) suggests an enormous variation in experience from firm to firm, with over 36 per cent of enterprises obtaining over half their material inputs intra-firm being set against over 40 per cent obtaining none. Hoare's (1978a) findings from Northern Ireland show how multi-plant firms have a wide range of attitudes in this respect, with over 50 per cent of the relevant sample maintaining they had no formal policy to give preference to intra-firm partners for linkage decisions. Perhaps here we have an example of the very wide diversity of experience of the management of subsidiary units in multi-locational companies over decision-making autonomy in general (Dicken, 1976; Townroe, 1975).

A final geographical aspect of this theme is that the role of intra-company linkage flows seems to become more important for multi-plant firms in the peripheral parts of economic space. There is some support for this from both sides of the Atlantic. Thus in the Toronto region Britton's (1978) sample of 87 engineering and metals firms tended to substitute intra- for inter-company links as their distance from Toronto increased, while in the United States Schmenner (1982) notes that manufacturing plants in the Sun Belt of the south and western states have more intra-firm linkage dependence than those back in the Frost Belt of the north and east. (Here we make the added assumption, on which Schmenner keeps his silence, that many Sun Belt plants are controlled from Frost Belt bases). Similarly, in Britain the ILAG survey (DTI, 1973) covering firms throughout the industrial spectrum, suggested that intra-company linkages were more important to branch plants located in the peripheral regions than in the South East. What none of this work tells us, though, is whether the linkage patterns are a *response* to the degree of linkage poverty of their local areas or whether the types of manufacturing activities directed towards the peripheral sites are those planned from the outset as being tied into the linkage umbilical cord of the parent firm.

(c) *Actual and Potential Linkages.* Much of this sort of linkage work reviewed above cries out for some attention to the geography of *potential* linkage partners. If a factory obtains 60 per cent of its inputs of a particular sort from its local area the significance of this will be very different if the town itself contains only 10 per cent of all possible such suppliers (an indication here of local preference) rather than 60 per cent (in which case no local preference need apply) or even 80 per cent (when there is even some underuse of local potential contacts); see Hoare (1978b). Following Huff's well-known formulation of shopping behaviour, the probability of a firm at X establishing a link with another at Y (P_{xy}) may depend on the number of potential contacts at Y as set against the overall distribution of possible contacts at varying distances from X, thus

$$P_{xy} \propto ([c_y/d_{xy}^b] / \textstyle\sum_y [c_y/d_{xy}^b])$$ When c_y = potential contacts at y
d_{xy} = distance from x to y
b = constant exponent term

Thus Boeing's contact partners in 'distant' Connecticut may have no rivals in more accessible and hence attractive locations to Seattle (Ericksson, 1975) while the tendency is for mundane, commonplace, tasks to be undertaken locally where there is an abundant supply of contacts (e.g. Britton, 1978).

In practice this sort of formulation is far from easy to put into practice. Partly it involves the familiarity of researchers with the often highly specific needs of manufacturing firms (Gilmour, 1974; Hoare, 1978b) and partly it runs up against a plethora of data problems (see Taylor, 1973). Even so, Taylor (1973, 1978a) has experimented with this type of approach among iron foundry firms in England and a range of industries selling from a base in Auckland, New Zealand. In both cases predictions broadly accord with the actual contacts found at varying distances from base, although interesting deviations, especially in the local environment where prediction often falls well below reality, led to his interpretation of the parochial dependence of certain firms on local trade, cited earlier. Using a rather different approach, engineering plants in Northern Ireland had their actual backward linkages for four fairly commonplace material and service inputs compared with the geographical pattern of all possible such contacts in that region. But here, if there is any 'parochialism' it belonged to the more sophisticated organisational sub-set of 'outside' controlled firms which showed a slightly greater tendency to use nearer rather than further potential contacts than did Ulster-based companies, a difference tentatively attributed to the latter's greater experience of operating in, and wider mean information field of, the pool of possible contact partners (Hoare, 1978a).

(d) *Time and Linkages.* As firms change internally and as their external environments also change so we might expect their linkage geographies to change in sympathy. This literature divides neatly into two. The first examines linkage changes by plants *in situ.* An interesting early study by Steed (1970) used a variety of official data from Northern Ireland to estimate changes in the internal linkages in that region's linen industry between 1950 and 1964, a period during which it suffered a major decline. His findings show the industry as much less integrated on a regional scale in the later year — the various firms depend more on outside sources for inputs and outside outlets for sales, and his estimates for the employment multiplier effect of the final 'making up' stage on those stages below it suggest this fell from 3.76 to 2.01. His concern with aggregated industrial data makes it impossible to decide how much of this is due to increased mechanisation in the industry rather than the shifting geography of linkage: later studies, in contrast, have shifted the focus to individual firms considered at two or more points in time.

Thus Lever (1974) demonstrates how backward and forward linkage change among a fairly small set of 24 plants in west central Scotland is greater among newly established plants, among those not based in the region and, especially so, among rapidly growing plants. This does not necessarily mean that these are becoming more or less dependent upon their local community over time, but it certainly seems reasonable that firms still 'settling in' to a new environment and those undergoing major changes in growth (involving new markets and more supplies) will be more volatile in their linkage partners. Taylor's (1978b) own work among his West Midlands ironfounders takes a longer time perspective (1968-76) but in a period of regional (and national) recession. Overall, there is some reduced dependence on local linkages over time, and especially so for firms undergoing an increase in organisational complexity (as the static studies would lead us to expect), although some types of linkages also show a slight increase in local dependence. Given the recessed nature of the regional economy, and the lack of major technological change exhibited by these firms over this period, this slightly 'choppy' picture may not be surprising — rather than being masters of their own destiny many of his firms will be buffeted around by chill economic gales over which they have no control. Finally, LeHeron and Schmidt's (1976) 'exploratory' account of linkage adjustments accompanying growth and technological change among plywood and steel-making firms in the Pacific North West of North America showed there were some relationships between these variables, but these did not always occur in the ways expected, and only sometimes resulted in changes in the geographical scale of linkage interaction.

A rather different sort of change comes about when firms are taken over by other companies, as here the form and structure of management and decision-making will alter without necessarily any changes in technology or types and levels of output. Leigh and North's (1978) study of 61 British companies so acquired in 1973/4 tested *inter alia* the possibility that these linkages may change after acquisition. In practice, experience was mixed, not just from case to case but from linkage to linkage. Forward linkages expanded geographically as the acquired firms now had access to the wider marketing resources of a larger organisation, backward service linkages were usually 'lost' to the suppliers of parallel services already used by the new parent firm (usually with a net advantage to south east England, where the bulk of the acquirers were based) while input material linkages were usually left intact, being considered matters best decided by the management of the acquired plant 'on the spot'.

The second group of dynamic studies looks at linkage consequences of firms changing their locations. On 'distance minimisation' grounds alone we might expect firms establishing new manufacturing capacity away from their previous 'base', to look for new linkages in the vicinity of the new plant. Practice seems very different. In the ILAG survey cited earlier, for example, (DTI, 1973) on average over 80 per cent of all such firms had 'largely relied on the same sources of materials and components at the new location as at the old'. While slightly lower in the peripheral regions, the figure never fell below 60 per cent for any region, and in relatively peripheral Wales was even as high as 97 per cent, despite the fact that the lion's share of the moves covered had originated in the more central regions. Only a relatively small part of this linkage stability could be attributed to intra-firm supplies. Moseley and Townroe's (1973) study of backward linkage effects of movement to East Anglia and northern England covering a roughly similar period confirmed the stability and 'stretchability' of linkages over space with well over half their respondents reporting 'no change', a figure that, paradoxically, was highest with the longest-distance movers (those settling in the north reported a 67 per cent stability score). For such changes as did occur those favouring the new local region were outnumbered by those to other regions by over two to one. They did not also examine the marketing side of the linkage coin, but here ILAG confirmed the generally low level of linkage to the new region: overall 70 per cent of its movers sold less than 20 per cent of output within 40 miles, with figures being highest (i.e. local linkage lowest) among those moving to the peripheral regions.

In part this lack of linkage integration with the new host region may reflect its inability and reluctance to supply the input needs for and purchase from the in-migrant (as James, (1964) illustrated on the 'input' side), yet when set against the high level of satisfaction of ILAG firms with their new locations, and with little or no regional variation (Northern Ireland apart, for reasons presumably linked to the 'troubles'), it seems likely that many moves were designed from the outset to have only a low level of local linkage.

Finally, large corporations can adjust to changing needs and circumstances both through the opening (and closing) of locations and also through the reorganisation of production at existing locations. Bloomfield (1981) for example, discusses how the world's motor car producers have had to face major changes in trade conditions, energy supplies and prices, technological innovation and government involvement in the 1970s. In spatial terms, his work shows how the response in companies like Volkswagen produces a different inter-plant linkage pattern in 1977 from that five years earlier: Nigeria has arrived as an assembly location and Australia has disappeared, and the network of international flows has become more intricate. There will probably be inter-firm linkage adjustments running alongside these, but what they are we can only guess. Here, as in the other 'dynamic' aspects of linkage geography, comparative work has yet to be done, not least because of the obviously greater data problems in this field.

(e) The Role of Linkages in Locational Evaluations. Most of these field studies are concerned with measuring the quantity of linkage flows in some way or other, yet we saw earlier how this may not necessarily be a good measure of the perceived importance of access to suppliers and customers to the management of the same firms. A number of studies suggest that proximity to markets and suppliers figures prominently in the minds of managers when assessing their present locations, and that its importance has a fairly clear geographical pattern. Thus two different surveys of manufacturers in London and the western Home Counties, adjacent to London, both found market access and supplier access ranked respectively 1st and 3rd out of 15 possible factors (Hoare, 1983), and in the London case the former also ranked first in dissuading firms from decentralising, and the latter 4th (Hoare, 1973). In contrast, Begg (1972) noted that Tayside's remoteness was the major *problem* experienced by its industrialists, with customer and supplier access mentioned as specific instances of this. Law (1964) found transport-related difficulties were the paramount industrial drawback of Northern Ireland and Cameron and Reid (1966) that unsatisfactory access to markets, to suppliers and to 'linked companies' were far and away the major reasons for migrant factories considering but rejecting Scotland in comparison with other British regions. While we must be wary about drawing too close parallels between different surveys, a similar centre-periphery pattern emerges from those few which examine the relative locational advantages of different locations within our study. Thus the ILAG survey (DTI, 1973) also showed how access to suppliers and to markets were both more significant location factors for their 1964-67 cohort of migrant factories settling in the Midlands and South of the United Kingdom than in the peripher-

ies and were also important reasons for rejecting certain peripheral regions. Similarly Green's survey of factories moving from the South East and West Midlands to the Development areas in the same period (quoted in Keeble, 1976) showed how the quality of their locations' market and supply accessibility had declined in the opinions of management both in their overall 'favourableness' and, in relative terms, from ranks 1 and 3 (out of 15) in the old location to 7 and 8 in the new.

Contemporary surveys from outside Britain add a further, metropolitan, dimension to this perception of linkages advantage. Thus manufacturers in Michigan rate market access and supply access as (again) 1st and 3rd in importance to their locations but with the first noticeably higher in metropolitan Detroit than among respondents elsewhere in the state (Katona and Morgan, 1952). McDermott and Taylor (1976) similarly showed how 'potential of the local market' and 'supplies from local manufacturers' were not only the two advantages of Auckland most prized by its manufacturers but were also considerations where that city had a clear edge over smaller New Zealand towns, in contrast to managements' attitudes towards labour, land and local authority-related factors which were more favourable outside Auckland than within it.

In all, then, it seems as if linkage access is not only still important in the present-day assessment of locations by manufacturers, but is especially so in larger cities and agglomerations. Two notes of caution, though. First, some of these 'big city' advantages might be through its providing not just a *local* market but also access to wider national and international ones. Second, these bland locational categories used by almost all surveys of this kind generally allow us little chance to discriminate among particular *types* of markets and suppliers, so tracing out the relative importance of the various sub-groups identified in Figure 2.1.

Conclusions

The last few years have seen a sustained impetus in industrial linkage studies, including and illustrated by a recent review article by Scott (1983a). On the conceptual front, the same author has examined the illumination cast by linkages on the workings of capitalist production within cities (Scott, 1982, 1983b), and McDermott and Taylor (1982) have used linkage evidence to exemplify the ways in which organisational and locational theory might be brought together. Clearly, the death of geographical investigation of linkages forecast by Moseley and Townroe (1973) has, like that of Mark Twain, been much exaggerated. And equally clearly, in a field where much is still being done, it would be as unwise as it would be difficult to draw too many definitive conclusions. But two final points do seem worth underlining. The first is that recent experience has seen both a whittling away of the Marshallian model of agglomeration-through-linkage in the minds of geographers and in the evolution of linkage patterns on the ground. Without denying the importance for some linkage partners of being close to one another, such proximity is not now as necessary as it was on such a localised scale for much of the economy. Opportunities are there for linkages to exist over greater distances than before, even if not all manufacturing firms *want* to take advantage of this, *need* so to do, or are *able* to exploit this potential. Manufacturing trends as a whole are moving away from those agglomerations frequently 'explained' in Marshallian linkage terms. Significantly, too, in Townroe and Robert's (1980) pioneering attempt to explain geographical variations in levels of industrial performance in Britain through their correlation with external economies of agglomeration, the input-output based linkage measure was *dropped* as its correlations with their three performance variables were so low. If industry does not have *carte blanche* in linkage terms as to where it locates, it is also probable that such spatial and industrial linkage associations as remain will contain more than a pinch of inertia. When they come under challenge through such jolts as relocation, organisational change, technological innovation, growth or contraction, they can either survive over much greater distances, or be reformulated with much less attention to geographical distance than before.

Secondly, the importance of manufacturing linkage to firms cannot be understood simply in terms of the quantities of material being moved. Access between linked firms may mean access between the buying and selling offices of big manufacturers, rather than the origin and destination depots and factories between which the goods ultimately move (Crum and Gudgin, 1977). In such ways as this, the 'human content' of linkage flows may now be the dominant locational ingredient in an age of efficient low cost freight transport. The other key ingredient may be *unpredictability* — breakdowns, surges in demand, fluctuating market conditions —

which also places far more of a premium on short distance linkages than regular, predictable, mass movements of standardised inputs and products.

There is still a geography of linkages (everything happens somewhere) but it is no longer a geography that could be analysed simply with the geographer's kit of distance-based tools. As with other aspects of industrial space reviewed in this volume, we have to see this geography in a wider context (Massey and Meegan, 1982), whose understanding takes us inside the manufacturing firms and into topics geographers have not seen as their natural hunting ground (Scott, 1983a). This may make it much more difficult to understand such an integral part of the modern manufacturing process as industrial linkage in isolation, but at least we will be starting from a more realistic base.

References

Bale, J. (1973) *The Location of Manufacturing Industry*, Oliver and Boyd, Edinburgh

Barlow, Sir M. (1940) *Report of the Royal Commission on the Distribution of the Industrial Population*, (Chairman Sir Montague Barlow) Cmnd. 6153, HMSO. London

Bater, J.H. and Walker, D.F. (1974) 'Aspects of industrial linkage: the example of the Hamilton metal making complex, Ontario,' *Revue de Geographie de Montreal*, 28, 233-43

Begg, H. (1972) 'Remoteness and the location of the firm,' *Scottish Geographical Magazine*, 88, 48-52

Bergman, J., Greenston, P. and Healy, R. (1972) 'The agglomeration process in urban growth,' *Urban Studies*, 9, 263-88

Bergman, J., Greenston, P. and Healy, R. (1975) 'A classification of economic activities based on location patterns,' *Journal of Urban Economics*, 2, 1-28

Berry, B.J.L., Conkling, E.C. and Ray, D.M. (1976) *The Geography of Economic Systems*, Prentice-Hall, Englewood Cliffs, N.J.

Bloomfield, G.T. (1981) 'The changing spatial organisation of multinational corporations in the world automative industry' in F.E.I. Hamilton and G.J.R. Linge (eds.), *Spatial Analysis, Industry and the Industrial Environment*, Vol. 2. Wiley, Chichester, pp. 357-94

Bora, G. (1979) 'The stages of development in the industrial system of Budapest' in F.E.I. Hamilton and G.J.R. Linge (eds.), *The Spatial Structure of Industrial Systems*, Wiley, Chichester, pp. 41-61

Boyce, R.R. (1974) *The Bases of Economic Geography*, Holt, Rinehart and Winston, New York

Britton, J.N.H. (1976) 'The influence of corporate organisation and ownership on the linkages of industrial plants: a Canadian enquiry,' *Economic Geography*, 52, 311-24

Britton, J.N.H. (1978) 'Influences on the spatial behaviour of manufacturing firms in

Southern Ontario' in F.E.I. Hamilton (ed.), *Contemporary Industrialization*, Longman, London, pp. 110-21

Britton, J.N.H. and Gilmour, J.M. (1978) *The Weakest Link: a Technological Perspective on Canadian Industrial Underdevelopment*, Science Council of Canada, Ottawa

Brooks, S., Gilmour, J.M. and Murricane, K. (1973) 'The spatial linkages of manufacturing in Montreal and its surroundings,' *Cahiers de Geographie de Quebec*, *17*, 107-22

Cameron, G.C. and Reid, G.L. (1966) *Scottish Economic Planning and the Attraction of Industry*, University of Glasgow Science and Economic Studies, Occasional Papers, No. 6

Campbell, J. (1974) 'Selected aspects of the inter-industry structure of the State of Washington, 1967,' *Economic Geography*, *50*, 35-46

Chapman, K. (1970) 'Oil-based industrial complexes in the United Kingdom,' *Tijdschrift voor Economische en Sociale Geografie*, *61*, 157-72

Chisholm, M.D.I. and O'Sullivan, P. (1973) *Freight Flows and Spatial Aspects of the British Economy*, Cambridge University Press, Cambridge

Cohen, Y.S. and Berry, B.J.L. (eds.), *Spatial Components of Manufacturing Change, 1950-1960*, University of Chicago, Department of Geography, Research Paper No. 172

Crompton, D., Barlow, A.T. and Downing, S. (1976) *Component Suppliers to the Car Industry*. Department of Industry (West Midlands Regional Office), Birmingham

Crum, R.E. and Gudgin, G. (1977) *Non-productive Activities in UK Manufacturing Industry*. Commission of the European Communities, Regional Policy Series No. 3, Brussels

Czamanski, S. (1971) 'Some evidence of the strengths of linkages between groups of related industries in urban-regional complexes,' *Papers of the Regional Science Association*, *27*, 137-150

Czamanski, S. and de Ablas, L.A. (1979) 'Identification of industrial clusters and complexes: a comparison of methods and findings,' *Urban Studies*, *16*, 61-80

Czamanski, D. and Czamanski, S. (1977) 'Industrial complexes: their typology, structure and relation to economic development,' *Papers of the Regional Science Association*, *38*, 93-111

Daniell, P.N. (1982) *Subcontracting in the aerospace industry: a geographical perspective*, University of Bristol, Department of Geography, Unpublished B. Soc. Sci. Dissertation

Dennison, S. (1939) *The Location of Industry and the Depressed Areas*, Oxford University Press, Oxford

Dicken, P. (1976) 'The multiplant business enterprise and geographical space: some issues in the study of external control and regional development,' *Regional Studies*, *10*, 401-12

DTI (Department of Trade and Industry) (1973) *Memorandum on the inquiry into location attitudes and experience, Minutes of Evidence*, Trade and Industry Sub-committee of the House of Commons Expenditure Committee, Session 1972-3, HMSO, London

Edwards, S.L. (1970) 'Transport costs in British industry,' *Journal of Transport Economics and Policy*, *4*, 1-19

Erickson, R.A. (1975) 'The spatial pattern of income generation in lead firms, grant area linkage system,' *Economic Geography*, *51*, 17-26

Estall, R.C. (1983) 'The decentralization of manufacturing industry: recent American experience in perspective,' *Geoforum*, *14*, 133-47

Estall, R.C. and Buchanan, R.O. (1980) *Industrial Location and Economic Activity*, Hutchinson, London

Field, N.C. and Kerr, D.P. (1968) *Geographical aspects of industrial grants in the*

Metropolitan Toronto Region, Government of Ontario Regional Development Branch (Department of Treasury and Economics), Toronto

Fredriksson, C.G. and Lindmark, L.G. (1979) 'From firms to systems of firms: a study of inter-regional dependence in a dynamic system' in F.E.I. Hamilton and G.J.R. Linge (eds.), *Spatial Analysis, Industry and the Industrial Environment*, Vol. 1 — *Industrial Systems*, Wiley, Chichester, 155-86

Friedman, A.L. (1977) *Industry and Labour: Class Struggle at Work and Monopoly Capitalism*, Macmillan, London

Gilmour, J.M. (1974) 'External economies of scale, inter-industrial linkage and decision-making in manufacturing' in F.E.I. Hamilton (ed.), *Spatial Perspectives on Industrial Organization and Decision-making*, Wiley, Chichester, 335-62

Goddard, J.B. (1975) *Office Location in Urban and Regional Development*, Oxford University Press, London

Goodwin, W. (1965) 'The structure and position of the British motor vehicle industry,' *Tijdschrift voor Economische en Sociale Geografie, 56*, 145-56

Harrigan F.J. (1982) 'The relationship between industrial and geographical linkages: a case study of the United Kingdom,' *Journal of Regional Science, 22*, 19-31

Harrigan, F.J., McNicoll, I.H. and McGilvray, J.W. (1980) 'A comparison of national and regional; technical structures,' *Economic Journal, 90*, 795-810

Harrison, R.E.T., Bull, P.J. and Hart, M. (1979) 'Space and time in industrial linkage studies,' *Area, 11*, 333-8

Hoare, A.G. (1973) 'The spheres of influence of industrial location factors,' *Regional Studies, 7*, 301-14

Hoare, A.G. (1975) 'Linkage flows, locational evaluation and industrial geography: a study of Greater London,' *Environment and Planning, A, 7*, 41-58

Hoare, A.G. (1978a) 'Industrial linkages and the dual economy: the case of Northern Ireland,' *Regional Studies, 12*, 167-80

Hoare, A.G. (1978b) 'Three problems for industrial linkage studies, *Area, 10*, 217-21

Hoare, A.G. (1983) *The Location of Industry in Britain*, Cambridge University Press, Cambridge

Huggett, R. and Meyer, I. (1981) *Industry*, Harper and Row, London

Hurst, M.E. (1972) *A Geography of Economic Behaviour: an Introduction*, Wadsworth, Belmont, Calif.

James, B.G.S. (1964) 'The incompatibility of industrial and trading cultures,' *Journal of Industrial Economics, 2*, 184-192

Jarrett, H.R. (1977) *A Geography of Manufacturing*, MacDonald and Evans, Plymouth

Johnston, R.J. (1981) (ed.) *The Dictionary of Human Geography*, Blackwell, Oxford

Karaska, G.J. (1969) 'Manufacturing linkages in the Philadelphia economy: evidence of external agglomeration forces,' *Geographical Analysis, 1*, 354-69

Katona, G. and Morgan, J.N. (1952) 'The quantitative study of factors determining business decisions,' *Quarterly Journal of Economics, 66*, 73-81

Keeble, D.E. (1969) 'Local industrial linkage and manufacturing growth in outer London,' *Town Planning Review, 40*, 163-188

Keeble, D.E. (1976) *Industrial Location and Planning in the United Kingdom*, Methuen, London

Kenyon, J.B. (1975) 'An interindustry gravity model applied to southern Ontario,' *Canadian Geographer, 19*, 235-50

Kipnis, B.A. (1976) 'Local versus national coefficients in constructing regional input-output tables in small countries: a case study of northern Israel,' *Journal of Regional Science, 16*, 93-9

Kortus, B. and Kaczorowski, W. (1981) 'Polish industry forges external links' in F.E.I. Hamilton and G.J.R. Linge (eds.), *Spatial Analysis, Industry and the*

Industrial Environment: Vol. 2 International Industrial Systems, Wiley, Chichester, 119-53

Kuklinski, A. (1981) (ed.), *Polarized Development and Regional Policies*, Mouton, The Hague

Latham, W.R. 3 (1976) 'Needless complexity in the identification of industrial complexes,' *Journal of Regional Science, 16*, 45-55

Law, D. (1964) 'Industrial movement and locational advantage,' *Manchester School of Economic and Social Studies, 32*, 131-54

Le Heron, R.B. and Schmidt, C.G. (1976) 'An exploratory analysis of linkage change within two regional industries,' *Regional Studies, 10*, 465-78

Lee, C.H. (1979) *British Regional Employment Statistics*. Cambridge University Press, Cambridge

Leigh, R. and North, D.J. (1978) 'Acquisitions in British industries: implications for regional development' in F.E.I. Hamilton (ed.), *Contemporary Industrialisation*, Longman, London, 158-81

Lever, W.F. (1974) 'Manufacturing linkages and the search for supplies and markets' in F.E.I. Hamilton (ed.), *Spatial Perspectives in Industrial Organisation and Decision-making*, Wiley, Chichester, 309-34

Lever, W.F. (1975) 'Mobile industry and levels of integration in subregional economic structures,' *Regional Studies, 9*, 265-78

Linge, G.J.R. and Hamilton, F.E.I. (1981) 'International industrial systems' in F.E.I. Hamilton and G.J.R. Linge (eds.), *Spatial Analysis, Industry and the Industrial Environment, Vol. I: International Industrial Systems*, Wiley, Chichester, 1-117

Linge, G.J.R., Karaska, G.J. and Hamilton, F.E.I. (1978) 'An appraisal of the Soviet concept of the Territorial Production Complex,' *Soviet Geography, 19*, 681-97

Livesey, F. (1972) 'Industrial complexity and regional economic development,' *Town Planning Review, 43*, 225-42

Lloyd, P.E. and Dicken, P. (1977) *Location in Space*, Harper and Row, London

McDermott, P.J. (1979) 'Multinational manufacturing firms and regional development: external control in the Scottish electronics industry,' *Scottish Journal of Political Economy, 26*, 287-306

McDermott, P.J. and Taylor, M.J. (1976) 'Attitudes, images and location: the subjective context of decision-making in New Zealand manufacturing,' *Economic Geography, 52*, 325-47

McDermott, P.J. and Taylor, M.J. (1982) *Industrial Organisation and Location*, Cambridge University Press

Malecki, E.J. (1983) 'Technology and regional development: a summary,' *International Regional Science Review, 8*, 89-125

Marshall, A. (1898) *Elements of Economics of Industry*, Macmillan, London

Marshall, J.N. (1979) 'Ownership, organization and industrial linkages: a case study in the northern region of England,' *Regional Studies, 13*, 531-57

Massey, D. and Meegan, R. (1982) *The Anatomy of Job Loss: the How, Why and Where of Employment Decline*, Methuen, London

Moseley, M.J. (1974) *Growth Centres in Spatial Planning*, Pergamon, Oxford

Moseley, M.J. and Townroe, P.N. (1973) 'Linkage adjustment following industrial movement, *Tijdschrift voor Economische en Sociale Geografie, 64*, 137-44

O'Farrell, P.N. and O'Loughlin (1981) 'New industry input linkages in Ireland: an econometric analysis,' *Environment and Planning A, 13*, 285-308

Pallot, J. and Shaw, D. (1981) *Planning in the Soviet Union*, Croom Helm, Beckenham

PEP (Political and Economic Planning) (1939) *Report on the Location of Industry*, PEP, London

Prais, S.J. (1976) *The Evolution of Giant Firms in Britain*, Cambridge University Press, Cambridge

Richter, C.E. (1969) 'The impact of industrial linkages in geographic association,'

Journal of Regional Science, 9, 19-28

Riley, R.C. (1973) *Industrial Geography*, Chatto and Windus, London

Rodgers, A. (1979) *Economic Development in Retrospect: the Italian Model and its Significance for Regional Planning in Market Oriented Economies*, Wiley, New York

Roepke, H., Adams, D. and Wiseman, R. (1974) 'A new approach to the identification of industrial complexes using input-output data,' *Journal of Regional Science, 14*, 15-29

Schmennor, R.W. (1982) *Making Business Location Decisions*, Prentice-Hall, Englewood Cliffs, N.J.

Scott, A.J. (1982) 'Production system dynamics and metropolitan development,' *Annals of the Association of American Geographers, 72*, 185-200

Scott, A.J. (1983a) 'Location and linkage systems: a survey and reassessment' *Annals of Regional Science, 17*, 1-39

Scott, A.J. (1983b) 'Industrial organisation and the logic of intra-metropolitan location: 1 Theoretical considerations, *Economic Geography, 59*, 233-50

SEJPT (South East Joint Planning Team) (1971a) *Strategic plan for the South East: Studies Volume 1 (Population and Employment)*, HMSO, London

SEJPT (South East Joint Planning Team) (1971b) *Strategic plan for the South East: Studies Volume 5 (Report of Economic Consultants Ltd.)*, HMSO, London

Slater, P.B. (1977) 'The determination of functionally integrated industries in the United States using a 1967 inter-industry flow table,' *Journal of Empirical Economics*, 1977, 1-9

Smith, D.M. (1981) *Industrial Location: an Economic Geographic Analysis*, Wiley, Chichester

Soderman, S, (1975) *Industrial Location Planning: an Empirical Investigation of Company Approaches to the Problem of Locating New Plants*, Almquist and Wiksell Institute, Stockholm

Steed, G.P.F. (1970) 'Changing linkages and internal multipliers of an industrial complex, *Canadian Geographer, 14*, 229-42

Streit, M.E. (1969) 'Spatial association and spatial linkages between industries,' *Journal of Regional Science, 9*, 177-88

Taylor, M.J. (1973) 'Local linkage, external economies and the iron foundry industry of the West Midlands and the East Lancashire conurbations,' *Regional Studies, 7*, 387-400

Taylor, M.J. (1975) 'Organisational growth, spatial interaction and location decision-making,' *Regional Studies, 9*, 313-23

Taylor, M.J. (1978a) 'Spatial competition and the sales linkages of Auckland manufacturers', in F.E.I. Hamilton (ed.), *Contemporary Industrialisation*, Longman, London, 144-57

Taylor, M.J. (1978b) 'Linkage change and organisational growth: the case of the West Midlands iron foundry industry,' *Economic Geography, 54*, 314-36

Taylor, M.J. (1980) 'External economies and agglomeration: an appraisal of macro-scale studies of polarization,' *Tijdschrift voor Economische en Sociale Geografie, 71*, 264-76

Taylor, M.J. and Thrift, N.J. (1982) 'Industrial linkage and the segmented economy: 1,' *Environment and Planning A, 14*, 1601-13

Taylor, M.J. and Wood, P.A. (1973) 'Industrial linkage and local agglomeration in the West Midlands metal industries,' *Transactions of the Institute of British Geographers, 59*, 129-54

Townroe, P.N. (1975) 'Branch plants and regional development,' *Town Planning Review, 46*, 47-62

Townroe, P.N. and Roberts, N.J. (1980) *Local-external Economies for British Manufacturing Industry*, Gower, Farnborough

Tybout, R.A. Mattila, J.M. (1977) 'Agglomeration of Manufacturing in Detroit,'

Journal of Regional Science, 17, 1-16
Vernon, R. (1979) 'The product cycle hypothesis is a new international
    environment,' *Oxford Bulletin of Economics and Statistics, 41,* 255-67
Watts, H.D. (1980) *The Large Industrial Enterprise,* Croom Helm, London
Wise, M.J. (1949) 'On the evolution of the jewellery and gun quarters in
    Birmingham,' *Transactions of the Institute of British Geographers, 15,* 57-72

3 INTRA-URBAN INDUSTRIAL GEOGRAPHY

P.J. BULL

Introduction

This essay is concerned with the changing geography of intra-urban industrial activity, that is with the changing locations secured by industrial establishments in cities and the different spatial patterns their aggregate behaviour creates. Despite the dominance and increasing importance of the service sector in cities — accounting for almost 68 per cent of employment in the UK conurbations in 1976 (Danson *et al.*, 1980) — the emphasis here will be on manufacturing activity simply because with a few notable exceptions such as Daniels (1977, 1982 and 1983), Damesick (1979), Gad (1979), Schwartz (1979), Damesick *et al.* (1982), and Ley and Hutton (1984), there has been very little published research on the geography of service employment in cities or its role in urban centre economies (Elias and Keogh, 1982). However, over the last ten years a large amount of research has been undertaken and published on the changing geography of intra-urban manufacturing activity, much of which has been concerned with describing in detail locational change at the establishment level. Most of this descriptive work has already been reviewed elsewhere (Bull, 1983; Lever, 1982a; Scott, 1982a; Thrift, 1979), and therefore only a brief contextural introductory statement is required here. What is far more important is the development of different approaches to the subject and different theoretical frameworks within which the changing geography of intra-urban industrial activity may be understood. It is on these aspects of recently published work that this essay will concentrate.

Intra-urban Locational and Spatial Change

Many of the recent detailed descriptions of the locational change of manufacturing activity in urban areas have made use of a 'components of change' establishment accounting system. With this technique employment change, for example, has been viewed as the outcome of four components:

1. *In situ* expansion or contraction.
2. The opening, or birth, of new plants which may include in-migrants to the study area.
3. The closure, or death, of existing plants, which may include transfers out of the study area.
4. Intra-urban transfers, or the 'lock-stock-and-barrel' movement of a plant from one location to another within the study area.

From the research on the components of change of manufacturing activity in North American, British and European cities few general points have emerged on the relationships between the components of change and aggregate employment change. American research, for example, has demonstrated that one cannot assume that a city with an expanding labour force will record a relatively high plant birth rate, or that relatively high closure rates will be associated with cities losing jobs. In some cases *in situ* employment change may be the most important component accounting for employment expansion or contraction (Struyk and James, 1975). In the UK variable results between cities have also been found (Bull, 1983; Thrift, 1979). However, Fothergill and Gudgin (1982) have argued that when adjustments are made for variations in plant size, industrial structure and the operation of regional policy (see Mason (1980) on this last point) much of the recent decline in the UK conurbations relative to smaller settlements can be explained in terms of *in situ* employment change. Perhaps if a rigorous comparative analysis along these lines were undertaken on the major cities of the UK or the USA some of the variation in their recent components of change experience would become more apparent than real.

In terms of aggregate spatial change within urban areas, decentralisation or suburbanisation has been the general trend in all cases. However despite massive employment and establishment losses from central urban areas, cities still remain core dominated. That is, the greatest density of manufacturing plants and employment is still to be found in relatively central urban locations. However, it is important to note that this is merely a description of the spatial pattern of manufacturing activity in urban areas and it is not intended to suggest that the inner city is an important contemporary focus for industrial growth. The components of change research has also demonstrated that the suburbanisation of manufacturing activity can be generated in a number of different ways. In Clydeside (1958-68) and Greater London (1966-74) for example, employment and establishment closure rates were found to be spatially invariant with respect to distance from the urban core and suburbanisation was principally the result of increasing birth rates towards the suburbs (Cameron, 1973; Dennis, 1978). In Greater Manchester (1966-75), however, suburbanisation was primarily the result of a marked downward gradation of closure rates with distance from the city centre (Mason, 1981). Whereas in both Greater Leicester (1957-70) and Merseyside (1966-75) both the spatial distributions of birth rates and death rates were tending to foster suburbanisation (Fagg, 1980; Lloyd, 1979). Interestingly in this last conurbation *in situ* employment shrinkage accounted for approximately 50 per cent of employment loss in the central area (Lloyd, 1979). Only on one point do all the recent component of change investigations appear to agree, namely the minor role played by intra-urban transfers in the suburbanisation process. It may well have been the case that in the past the transference of establishments from central to relatively suburban places was important in changing the geography of intra-urban manufacturing activity (Hoover and Vernon, 1959; Wood, 1974), but this has not been the case during the last 25 years.

The Conceptualisation of Industrial Change

Industrial change may be usefully conceptualised in terms of successive rounds of investment (and disinvestment) through time in which each new round of investment alters the industrial geography of an area — a change which itself is strongly influenced by the existing distribution of investment from previous time periods (Massey, 1979, 1983). Thus, although it may be possible for general spatial trends to be observed in urban areas — especially in simply space filling terms such as suburbanisation — the underlying locational events which cause such changes may differ quite markedly between places. Indeed this has already been demonstrated above in terms of the different combinations of components of change generating suburbanisation in different cities. And given the different economic histories and built environments of these places this should have been expected and should in no way be regarded as exceptional. The unique qualities of different cities will play an important part in moulding the local impacts of different rounds of investment to create new unique local urban geographies. At any point in time, therefore, a particular city presents an extremely complex mix of plants, firms and industries existing from many previous rounds of investment, whose original locational decisions will have varied markedly in response to different urban geographies and to different national and international economic situations. An investigation of the changing industrial geography of any city will require a detailed understanding of such complexities. However, all that can be achieved in this essay is a discussion in very general terms of the impact of different rounds of investment on the changing geography of intra-urban manufacturing activity.

To begin to understand the locational and spatial dynamics of intra-urban manufacturing activity it is first necessary to understand the pressures faced by firms which can generate changes in their mix of factors of production at existing locations and which ultimately may lead to locational change. The majority of firms in western capitalist countries operate in competitive markets in which profits have to be made to satisfy two demands. First, to satisfy the financial demands of their shareholders, and second in order to reinvest and innovate and thereby attempt to maintain an economic advantage over their competitors. Reinvestment in new capital equipment is of course required not only to reduce the cost of the ways in which existing product lines are manufactured, and thereby improve competitiveness and profitability, but also to introduce new products to replace those for which demand is on the wane or whose profitability is in decline. When reinvestment or new capital investment is being planned two sets of factors must be considered. First, changes in the external geographical environment. For example, the availability of suitable premises or labour may necessitate a completely new location and the vacation of existing premises. Similarly, changes in the relative accessibility of places by, say, the construction of new routeways may make a new location far more profitable than an existing one. Second, changes in production techniques. The adoption of best practice production techniques may lead almost invariably today to employment reductions and may necessitate completely new premises. Indeed the importance of technological change in the stimulation of locational change in all the economic activities of urban places needs to be strongly emphasised, and its realisation leads directly to the necessity of an understanding of the locational demands of different production processes for an understanding of the geography of intra-urban industrial change. Indeed the geography of industrial change has been viewed by many in these terms as the outcome of a temporal process whereby best practice production methods replace older technological forms (Bull, 1983; Community Development Projects, 1977; Firn, 1976; Massey, 1979; Scott, 1982a). Unfortunately for many localities the sites favoured by previous forms of production are not demanded by the new. Thus for some areas industrial decline will ensue as soon as existing industrial operations cease to be profitable. In north west Europe and North America such a process has already occurred in many towns dominated by traditional industries such as textiles, shipbuilding and steel manufacture as well as in many inner-city areas.

The Conceptualisation of the Spatial Change of Intra-urban Manufacturing Activity

In the intra-urban case such an historical process of industrial change is often stereotyped in terms of a 'dual economy' with small indigenous establishments in declining or static industries in the city core and with the periphery populated by the branches of large multi-regional and multinational firms predominantly in the growth sectors of the economy. If such a view — termed urban dendrochronology by Firn (1976) — is appropriate then it should perhaps best be viewed not in terms of particular plants, firms or even industries, but more in terms of a decline in the usefulness and profitability of the urban fabric: the size and layout of premises and the transportation systems in inner-city areas becoming increasingly obsolete as changes in marketing, production and communication methods alter the most profitable ways, and therefore locations, in which goods can be produced (Bull, 1983). However, this is making a major leap ahead in the argument to be developed here.

An important set of ideas making use of such a dualism of industrial establishments has been developed by Scott (1980, 1981, 1982a, 1982b). He suggests that the locational trends of industrial activity in metropolitan areas have become differentiated into two components. The first component is the tendency of labour intensive firms to cluster together at the centre of the metropolitan labour market, and the second is the tendency of capital intensive firms to seek out cheap land at relatively inaccessible (to the city as a whole) peripheral urban locations. 'Accordingly, as the historical process of the displacement of labour by capital in manufacturing industry has gone forward, so firms have steadily dispersed away from core areas within the metropolis.' (Scott 1982a, p. 125) Thus the spatial change of intra-urban manufacturing activity takes place by the addition of new establishments (and not firms as Scott suggests) to the outskirts of urban areas, and as the urban area expands through time these locations will become increasingly less suburban and absorbed into the main body of the urban complex in a fashion rather similar to Whitehand's (1972, 1974) conceptualisation of the locational development of major urban institutions. At the same time the number of establishments in central urban areas will decline. Scott's mechanism for change is the matching of the capital or labour intensive nature of establishments with variations in factor costs within the metropolis. Land costs and the costs of construction are regarded as being much higher in the central areas of cities and therefore capital intensive (which usually implies space extensive) operations are repelled from these areas. Meanwhile Scott suggests that labour costs over the post-Second World War period have become lower in the centres of cities than in the suburbs. Thus labour intensive establishments will locate in the urban cores.

This latter point requires further explanation. Scott (1981) argues with reference to empirical evidence from Toronto in the early 1970s that although wage rates are variable across urban areas they exhibit a strong tendency to rise as the local demand for labour rises relative to supply. Because population densities decline towards the suburbs and because urban transport systems are orientated towards urban centres, upward pressure on wages will take place as increases in labour demand move further from the urban centre. Thus it becomes possible for wage rates in less central locations to rise higher than those in urban cores. Evidence for such a trend has been found in New York since the mid-1950s (Hoover and Vernon, 1959) and more recently for the British conurbations in the 1960s (Tyler, Moore and Rhodes, 1980, quoted in Lever, 1982b).

Thus according to Scott industrial decentralisation in cities can be explained in terms of a switch by industry from labour intensive to capital intensive production systems dictated by the development of new technologies that have raised productivity and eliminated jobs. While these ideas certainly encapsulate much that is of use for an understanding of industrial decentralisation there is still a great deal more that needs to be added. Norcliffe (1984), for example, points out that during the last 20 years increasing numbers of manufacturing establishments which in the immediate post-Second World War era might have located in the suburbs of the major cities have located in non-metropolitan locations. As one moves towards more rural settlements both capital and labour costs will tend to decline. Thus, Norcliffe argues, Scott's basic theoretical framework should lead ultimately to all industry leaving the major urban areas for more rural environs. While the non-metropolitan areas of all western societies have experienced remarkably favourable levels of employment growth over the last two decades (Fothergill and Gudgin, 1982; Keeble, 1984; Lonsdale and Seyler, 1979) it is clear that a mass exodus of industry from urban areas has not taken place. In order to account for this observation in theoretical terms Norcliffe (1984) distinguishes between two types of capital costs: fixed and circulating. Fixed capital is invested in land, plant and vehicles whereas circulating capital is represented by primary, intermediate or even fully manufactured inputs that are needed to produce further commodities or are held as inventory. The cost of these inputs and inventories includes the cost of assembling them on a c.i.f. (cost, insurance, freight) pricing basis. As in Scott's model fixed capital costs are high in the urban core and decline towards the outer limits of the city and beyond. They will probably only begin to rise again in the most remote and inhospitable parts of a country. Circulating capital costs (which include the delivery costs in the price of the finished products), will tend to be low in central areas of cities and rise only slowly towards the suburbs. From the outskirts of the urban area circulating capital will rise at a faster rate.

One possible configuration of the circulating and fixed capital cost curves along with a labour cost curve with respect to distance from the urban core for a contemporary city is given in Figure 3.1c. The result of this argument, according to Norcliffe, is a more realistic division of manufacturing activity in contemporary urban areas into three groups:

Figure 3.1: The Distribution of Labour, Fixed Capital and Circulating Capital Costs with Respect to Distance from the City Centre of a Hypothetical Urban Area at Three Points in Time

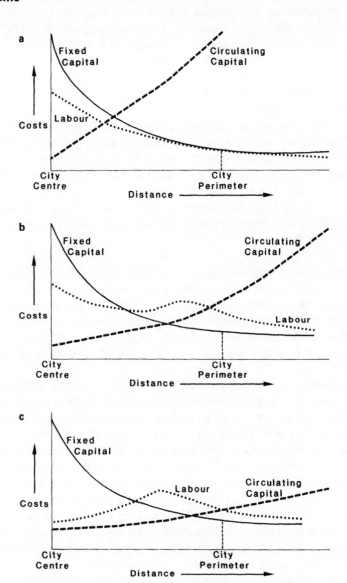

1. City centre occupiers — low labour and circulating capital costs and relatively high fixed capital costs — an area favoured by space intensive and labour intensive establishments.

2. The occupiers of relatively suburban locations — low fixed and circulating capital costs and relatively high labour costs — attractive for capital intensive operations such as automated assembly plants, warehousing and distribution which carry large stocks and need a lot of space. Such establishments are unlikely to be orientated solely to the local urban complex and therefore a suburban location may help to minimise overall accessibility to suppliers and markets.

3. The occupiers of non-metropolitan areas — low labour and fixed capital costs with the costs of circulating capital rising with increased distance from urban areas. Favourable for processing and fabricating plants which require substantial labour, and those producing high value goods which are easy to transport. The cost of circulating capital could also be minimised by the careful programming of deliveries and by the carrying of low inventories.

One of the disturbing features of this schema for the future employment opportunities of the major urban areas is that the kinds of industries likely to favour non-metropolitan locations such as light engineering, pharmaceuticals and electronics are the same as those identified by some academic futurologists as forming the next major growth impulse in western capitalist economies (Hall, 1981).

In general terms it is probably reasonable to suggest that the fixed capital cost curve has remained relatively stable throughout the last century as demand for central urban space has remained buoyant. Although initially this demand came from all forms of urban economic activity the demands of the tertiary sector now dominate. However, with the increased use of sophisticated information technology this may not be so in the future as it becomes increasingly possible to decentralise office occupations and functions to people's own homes. The circulating capital and labour cost curves have changed substantially over the last hundred years. In cities of the mid-nineteenth century, given only horse and cart and limited canal and early railway transportation systems, circulating capital would rise steeply from the centre of urban areas for most industrial activities. As a result central urban space would be at a premium and labour demand would be focused on these areas resulting in high labour costs. This situation is depicted in figure 3.1a. Figure 3.1b represents an intermediate stage. As technological improvements began to permit a combination of larger factories, a more efficient transportation system and larger market areas, then the rise of circulating capital costs from urban centres became less steep and the decentralisation of the more capital intensive forms of manufacture tended to increase suburban labour costs.

As the above discussion has already begun to make clear, changes in production technologies alone are not enough to account for the suburbanisation of manufacturing activity in western cities. A number of other technological as well as some societal developments must also be taken into account. For example in the post-Second World War period average plant size in employment and particularly in output terms has risen substantially (Prais, 1976) as firms have taken advantage of the potential economies of scale in production. However, such developments only became possible when a country's population became affluent enough to afford mass produced commodities such as clothes and magazines. In the clothing industry, for example, the off-the-peg, factory produced goods reached a much larger, and a somewhat different market, than the bespoke trade. However, in part owing to their lower cost, they helped to lead to the post-1940 decline in the made-to-measure clothes industries in western capitalist economies. In other industries such as brewing the growth of large scale establishments led more directly to the closure of competing establishments. In a market that was already substantially spatially saturated the only possible way of exploiting economies of scale was via the take-over and closure of existing smaller breweries. In the UK, for example, between 1951 and 1980 beer output increased, yet principally as a result of the acquisition and closure activity of eight rapidly growing firms the number of breweries declined from 539 to 145 (Watts, 1981).

The brewing example raises two further relevant issues. First, the growth and behaviour of large organisations about which more will be said later, and secondly the need for the development of communication systems to permit the distribution and organisation of production at an inter-regional scale. Improvements in road transport in particular through the building of motorways and inter-state highways along with the increasing fuel-efficiency of large trucks has led to a reduction in transport costs as a proportion of net output, and to a greater flexibility in delivery locations and load sizes. Containerisation has also helped to improve the efficiency of transportation systems at all scales. Thus market areas have been increased allowing establishments both to increase in size and to specialize in the goods they manufacture. In terms of intra-urban locational change it is clear that these changes all lead to a demand for larger premises and therefore to a demand for relatively suburban sites.

There are two further potential locational ramifications of these developments. First, the arrival of a large manufacturing establishment in an industry may lead to the closure of existing smaller units either indirectly in a competitive way by producing cheaper goods as in the clothing industry, or more directly by acquisition and closure as in brewing. It is highly likely that the plants closed will be in relatively central urban locations simply as a function of their earlier existence. Thus suburbanisation will be promoted. Second, and of greater importance in an inter-urban context, is the actual size in terms of market share of the new unit. In the extreme case of the new plant being able to satisfy the demand of a whole country or group of countries, and by initial price cutting being able to eliminate a large proportion of the potential competition, then a number of urban places could lose both employment and plants and only one place would gain. Furthermore, there is no guarantee that the new site will be in a city. A location in a relatively small settlement yet central to the whole potential market could be chosen. Thus, in part as a result of technological changes permitting increases in plant size, cities may be losing manufacturing establishments and employment to be left with at best local depots and distribution points. Some of the new manufacturing capacity will of course be created on the peripheries of existing cities but as already pointed out more may locate in smaller settlements in more rural locations.

According to Lever (1984) non-metropolitan locations may also offer distinct advantages to relatively large establishments in terms of risk avoidance, especially if the area has a high rate of unemployment and the plant, by virtue of its size, dominates the local labour market. In such a situation the firm to which the large plant belongs may be able to exercise considerable power in minimising the potential negative impacts of changes in the local external environment. Its dominance of the economy of a small settlement could lead to compliant Local Authorities, local linkage clients, and local labour markets, such that planning permissions for future developments could be easily obtained, wage rates controlled and favourable discounts obtained from local suppliers. These conditions are unlikely to apply to such an extent in large urban areas where no one manufacturing unit can hope to dominate. They therefore provide another set of reasons why contemporary manufacturing activity may be locating in non-urban places.

The post-Second World War period has not only been characterised by growth in plant sizes but, of far greater importance, by a growth in the concentration of all manufacturing activity into larger firms by merger and acquisition activity and by the setting up of new branch plants (see below). In this process plant size increases have played only a minor role. However to a large degree this has only become possible because of technological developments in inter-personal contact systems such as the telephone and telex which have permitted a central headquarters unit to exercise a high degree of control over many locationally distinct manufacturing establishments. Thus firms can benefit from growth economies (Penrose 1963) by setting up branches and acquiring existing firms without losing control over their operations. Indeed it has permitted the integration of the production of many spatially separate establishments into increasingly sophisticated product systems. Thus, and this is an important point for many urban economies, the replacement of locally owned industry by branches of multiplant corporations may in some cases lead increasingly to a corresponding replacement of the traditional external economies of an urban location by in-house linkages between the plants of these larger firms for components and services of all kinds (Lever, 1974). Clearly such a development could have a damaging effect on existing urban manufacturing establishments.

As production becomes increasingly concentrated into integrated systems of branch plants, and as deliveries between branches become larger and more carefully planned then, as Hoare (1975) has suggested, a consequence of a reduction in transport costs as a proportion of overall costs has been a corresponding reduction in the need for the spatial proximity of linked establishments. However, at the same time the inter-urban transportation of goods increases, and therefore motorway access points have assumed a particular significance for new plant locations. Clearly for establishments involved in multi-unit production systems central urban locations where roads are often congested — although admittedly some cities do now possess their own expressways and motorways — do not tend to offer advantageous locations. It is only when contacts between businesses and their customers are irregular that close proximity is advantageous. It is typically in parts of the clothing, leather goods, printing and publishing, furniture and instrument engineering industries in which irregular quantities of a specific good have to be produced because of irregularly changing demand specifications that close proximity between the interested parties is required for consultation purposes. In the past this proximity requirement has in part led to the development of large concentrations of interlinked establishments in some industries in relatively central urban locations. However, given the trend away from this small scale, craftsmen and labour intensive form of production, most post-1940 urban industrial research has tended to record the contraction of these once important urban industrial complexes. Examples include the gun and jewellery quarters of Birmingham (Wise, 1951), printing, publishing and clothing in Montreal and Toronto (Steed, 1976a, 1976b, 1976c), furniture, printing and clothing in London (Hall, 1962) and the garment industry in New York (Hall, 1959). Important remnants of these industries of course still remain in the central areas of some cities. However, their gradual contraction since the turn of the century has added an important decentralising component to the geography of intra-urban economic activity.

An important point often ignored by theories of intra-urban industrial change is that the majority of manufacturers rent their industrial premises, they do not buy them and they rarely build them. Therefore in the short to medium term the existing stock of industrial property available for rent places an important constraint on the locational dynamics of manufacturing activity in urban places. However, the existing stock of property in any city will vary markedly, from large warehouses in derelict docklands to newer flatted factories in suburban industrial estates and from new nursery units for small firms to loft-workshops in down-town tenements. Technological changes in best practice production methods may lead to changes in the types of industrial property demanded. Such changes have been particularly dramatic during the last 20 years. In recent rounds of investment labour saving devices and work practices have tended to be introduced and as a result, despite possible output increases, jobs have been lost (Massey and Meegan, 1982). This has happened throughout urban areas but especially in urban cores. In many cases existing premises have simply been unable to accommodate the space requirements of the latest profitable production methods, and the congested nature of many intra-urban sites may leave no adjacent room for the physical expansion of the existing building. Plants in urban areas have often faced a ceiling to *in situ* expansion (Keeble, 1968) but more recently, according to the 'constrained location' ideas of Fothergill and Gudgin (1982) they now face similar problems when merely considering re-equipping with modern production technologies. In buildings where these new production methods are adopted employment/floorspace ratios will fall. However, in many cases older industrial premises may have to be vacated altogether in favour of more modern and probably less centrally located urban factory accommodation. Given the preponderance of older industrial property in the central areas of cities it is clear that both these trends will tend to encourage the suburbanisation of manufacturing activity, the first in terms of employment and the second in terms of establishments. However, this must be tempered by the knowledge that the vacated central urban property will probably not move out of industrial usage. The stock of central urban industrial premises, although often seriously altered by redevelopment schemes (Bull, 1979), will probably have a much longer life span than any of its industrial inhabitants. Indeed much of this property will have a history of occupancy of probably increasingly marginal and transitory establishment until its eventual redevelopment or dereliction. The reoccupancy of industrial premises will clearly reduce the rate of suburbanisation.

The types of industrial property in a city will clearly be dependent upon its role in previous rounds of investment. However, because manufacturing establishments have shorter lives than their industrial buildings, these buildings will influence the types of future establishments attracted to the city. In some cases the effects of the vacation of industrial property may be economically relatively benign. For example, cheap small-scale central urban industrial property is often demanded by new businesses and therefore the closure or departure of its initial occupants may have few local economic impacts. Unfortunately in cities dominated by large establishments, such as Liverpool (Lloyd, 1979), and by those with specialised capital equipment then the departure of the initial occupiers may leave very little opportunity for reoccupation by other firms, and could lead to serious local unemployment. Thus, for an understanding of the potential economic stability of a city as well as for an understanding of the spatial and locational changes of manufacturing activity within it, it is important to have a detailed knowledge of its stock of industrial premises and the ways they may constrain the adoption of the most profitable forms of production.

The above discussion should lead to one principal conclusion: that during the last two or three decades manufacturing establishments in central urban areas should have been less profitable than those in other urban locations. It may also be tempting to suggest that many of the economic problems suffered by inner-city areas were a consequence of the secular decline of the industries, such as clothing, textiles, printing, and woodworking in which they often possessed large concentrations. An explanation of recent inner-city decline in terms of the industrial structures of these areas has, however, been shown to be false (Danson *et al.*, 1980). Inner-city areas tend to possess very diverse industrial structures (Bull, 1983) and therefore one would expect them to fare relatively favourably at all times, with local employment expansions in nationally growing industries counterbalancing the employment contractions of those in national decline. Unfortunately this has not been the case. For example, in terms of all industries between 1952 and 1976 the inner areas of the eight major UK conurbations declined by over 2.5 million jobs more than would have been expected given national growth rates and their own industrial structures (Danson *et al.*, 1980). The decline of central urban areas has occurred in nearly all manufacturing industries and its origins lie in the changing requirements of profitable production across all sectors.

In terms of the profitability of urban establishments there is a growing amount of evidence supporting the contention that firms in conurbations were not as profitable as either firms in smaller settlements (Fothergill *et al.*, 1984) or with national averages controlled by industrial sector (Lever, 1982b). However, for within urban areas the evidence is less convincing. Tyler, Moore and Rhodes (1980, quoted in Lever, 1982b) have used census data for the periods 1958-63 and 1963-68 to compare the UK conurbations with their hinterlands. Their results demonstrate that in general the British conurbations, excluding South Yorkshire, had a lower level of profitability (profit/employee) than their hinter-

lands, with Merseyside in 1963 and London in 1968 being exceptions. Although indicative of the anticipated trend this study again
is at a rather smaller spatial scale than required. The investigation
nearest to our needs is by Wellbelove *et al.* (1981) who used the
1974-77 accounts of firms in the central London borough of
Islington and compared them with equivalent national enterprises.
Unfortunately a marked discrepancy in profitability between
inner-city and similar national firms was not discovered. Indeed
when specific industries were considered, printing and publishing
and metal trades recorded higher levels of profit in Islington, this
being counterbalanced by lower local levels of profit in engineering
and clothing. It is not the case therefore that all inner-city firms
record lower levels of profit than their equivalent national-scale
enterprises. The authors account for this result by suggesting that
perhaps because of earlier pressure on operating costs fewer marginal enterprises existed in central London by the mid-1970s than
could have otherwise been expected. And this earlier closure of
marginal enterprises may have left in its wake a larger market for
those remaining in existence which could have temporarily
improved their profitability. For a short period of time therefore
the locational comparative disadvantage of inner London may
have come to an end.

In this essay the changing geography of intra-urban manufacturing activity has tended to be discussed in terms of manufacturing establishments or plants. Unfortunately, the evidence just
reported, including the work by Wellbelove *et al.* (1981) has been
in terms of firms. While many of the individual firms included in
this latter piece of research were small in financial terms and may
have been principally single-plant enterprises, some will have had
more than one establishment. This will also have almost certainly
been true of the national sample of firms adopted by this work.
Thus none of the research quoted above accords directly with the
parameters of the original inner-city profitability proposition. Of
course given that usually a firm only has to file its public accounts
for the enterprise as a whole and not for its constituent establishments this problem is unlikely to be resolved. Nevertheless, this
observation raises a fundamentally important point for an understanding of the behaviour of intra-urban manufacturing activity.
While it may be most appropriate to investigate spatial and locational change in terms of individual plants or establishments
because of their discreet locational nature, the behaviour of a plant

is of course controlled by the firm to which it belongs. To understand this behaviour one must have a knowledge of the strategies and plans pursued by the controlling firms. For any city under investigation the majority of firms encountered will probably be single-plant enterprises whose locus of decision making will clearly lie within the city and whose behaviour will be severely constrained by local conditions. However, for a large minority, and probably for those controlling most output and employment, their operations may be organised on a supra-urban scale with the strategic decision makers located in another city and with the local external environment having a relatively modest influence on their behaviour. In some cities these multiplant corporations may assume an alarming importance. In Merseyside, for example, the most extreme case in the UK, 90.7 per cent of all manufacturing employment in 1975 was controlled directly by multiplant firms and 85.8 per cent was headquartered outside the conurbation (Lloyd and Dicken, 1983). It is to a consideration of this corporate dimension on the geography of intra-urban manufacturing activity that this essay now turns.

The Corporate Dimension

One of the most prominent characteristics of the control and organisation of manufacturing activity throughout this century and especially in the post-Second World War period has been the increased economic concentration of production and employment, not only within nations but also on an international basis, by the growth of multiplant firms (Hannah and Kay, 1977; Lloyd and Dicken, 1977; Prais, 1976). This in turn has led to the development of multi-establishment production systems, sometimes involving plants and subsidiaries in many different countries (Hamilton and Linge, 1981). Thus the comparison of production costs for suitable plant locations may now increasingly be considered not only on an inter-regional basis within particular nations but also on an international basis (Dicken 1977). Furthermore, with the expansion of markets internationally companies may choose to operate in a number of countries to reduce the risks of national strikes, high interest rates, exchange and currency fluctuations, etc. even though it may be operating at a lower level of efficiency than if all production were on the same site (Lever, 1984).

By definition multi-unit firms are less constrained locationally than single-plant firms and have the opportunity to move production between existing units unlike the single-plant enterprise which must either change *in situ* or transfer to a new location. Thus, for the multi-unit firm adverse conditions in any one location could lead to a very rapid shift of production elsewhere, either within or between countries. In addition, decisions on the continuance of any one establishment within a multi-unit enterprise may no longer be in terms of its individual profitability but on how it fits into the corporate plan for the overall profitability of the business.

The growth of multiplant firms creates a number of problems for an understanding of industrial change within cities. As the manufacturing units within an urban area become increasingly absorbed and integrated into an extensive range of different sectoral and spatial production systems, then the reasons for spatial change become increasingly less local in origin. Local conditions, no matter how favourable for manufacturing activity, may not have the slightest impact on the continuance or expansion of a branch plant within an area. This is not just in terms of whether a firm is locally headquartered — that is, the strategic decision making unit is within the city investigated — but whether it is spatially organised on a local or an inter-regional/international basis. To understand industrial change in cities therefore one also has to begin to understand the spatially extensive production systems within which some plants in the city will be integrated. In addition, in terms of the behaviour of multiplant enterprises, cities must be viewed in many ways as no more than the recipients of decisions handed down by the major corporate decision makers, which in turn are conditioned by the exigencies of either national or international profitability. Clearly this makes a detailed explanation of industrial change within cities an extremely difficult task.

Within the branch plant and corporate affiliate sector in any major city there is a great deal of variation in the characteristics of the manufacturing units. They will differ in terms of, for example, industrial sector, their country of origin and ownership and in the size and spatial extent of the production systems to which they belong. As a result there may be many factors — international, corporate, technological, sectoral as well as local — impinging simultaneously upon decisions to close or open, or expand or contract, any individual plant belonging to a multi-unit enterprise within a city. Thus, as Lloyd and Shutt (1983, p. 32) point out 'while outcomes with respect to employment in the region are relatively easy to describe ... the processes at individual firm or sector level which gave rise to them are far more difficult to categorise.' One way of attempting to overcome some of the seemingly intractable problems posed by the multiplant corporate sector in cities is to concentrate on the behaviour of the most important, or 'prime-mover' firms in the area under investigation. That is, to begin by investigating the firms whose branches and subsidiaries are vital for the future well-being of the economy, labour market and levels of investment of the urban area, and whose future behaviour could have the most marked local structural and spatial impacts. In this area of research the work of the North West Industry Research Unit at the University of Manchester has been pioneering. Lloyd and Shutt (1983), for example, have demonstrated that 54 firms controlled almost 42 per cent (320,000 jobs) of the manual workforce in manufacturing in 1980 in the North West region of England, and that over the period 1975-80, as the recent recession deepened, these firms shed over 90,000 manual jobs. What is more, this loss was at a faster rate than in the other firms in the North West region. This work has also gone some way towards putting this employment loss into the context of the different corporate strategies adopted by firms with plants in the region to deal with the three dominant and interdependent economic imperatives of the time: corporate restructuring in the face of world recession and over-capacity, the introduction of new technologies, and the internationalisation of production.

Within the last 20 to 30 years the development of multi-unit firms has passed through probably two major phases, although of course they vary between corporations sectorally, spatially and in their precise timing. First the years of economic growth in the late 1950s and the 1960s witnessed a period of corporate growth, involving the establishment of branches and subsidiaries and acquisition and merger activity. For example, simply in terms of acquisitions and mergers, the Federal Trade Commission in the USA has estimated that the top 200 corporations in the country increased their share of total manufacturing assets by as much as 15 per cent between 1947 and 1968 (Lloyd and Dicken, 1983). The setting up of branch plants became part of the process whereby corporate functions could be split into different locations. Many branches became simply production (fabrication and assembly) units with only minor research and development and office functions. Frequently the latter functions were located in the major metropolitan urban centres, with the production units, it has been argued, being increasingly directed towards towns and cities where relatively cheap labour, and especially unskilled and female labour was available. Such locations have often been in the 'problem' or 'development' areas of countries which have usually had the added attraction of capital and development grants. Thus according to Massey (1979) and Dunford (1979) some cities which may once have specialised in certain products such as ships, textiles, or iron and steel may now be tending to specialise in certain types of labour, resulting in a general deskilling of the urban labour force (Thrift, 1979). At the same time the setting up of branch plants along with acquisition and merger activity was opening urban economies much more directly to the vagaries of international competition between transnational corporations.

In specific locational terms, given the above average size of many of the branch plants of the 1960s and their association with regional development assistance, suburban locations usually resulted, often in publicly or privately developed trading estates or industrial parks. This behaviour added an important decentralisation impulse to the geography of intra-urban manufacturing activity during this period of time.

The 1960s, however, were not a period of expansion for all major corporations. Those in industries with outmoded products and technologies, and partly as a consequence suffering from over-capacity, carried out rationalisation and disinvestment strategies as Massey and Meegan (1978) have shown for the 25 major firms in the British electrical and electronics industries between 1966 and 1972. The important point for the major cities of London, Liverpool, Manchester and Birmingham, encompassed by these firms was that although they only possessed 32 per cent of their employment at the beginning of 1966 they suffered 84 per cent of the jobs lost during the restructuring process. The 30,365 jobs lost in the major cities were either the result of *in situ* contraction, closure, location-loss to other factories, or in-transit loss. (The latter category recognises the fact that in the process of plant trans-ference in major companies jobs will be lost as a result of the rationalisation of production processes by machines replacing labour.) Only 11 per cent were the result of location loss — that is, jobs being diverted to other factories. The rest were lost to the economy as a whole. Clearly this represents the inability of cities in Britain to offer favourable locations and premises to many manufacturers during the reorganisation of large multiplant production systems.

More recently attention has been focused even more sharply on the rationalisation of major corporations during the recessions of the 1970s and 1980s (Hood and Young, 1982; Lloyd and Shutt, 1983; Townsend, 1983). The last decade has emphasised the need for corporations to invest in new process technologies, especially labour saving devices to lower production costs, and the need to operate internationally not only to reduce factor costs in western countries but, perhaps more importantly, to manufacture abroad so that foreign markets can be served without incurring tariff penalties as home demand declines. In some sectors such as electronics, for example, competition has been so severe and technological developments so rapid that individual manufacturing establishments may be in operation for only a few years until a new production process is brought into play which will demand a new factory. Lloyd and Shutt (1983), for example, cite the case of ICL which established a plant producing printed circuit boards in Manchester in 1979 that was closed in 1982 with over 300 redundancies as a consequence of technological developments.

The consequences for all urban areas of the recent recession have been particularly serious with establishments in many different locations and of all vintages being contracted or closed. As we have already described, throughout the latter half of the 1960s and during the first half of the 1970s the inner areas of the major metropolitan areas in most western countries lost many manufacturing jobs and establishments. The recession of the last decade would seem, although as yet there is little definitive evidence, to have had a more general impact. The behaviour of the larger firms in cutting capacity would appear to have been unpredictable with in many cases relatively modern premises being closed often in suburban industrial estates and often in the problem development areas of countries: that is, the loss of government assisted plants which have now added to the problem they were supposed to help overcome. This has been particularly true in the UK where since 1977 all the major industrial/urban areas except London have suffered faster rates of decline in employment than the country as a whole. The cities in severe decline therefore included the Birmingham-based industrial complex in the West Midlands, which in the 1960s was regarded as one of the major industrial growth regions of the nation (Keeble, 1985; Martin, 1982). However, as yet no detailed intra-urban analyses of the impact of the deep recession of the last decade have been published.

At the other end of the enterprise size spectrum much attention has been lavished recently by both politicians and academics on the role of small firms in generating new employment opportunities (Aydalot, 1984; Birch, 1979; Storey, 1982). In many western nations during the post-Second World War period the small firm sector has been in decline. However although marked variations exist between nations, since the decade of the 1960s the importance of the small firm sector has tended to be on the increase. Keeble (1985), for example, notes that between 1970 and 1980 in the UK the number of small manufacturing plants — those with one to ten employees — increased by 58 per cent and the number employed in this sector increased by 23 per cent in a period when manufacturing employment as a whole declined by 20 per cent. Keeble argues that this increase is not principally due to larger plants contracting into smaller ones, but much more to a relatively high rate of new small firm formation. Some of these firms have resulted from the unemployed attempting to become self-employed in the absence of any other form of gainful employment in the areas most severely affected by the recent recession. However, many more, and especially those in the growing sectors such as the high technology electronics industry, have shown a quite specific locational preference for the smaller towns and cities in the south and east of England. Many of the large traditional industrial cities of the north and west of the UK appear to be producing fewer of the more dynamic new businesses. In these cities, where of course large numbers of new firms are still being generated, far more are based on existing industrial practices, using second-hand equipment and existing on a sub-contracting and jobbing basis (Lloyd, 1980). It has been argued elsewhere that small firms cannot hope to generate enough employment in the short or medium term to begin to compensate for the loss of jobs from the rationalisation and closure of larger firms (Bull, 1983; Fothergill and Gudgin, 1979). There are simply not enough of them being created. And even in the more successful regions of the UK such as South Hampshire too few grow rapidly enough in the short to medium term to generate a significant number of new jobs (Mason, 1984). What is important here for most of the major urban areas in the UK and probably for the majority of large industrial cities in other western nations is that the most successful new firms which may begin to generate significant numbers of new jobs in the long term are unlikely to be located in the urban areas which most desperately need new employment opportunities.

Conclusion

This essay, after describing briefly some of the important points concerning the locational and spatial changes of intra-urban manufacturing activity, went on to begin to develop an explanation of the suburbanisation of manufacturing activity. This explanation was based on the ways in which improvements in technology have permitted through time major changes in the most profitable ways in which goods can be manufactured and distributed and in the ways in which this activity can be organised. In very broad terms these changes have led to a lowering in the demand for traditional industrial property in the central areas of cities in favour of the suburbs, and more recently non-metropolitan areas. The changing characteristics of manufacturing establishments, however, which have led to suburbanisation have not in general been the result of individual plants moving through a series of different forms of production, and therefore locations. It has resulted far more from plants with unprofitable characteristics being contracted and closed in relatively central urban areas and new plants being opened and expanded elsewhere. In New York in the late 1950s Hoover and Vernon (1959) observed a large number of centrally located establishments moving to more suburban locations to accommodate employment growth, and as a result they suggested that intra-urban transference was the principal motor behind the suburbanisation phenomenon. However, for the post-1960 period this has not been found to be the case in the majority of cities investigated (Bull, 1983; Fagg, 1980; Leone and Struyk, 1976; Nicholson *et al.*, 1981). Despite seemingly high establishment birth rates in central urban areas and high rates of intra-urban transference few plants during the last 20 years appear to have developed sufficiently to demand larger and more sophisticated premises, and as a result few have transferred to less central locations. Why is this? One way of approaching this question is to consider the way in which businesses in contemporary western societies are segmented into different groups; that is into unequal groups with distinctly different levels of economic power, being similar not in what they produce but in the organisation behind the production, that is, in terms of economic objectives, labour processes, technological usage, organisational structures and resources controlled (Taylor and Thrift, 1982, 1983). For the present period of time Taylor and Thrift divide the business world into two main segments: small firms and the large business organisations (see Figure 3.2). Size is not meant simply in terms of output or employment, although this is part of the distinction, but in terms of an inter-relationship of the above criteria for segment differentiation. What is important here is that although there will be connections across the corporate/ small firm divide in terms of sales, purchases, subcontracting, licensing, the departure of staff from corporations to set up their own small businesses, etc., the transition across the divide for any small firm is fundamentally difficult, except by take-over. There are a series of organisational, product dependency and economic barriers which in the majority of cases cannot be overcome (Taylor and Thrift, 1982). Thus firms have tended to remain in their economic segment or niche and in some cases it may be possible to equate these segments with particular types of premises and locations.

Taylor and Thrift (1982, 1983) divide the contemporary small firm segment into four groups

1. Leaders, firms in which a new unique product or process is exploited, often by an enthusiastic and entrepreneurial management.
2. Intermediates or dependent subcontractors.
3. Laggards which include (a) Businesses which are deliberately kept small by their owners in order to maintain control. If successful they may exist until the retirement of the proprietor; (b) Craftsmen based firms, often run by skilled workers producing small quantities of goods and often in industries with a long history.
4. Loyal opposition, firms, often with large plants in relatively stagnant markets with low profitability, and therefore unlikely to be taken over by growing corporations.

With the exception of this last group many of these firms will be single plant units demanding small scale premises. Within cities

Figure 3.2: The Segmentation of Contemporary Business Enterprises

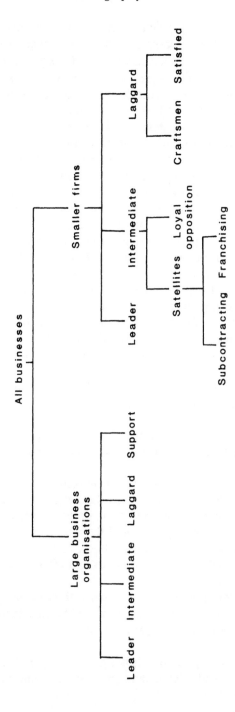

small scale industrial accommodation can of course be found in many locations. However, many of the largest western cities still possess major concentrations of this type of property to rent in relatively central locations. It is here that many of the intermediate and craftsmen type of small businesses may be found. It may be that for many of these firms to move from these locations and to be successful in more suburban sites would also necessitate a fundamental change in their behaviour, organisation and production techniques akin to crossing the major contemporary business segment divide. Thus few firms have in the last two to three decades made this transition. Instead they tend to remain in their economic niche, with the growth of any individual firm insufficient to make a serious impact on its economic status within the business world.

Figure 3.2 describes Taylor and Thrift's view of the segmentation of businesses in contemporary western societies. This typology is the outcome of the evolution of all previous segmentations as new ways of profitably organising production have developed. Taylor and Thrift (1983) suggest that the segmentation that exists today has its origins in the nineteenth century which was typified by factory-based businesses surrounded by constellations of small workshops. Elements of this earlier enterprise division may still be found in some cities today. Indeed large urban areas with industrial histories stretching back to the mid-nineteenth century could form useful arenas for furthering our understanding of the changing geography of intra-urban manufacturing activity because in these areas it would be possible to investigate in detail the locational ramifications of the progressive segmentation through time of business enterprise.

References

Aydalot, P. (1984) 'Questions for regional economy,' *Tijdschrift voor Economische en Sociale Geografie*, 75, 4-13

Birch, D.L. (1979) 'The job generation process,' MIT program on neighborhood and regional change, Cambridge, Mass.

Bull, P.J. (1979) 'The effects of central redevelopment schemes on inner-city manufacturing industry with special reference to Glasgow,' *Environment and Planning A*, 11, 455-62

Bull, P.J. (1983) 'Employment and unemployment,' in M. Pacione, (ed), *Progress in Urban Geography*, Croom Helm, London

Cameron, G.C. (1973) 'Intra-urban location and the new plant,' *Papers of the*

Regional Science Association, 31, 125-43

Community Development Projects (1977) *The costs of industrial change*, the CDP inter-project editorial team, London

Damesick, P. (1979) 'Office location and planning in the Manchester conurbation,' *Town Planning Review, 50*, 346-66

Damesick, P., Howick, C. and Key, T. (1982) 'Economic regeneration of the inner city: Manufacturing and office development in inner London,' *Progress in Planning, 18* (3), 137-267

Daniels, P.W. (1977) 'Office location in the British conurbations: trends and strategies,' *Urban Studies, 14*, 261-74

Daniels, P.W. (1982) 'An exploratory study of office location behaviour in Greater Seattle,' *Urban Geography, 3*, 58-78

Daniels, P.W. (1983) 'Business service offices in British provincial cities: location and control,' *Environment and Planning A, 15*, 1101-20

Danson, M.W., Lever W.F., and Malcolm, J.F. (1980) 'The inner-city employment problem in Great Britain, 1952-76: a shift-share approach,' *Urban Studies, 17*, 193-210

Dennis, R. (1978) 'The decline of manufacturing employment in Greater London: 1966-74,' *Urban Studies, 15*, 63-73

Dicken, P. (1977) 'A note on location theory and large business enterprise,' *Area, 9*, 138-41

Dunford, M. (1979) 'Capital accumulation and regional development in France,' *Urban and Regional Studies Working Paper, 12*, University of Sussex

Elias, P. and Keogh, G. (1982) 'Industrial decline and unemployment in the inner-city areas of Great Britain: a review of the evidence,' *Urban Studies, 19*, 1-15

Fagg, J.J. (1980) 'A re-examination of the incubator hypothesis: a case study of Greater Leicester,' *Urban Studies, 17*, 35-44

Firn, J.R. (1976) 'Economic microdata analysis and urban-regional change: the experience of GURIE' in J.R. Swales, (ed.), Establishment based research. *Urban and Regional Studies Discussion Papers*, 22, University of Glasgow, Department of Social and Economic Research

Fothergill, S. and Gudgin, G. (1979) 'The job generation process in Britain,' *Centre for Environmental Studies Research Series*, 32

Fothergill, S. and Gudgin, G. (1982) *Unequal Growth: Urban and Regional Employment Change in the UK*, Heinemann, London

Fothergill, S., Gudgin, G., Kitson, M., and Monk, S. (1984) 'Differences in the profitability of the UK manufacturing sector between conurbations and other areas,' *Scottish Journal of Political Economy, 31*, 72-91

Gad, G.H.K. (1979) 'Face-to-face linkages and office decentralization potentials: a study of Toronto' in P.W. Daniels, (ed.), *Spatial Patterns of Office Growth and Location*, Wiley, Chichester

Hall, M. (1959) (ed.), *Made in New York*, Harvard University Press, Cambridge, Mass.

Hall, P.G. (1962) *The Industries of London since 1861*, Hutchinson, London

Hall, P.G. (1981) 'The geography of the fifth Kondratieff cycle,' *New Society,* March 26, 535-7

Hamilton, F.E.I. and Linge, G.J.R. (1981) 'International industrial systems' in F.E.I. Hamilton, and G.J.R. Linge (eds.), *International Industrial Systems, Vol. 2, Spatial Analysis, Industry and the Industrial Environment*, Wiley, Chichester

Hannah, L. and Kay, J.A. (1977) *Concentration in Modern Industry*, Macmillan, London

Hoare, A.G. (1975) 'Linkage flows, locational evaluation and industrial geography: a case study of Greater London,' *Environment and Planning A, 7*, 41-57

Hood, N. and Young, S. (1982) *Multinationals in Retreat: the Scottish Experience,*

Edinburgh University Press, Edinburgh

Hoover, E.M. and Vernon, R. (1959) *Anatomy of a metropolis,* Harvard University Press, Cambridge, Mass.

Keeble, D.E. (1968) 'Industrial decentralization and the metropolis: the north-west London case,' *Transactions of the Institute of British Geographers, 44,* 1-54

Keeble, D.E. (1985) 'Industrial change in the United Kingdom' in W.F. Lever (ed.), *Industrial Change in the UK,* Longman, Harlow

Leone, R.A. and Struyk, R. (1976) 'The incubator hypothesis: evidence from five SMSAs,' *Urban Studies, 13,* 325-31

Lever, W.F. (1974) 'Manufacturing linkages and the search for suppliers and markets' in F.E.I. Hamilton (ed.), *Spatial Perspectives on Industrial Organization and Decision-making,* Wiley, Chichester

Lever, W.F. (1982a) 'Industry and employment,' *Unit 10 of Market processes II: the internal structure of the city,* Block 3 of urban change and conflict, Open University, Milton Keynes

Lever, W.F. (1982b) 'Urban scale as a determinant of employment growth or decline' in L. Collins (ed.), *Industrial Decline and Regeneration,* proceedings of the 1981 Anglo-Canadian symposium. Department of Geography and Centre of Canadian Studies Publications, University of Edinburgh, Edinburgh

Lever, W.F. (1984) 'Industrial change and urban size: a risk theory approach,' in B. Barr and N. Waters (eds.), *Proceedings of the 1983 Anglo-Canadian Symposium on Industrial Geography,* Calgary

Ley, D. and Hutton, T. (1984) 'Office location and public policy in a post-industrial city: the case of Greater Vancouver' in B. Barr and N. Waters (eds.), *Proceedings of the 1983 Anglo-Canadian symposium on Industrial Geography,* Calgary

Lloyd, P.E. (1979) 'The components of industrial change for Merseyside inner area: 1966-1975,' *Urban Studies, 16,* 45-60

Lloyd, P.E. (1980) 'New manufacturing enterprises in Greater Manchester and Merseyside,' *North West Industry Research Unit Working Paper No. 10.* School of Geography, University of Manchester

Lloyd, P.E. and Dicken, P. (1977) *Location in Space,* 2nd ed, Harper and Row, London

Lloyd, P.E. and Dicken, P. (1983) 'The components of change in metropolitan areas: events in their corporate context' in J.B. Goddard and A.G.Champion (eds.), *The Urban and Regional Transformation of Britain,* Methuen, London

Lloyd, P.E. and Reeve D.E. (1982) 'North-west England, 1971-1977: a study in industrial decline and economic restructuring,' *Regional Studies, 16,* 345-59

Lloyd, P.E. and Shutt, J. (1983) 'Recession and restructuring in the North-west region: the policy implications of recent events,' *North West Industry Research Unit Working Paper,* No. 13, School of Geography, University of Manchester

Lonsdale, R.E. and Seyler, H.L. (1979) (eds.), *Nonmetropolitan Industrialization,* Wiley, London

Martin, R.L. (1982) 'Job loss and the regional incidence of redundancies in the current recession,' *Cambridge Journal of Economics, 6,* 375-95

Mason, C.M. (1980) 'Industrial decline in Greater Manchester 1966-1975: a components of change approach,' *Urban Studies, 17,* 173-84

Mason, C.M. (1981) 'Manufacturing decentralization: some evidence from Greater Manchester,' *Environment and Planning A, 13,* 869-84

Mason, C.M. (1984) 'Small businesses in the recession: a follow-up study of new manufacturing firms in South Hampshire,' *Department of Geography, University of Southampton, Discussion Papers,* 25

Massey, D. (1979) 'In what sense a regional problem,' *Regional Studies, 13,* 233-43

Massey, D. (1983) 'Industrial restructuring as class restructuring: production decentralization and local uniqueness,' *Regional Studies, 17,* 73-89

Massey, D.M. and Meegan, R.A. (1978) 'Industrial restructuring versus the cities,' *Urban Studies, 15,* 273-88

Massey, D. and Meegan, R. (1982) *The Anatomy of Job Loss,* Methuen, London

Nicholson, B.M., Brinkley, I. and Evans, A.W. (1981) 'The role of the inner city in the development of manufacturing industry,' *Urban Studies, 18,* 57-71

Norcliffe, G.B. (1984) 'Non-metropolitan industrialisation and the theory of production,' *Urban Geography, 5*

Penrose, E.T. (1963) *The Theory of the Growth of the Firm,* Blackwell, Oxford

Prais, S.J. (1976) *The Evolution of Giant Firms in Britain,* NIESR, London

Schwartz, G.G. (1979) 'The office pattern in New York city, 1960-75' in P.W. Daniels (ed.), *Spatial Patterns of Office Growth and Location,* Wiley, Chichester

Scott, A.J. (1980) *The Urban Land Nexus and the State,* Pion, London

Scott, A.J. (1981) 'The spatial structure of metropolitan labour markets and the theory of intra-urban plant location,' *Urban Geography, 2,* 1-30

Scott, A.J. (1982a) 'Locational patterns and dynamics of industrial activity in the modern metropolis,' *Urban Studies, 19,* 111-42

Scott, A.J. (1982b) 'Production system dynamics and metropolitan development,' *Annals of the Association of American Geographers, 72,* 185-200

Steed, G.P.F. (1976a) 'Locational factors and dynamics of Montreal's large garment complex,' *Tijdschrift voor Economische en Sociale Geografie, 67,* 151-68

Steed, G.P.F. (1976b) 'Standardization, scale, incubation, and inertia: Montreal and Toronto clothing industries,' *Canadian Geographer, 20,* 298-309

Steed, G.P.F. (1976c) 'Centrality and locational change: printing, publishing, and clothing in Montreal and Toronto,' *Economic Geography, 52,* 193-205

Storey, D.J. (1982) *Entrepreneurship and the New Firm,* Croom Helm, London

Struyk, R.J. and James, F.J. (1975) *Intrametropolitan Industrial Location,* Lexington Books, Lexington, Mass.

Taylor, M. and Thrift, N. (1982) 'Industrial linkages and the segmented economy: I. Some theoretical proposals,' *Environment and Planning A, 14,* 1601-13

Taylor, M. and Thrift, N. (1983) 'Business organization, segmentation and location,' *Regional Studies, 17,* 445-65

Thrift, N. (1979) 'Unemployment in the Inner City: urban problem or structural imperative, a review of the British experience,' in D.T. Herbert and R.J. Johnston (eds.), *Geography and the Urban Environment. Vol. 2, Progress in Research and Applications,* Wiley, Chichester

Townsend, A.R. (1983) *The Impact of Recession on Industry, Employment and the Regions, 1976-81,* Croom Helm, London

Watts, H.D. (1981) *The Branch Plant Economy: a Study of External Control,* Longman, Harlow

Wellbelove, D., Woods, A. and Zafiris, N. (1981) 'Survival and success of the inner-city economy: the performance of manufacturing and services in Islington,' *Urban Studies, 18,* 301-13

Whitehand, J.W.R. (1972) 'Building cycles and the spatial pattern of urban growth,' *Transactions of the Institute of British Geographers, 56,* 39-55

Whitehand, J.W.R. (1974) 'The changing nature of the urban fringe: a time perspective' in J.H. Johnson (ed.), *Suburban Growth,* Wiley, Chichester

Wood, P.A. (1974) 'Urban manufacturing: a view from the fringe,' in J.H. Johnson (ed.), *Suburban Growth,* Wiley, Chichester

4 SERVICE INDUSTRIES: SOME NEW DIRECTIONS

P.W. DANIELS

Introduction

It may come as a surprise to discover a contribution on service industries in a text devoted to progress in industrial geography. For some reason the latter is invariably equated with manufacturing and most of the textbooks in economic geography published during the last 15 years do little to dispel this notion. Of course manufacturing industry makes a very important contribution to the socio-economic welfare and spatial organisation of both developed and less developed economic systems. But changes in the industrial distribution and occupational structure of employment during recent decades suggest that geographers must acknowledge and examine much more closely the significance of the expansion of service industries for the availability of employment opportunities and the morphological and development processes in the cities and regions which are ultimately exposed to the consequences of macro-scale economic and social trends.

In a review paper on the location of service activities Davies (1972, p. 125) noted that it 'is in the particular area of marketing geography, or retailing geography, that most substantive geographic work has been done. Alternative fields of enquiry, such as the geography of welfare and social services ... *and* ... Even distributive trades complementary to retailing, such as wholesaling and general office activities, have been relatively little investigated, although interest in the latter has recently gained considerable momentum'. There is no doubt that during the decade or so since Davies' observation the study of service industries by geographers has expanded to incorporate not just office location (Alexander, 1979; Goddard, 1975) but also health care delivery (Drury, 1983; Joseph and Phillips, 1984; Rosenberg, 1983; Shannon and Dever, 1974), recreation and tourism (Coppock and Duffield, 1975; Mathieson and Wall, 1982), public finance and service provision (Bennett, 1980; Kirby, Knox and Pinch, 1984) and, continuing work with the longest pedigree, studies in marketing and retail

111

location (Davies, 1976, 1979; Dawson, 1979, 1983; Guy, 1980; Sternlieb and Hughes, 1981). Issues associated with public welfare are also connected with service provision (Lea, 1979; Smith, 1977).

In this paper selected aspects of this recent work will be explored with a view to demonstrating the contention that there has been a recognisable diversification of the field of interest in service industry studies. It is suggested, however, that there is still a great deal of scope for much more research in which empirical and theoretical approaches could usefully be brought closer together.

Expansion of Service Industries

Services, which include transport and communication, retail and wholesale distribution, insurance, banking, finance, business services, professional services, a wide range of personal services and central and local government services, now account for some 75 per cent of non-agricultural employment in the United States and approximately 60 per cent in Britain (Davies and Evans, 1983; Dornbusch, 1983; Fox, 1984; Robinson and Wallace, 1983). Between 1974 and 1983 manufacturing employment in Britain decreased by almost 2.1 million jobs (−27.9 per cent) (Table 4.1) while employment in services increased by 765,000 (6.2 per cent); not enough to compensate for manufacturing job losses and rather different from the situation in the United States where manufacturing employment has remained stable but service employment (private sector services only) has increased by more than 5 million (31 per cent) during the same decade (Fox, 1984). The major increases in service employment have not occurred in retailing, which is the largest source of jobs within the service industries, but in professional and scientific services (12 per cent) such as legal/accounting services (34 per cent) and medical services (23 per cent), in insurance, banking and business services (20 per cent), and a wide range of miscellaneous services, especially entertainment, leisure, sport and clubs (37 per cent). Associated with these high growth rates for certain services has been growing specialisation of occupations and the displacement of blue- by white-collar workers in both manufacturing and service sectors. There has also been an increase in the level of part-time employment which seems to be associated with the growing proportion of females in the service sector labour force as well as an increase in the number of self employed, most of whom are engaged in providing services.

This is not the place to attempt an explanation for these clearly defined shifts in the structure of service employment, especially in advanced economic systems (see, for example, Bell, 1973; Blackaby, 1979; Gershuny and Miles, 1983; Singlemann, 1979; Stanback, 1979). It is sufficient to note that increases in productivity and output as a result of heavy capital investment by manufacturing industry have created a steady reduction in labour requirements while service industries, most of which are less capital intensive, require additional labour if they increase investment. This requirement is compounded by their lower productivity although, in practice, this is difficult to measure precisely because of the intangible attributes of much of the output (Smith, 1972). Whatever the causes of the expansion of services it seems especially important to know about the spatial patterns which they are

Table 4.1: Changes in UK Service Employment, 1974-83

Industry sector[a]	1974 (000's)	%	1983[b] (000's)	%	Change (%)
Transport and communication	1,483	12.1	1,305	10.1	−12.0
Wholesale distribution	829	6.8	829	6.4	0
Retailing	1,878	15.4	1,810	13.9	−3.6
Banking and finance	409	3.3	509	3.9	24.4
Insurance	262	2.1	287	2.2	9.5
Other business services	430	3.5	530	4.1	23.3
Medical and dental services	1,130	9.2	1,398	10.8	23.7
Education	1,693	13.9	1,740	13.4	2.8
Legal and accountancy services	187	1.5	250	1.9	33.7
Research and development	106	0.9	110	0.8	3.8
Other	168	1.4	170	1.3	1.2
Hotels and catering	795	6.5	923	7.1	16.1
Garages and motor repair	426	3.5	466	3.6	9.4
Recreation, sport and entertainment	277	2.3	380	2.9	37.2
Hairdressing	89	0.7	86	0.7	−3.4
Laundries and dry cleaning	86	0.7	60	0.5	−30.2
Other miscellaneous services	421	3.4	546	4.2	29.7
Public administration	1,551	12.6	1.540	11.9	−0.7
All services	12,220	100.0	12,985	100.0	6.2
Manufacturing industries	7,674		5,536		−27.9

Notes: a. Using Standard Industrial Classification, 1968.
     b. Estimates.
Source: Department of Employment Gazette and Census of Employment.

generating and the implications of these patterns for the planning and development of cities and regions (Marquand, 1979; Perry and Watkins, 1977; Stanback and Noyelle, 1982) or for models of the location of economic activity.

A Basic Dichotomy

In order to appreciate the case for the geographer's interest in service industries it is useful to distinguish immediately between two types of services. Firstly, there are those service industries that exist primarily to serve final demand and these are classified as consumer services (e.g. retailing, public transport, clubs, sport and recreation). Secondly, there are those service industries that provide specialist inputs which are used by other industries in the process of producing a final good or service; these are producer (or intermediate) services such as business services, research and development, advertising and market research, banking or bill discounting (Greenfield, 1966). While this basic classification greatly understates the problem of assigning individual service activities to either class because both final and intermediate demand may be met from the same establishment, and there are also occupational dimensions (see Gershuny and Miles, 1983 for a comprehensive overview), it draws attention to those services whose location is essentially dependent upon the distribution of population and those which are more dependent upon the spatial disposition of employment i.e. the manufacturing plants and office-based services which utilise their output.

Consumer services are therefore spatially ubiquitous and account for a large proportion of all service industry employment but producer services are much more footloose yet occupy certain kinds of location from which, given the structural and organisational changes in economic activity which are now taking place and in which knowledge is capital (Dicken and Lloyd, 1982), they exert considerable influence on the relative growth of cities, regions and even nations. Marquand (1979) has clearly demonstrated that there are spatial variations in the distribution of both consumer and producer services in the UK; even consumer services which are closely related to population distribution reveal varying degrees of under- and over-provision in different parts of the country and between cities of different sizes and location. Similar observations are made by Armstrong (1979) for the distribution of office employment and floorspace in the United States.

Local economic conditions, regional differences in the requirements of consumers, or variations in the willingness to invest, on the part of both retail and development companies, in different parts of the country (see, for example, Dawson, 1983) are just some of the factors leading to these spatial variations in service provision. However, the location decisions which give rise to discrepancies in the level of consumer services pose less of a threat to urban or regional economic, and to some extent social welfare than variations in the distribution of producer services. These services not only offer the prospect of substituting for the jobs shed by manufacturing as a result of de-industrialisation (Blackaby, 1978; Thirlwall, 1981) but also provide a lifeline to other economic activities wishing to adapt to the new opportunities for improved productivity or diversified product development made possible by the technological revolution. There is certainly some evidence for suggesting that the availability of producer services in regions influences the degree of innovation and product development in manufacturing (Oakey *et al.*, 1980) so that any deficits may retard the overall progress of a region or city.

Focus on Producer Services

Since there are many good state-of-the art overviews of retail location and planning (for example, Davies, 1976; Dawson, 1980, 1983), this chapter will concentrate on recent work on office-based and producer, rather than consumer, services. There are two prominent themes; firstly, studies of the locational behaviour and growth of office-based activities, many of which are producer services (although by no means exclusively) which have been subject to increasing research attention throughout the 1970s; and secondly, during the last five years there has been growing interest in exploring the locational and related behaviour of specific producer functions such as business or professional services. These two themes are to some extent interdependent in so far as some of the deficiencies in studies of office location have provided the lever for more specific analyses of individual producer services. Some of the output from these essentially empirical studies has also been utilised in more theoretical approaches to the location problem and some reference will also be made to examples of this work.

It is perhaps ironic that as the use and exchange of knowledge and information have become essential resources for the effective performance of contemporary economic activities, the activities and establishments which are the nodes in a complex web of inter-actions are still receiving relatively limited attention (Alexander, 1979; Armstrong, 1972; Goddard, 1975). Whether located in free-standing buildings in the CBD, in office parks in the outer suburbs (Hartshorn, 1973) or accommodated in office space inte-grated with production plants, office-based services are a much more intensive place for 'production' or for the deployment of manpower than industrial space. Therefore, despite the obvious physical impact of office buildings (Attoe, 1981) on selected parts of metropolitan areas, it is perhaps surprising that insufficient attention is given to their significance (and that of the producer services located in them) for urban economic development, the shaping and dynamics of the internal structure of urban areas, the demand which they generate for other services such as transport or retailing, or the changing relationships between areas within large cities and between metropolitan areas or regions at the national level (Corey, 1982; Goddard and Smith, 1978; Gottman, 1983; Pred, 1977). Office space now provides accommodation for at least 30-35 per cent of the labour force in advanced economies and producer services, such as financial services or advertising and computing services, which a recent estimate (Daniels, 1985) sug-gests occupy some 20-22 per cent of the UK labour force and probably more in the United States, are prominent occupiers.

An Historical Perspective

Prior to the mid-1950s the interest of geographers in office func-tions and their location was limited or non-existent. It was left to economists such as Haig (1927) to draw our attention to some of the locational considerations determining the place of the office function within the overall structure of the city. This interest was, of course, largely incidental to the attention given to the growth and location behaviour of manufacturing activities which per-formed essential basic functions in the economy. This early interest in office location was also largely to do with the way in which com-mercial office development fitted into neoclassical economic explanations for land use sorting in cities, especially within central areas where producer services have traditionally been prominent employers and competing users of space since the latter part of the last century. When geographers began to recognize the emergence of office functions they immediately considered them in a more explicit spatial context. Foley's (1956) work is a good example in that he traces changes, including shifts from the CBD to suburban locations, in the spatial distribution of administrative offices in San Francisco and offers some explanations. In many ways, Foley anticipated by several years an important motivation for office location studies, that of tracing the causes and consequences of locational change, during the 1960s and 1970s. In his study of linkages between activities in the centre of Philadelphia, Rannells (1956) also drew attention at an early stage to an important theme in subsequent analyses of office functions and their location.

Few urban and economic geographers followed these early leads. Given the early prominence of office space in American cities, there must have been a wealth of intelligence amongst developers and financiers about the location requirements of office-based activities and how these could be translated into suitable buildings. Unfortunately, such information tends to have restricted or at best, diluted, availability because of its 'value' to development companies and others who commission its collection but organisations such as the Building Owners' and Managers' Association in the United States have long kept records which might have provided a platform, however imperfect, for more research by geographers. The situation was little better in Europe until research burgeoned along a number of fronts when some applied geographical problems connected with imbalances in urban and regional development were recognised for the first time. This was especially true in Britain where, during the early 1960s, it was realized that office-based activities were making a significant contribution to the over-centralisation of economic activity in London and the South East.

This provided the spur for closer scrutiny of the characteristics and location of office activities: their spatial distribution (Armstrong, 1972; Goddard, 1975); the factors influencing their location behaviour (Alexander, 1979; Bennett, 1980; Cowan *et al.*, 1969; Damesick, 1979); the character and significance of meeting and telephone linkages (Gad, 1975; Goddard and Morris, 1976); the potential and actual mobility of office-based firms

(Code, 1983; Hall, 1972); the impact of mobile offices on their employees and the areas to which they had moved (Bateman and Burtenshaw, 1979; Daniels, 1980); or the effectiveness of the policy instruments used to attempt some redistribution of office functions between areas of over- and under-supply (Rhodes and Kan, 1971). All this work has its roots firmly implanted in efforts to better understand the office location pattern and process which has been viewed as imposing unacceptable costs on the population and infrastructure of, principally, large metropolitan areas while neglecting the changing needs of other regions experiencing the side effects of de-industrialisation.

As a result of the anxiety to monitor office location it is not surprising perhaps that empirical studies have been at the forefront. Such work provides valuable clues to the underlying processes but inevitably tends to rely heavily for explanations on the established tenets of neoclassical urban economic and industrial location theories. It is probably fair to say that this empirical tradition persists and is clearly evident in a number of publications during the mid- and late-1970s which attempted to provide a more systematic context for the study of office location (Alexander, 1979; Armstrong, 1972; Daniels, 1975). A trend apparent in recent studies of various facets of office location is the diversification of both their content and geographical coverage: from geographical analyses of trends in the location of corporate headquarters in the USA (Burns, 1977; Stephens and Holly, 1981), and in Canada (Semple and Green, 1983); to attempts to derive both normative (Clapp, 1983; Tauchen and Witte, 1983, 1984) and behavioural (Edwards, 1982, 1983) models of office location; and critiques of the assumption that relocation of office-based services from the CBD to the metropolitan suburbs or beyond is in some way an irreversible part of the dynamics of office location in Canadian or Australian cities (Code, 1983; Edgington, 1982).

Changing Directions

Modelling Office Location

An applied impetus has therefore been a very prominent characteristic of studies of office-based services. Although the number of attempts to develop models or to construct a theory of office/service location has been limited, interest in this facet of service sector research is growing. Partial models which incorporate behavioural approaches to decision-making (Edwards, 1982), employ economic equilibrium techniques (Clapp, 1980) or which rely on more descriptive approaches based on the costs and benefits of different location strategies (Alexander, 1979) represent the usual approach towards this problem. Economists are notable amongst the contributors to more specific theoretical work, largely through the application of equilibrium models. Thus far they have tended to concentrate on modelling office location at the microscale, such as the location of a firm within a square CBD (O'Hara, 1977) or an equilibrium model of office location and contact patterns in a hypothetical central area (Tauchen and Witte, 1983, 1984). This must be an important avenue for future work (see also Clapp, 1980; Malamud, 1971; O'Hara, 1977; Pritchard, 1975).

A notable feature of many of these models is the way in which they make use of assumptions about the contact behaviour of offices or the importance of agglomeration economies which are based upon existing empirical evidence. Good examples are the models developed by O'Hara (1977) and by Tauchen and Witte (1983). The former constructs an equilibrium model in which all the firms located in a square CBD derive equal benefit from access to the information assumed to be available because firms are centrally located relative to transport and other communications systems. Location is therefore resolved with reference to exogenously defined contacts and location decisions cannot be made on the basis of contacts between office firms in the CBD (endogenous contacts). The agglomeration economies derived from this interdependence are certainly influential in the location process so that in the Tauchen and Witte (1983) model location patterns are determined in circumstances where contact is defined endogenously by firms making profit-maximising decisions.

An important difference between this model and traditional industrial location models is that the latter assume that agglomeration economies are experienced simply by a firm being located in a city or industrial complex; in the Tauchen/Witte model firms only obtain the benefits of agglomeration through interaction with other office firms in the same area. Another strength of this model is that it makes use of the substantial empirical evidence about office contact behaviour and its heavy concentration within closely circumscribed areas to justify its emphasis on intra-urban rather than inter-urban modelling. The adoption of a square CBD (and city) is mathematically easier and well suited to many North American cities but is clearly less satisfactory for European cities. Market forces determine both the number and the entry and exit of firms into or from the city, office space can be constructed at any location, developers choose locations on the basis of profit maximisation in the same way as office firms also choose their location and volume of contacts in order to maximise their profits. The model ignores other benefits from agglomeration such as availability of a skilled labour pool or access to public services and, because of the emphasis on firm self-interest in location choice, the effects of public policies for land use zoning or limitations on the scale of development in specified areas are also overlooked.

The curves generated by the model for the relationship between distance from the centre of the CBD and rent or contact expenses are to some extent counter-intuitive. Contrary to traditional residential or industrial location models, the rent curves are concave rather than convex while the contact-expense curve is upwardly convex with increasing distance from the centre. These two curves are interdependent since the increased cost of maintaining contact from locations at the edge of the CBD (even if fewer contacts are involved) means that offices will be prepared to pay lower rents as distance from the centre increases. Tauchen and Witte (1983, p. 1323) conclude that the results of their work so far 'caution strongly against using industrial location models to address issues of office location'. There is therefore a good case for attempting to model the location of office-based services separately.

The application of normative theory to the location problem for office-based producer services does not only assume that the goal of profit maximisation is paramount but also assumes that decision makers, whether in single or multi-site organisations, are able to make wholly rational choices on the basis of complete information about the alternatives. There are those who would argue that this is an unrealistic way to explore the location problem and that it is more helpful to turn to the behavioural approach for more effective model construction (Edwards, 1983). Normative theory leaves many aspects of location behaviour unexplained, in particular the environmental context within which decision-makers must act and the internal attributes of the organisations of which they are a part. The latter means that organisational as well as individual choice is incorporated within the behavioural theory of office location.

Using existing empirical evidence about office location factors, together with data from two surveys of intra-urban office relocation in Liverpool and Manchester, Edwards (1983) has developed a hypothetical model of location choice for service sector establishments. The location decision process is divided into two stages; the stimulus to consider relocation (which may arise from conflict between the attributes of an office establishment and its environment) and the identification and evaluation of alternative locations. This is the core process model which is expandable to include, for example, the effects of factors internal and external to the organisation or the establishment. The external environment is a source of information which must be filtered and evaluated by decision-makers while the internal environment comprises personnel who must, in larger organisations, interact with each other as well as work within the constraints of company policy, budgets, operational characteristics and requirements.

A frequent element amongst the factors described by Edwards (1983) is the character of the establishment which is to relocate; it is therefore suggested that there is a relationship between the type of office establishment making a relocation decision and its decision profile. The hierarchy ranges from a branch without dependents of a large multi-site public company (Type I) to the sole office or small group of entrepreneurs at a single site (Type V). As one proceeds down the hierarchy informal incremental decision-making becomes more prominent because Edwards finds that entrepreneurs in small establishments (often acting on their own) are anxious to make location decisions which solve the immediate problem with minimal disruption to the day-to-day operation of their enterprise. Larger organisations (Type I) are more likely to seek the optimal location solution while type IV or type V organisations are only satisficers (Simon, 1955).

The choice of location by service establishments is rarely based only on the choice of suitable premises; other factors such as the attributes of their present location (whether CBD, inner or outer suburban for example), the residential distribution of decision makers, local initiatives to attract organisations, or improved access to existing or potential clients are just a few of the additional considerations. The heterogeneous character of service activities, in both the consumer and producer groups, also makes it difficult to derive a location decision-making model which is universally applicable. Perhaps it is significant, however, that despite 'the inherent potential for a range of processes, there is evidence of a recognisable insurance, banking and finance-sector identity from the communality of location requirements and modes of internal operation' (Edwards, 1982, p. 1341).

The location problem for service activities is not simply where to locate at the intra-urban level, there are also circumstances where an inter-urban location choice is necessary. This has attracted a good deal of empirical work, particularly on the location of headquarters offices (see, for example, Armstrong, 1979; Burns, 1977; Evans, 1973; Stephens and Holly, 1981) but only recently has an attempt been made to devise a model for inter-urban head office location (Coffey and Polese, 1983). The problem can be expressed in terms of the trade-off which head offices of multi-establishment firms must make between externalising inputs which they obtain on the open market from advanced corporate (producer) services and internalising inputs in the form of the skilled management required to perform tasks which would otherwise be contracted in. The principal assumptions of the model are: firstly, every head office produces a set of varied and variable outputs; secondly, it has a given and captive market for this output (other establishments within the same multi-regional organisation, for example); thirdly, the optimum location for the head office is not immediately obvious because of the multi-regional distribution of branches or other establishments; and fourthly, each head office seeks two major factor inputs which are advanced corporate services (ACS) and skilled management resources (SMR). The assembly of ACS and SMR will also entail communications costs (C).

After detailed validation of each of these assumptions, using documentary, interview, and existing empirical evidence, a typology of inter-urban head office orientation is suggested in relation to the distribution of total costs among communications (C) and the two principal factor inputs (ACS and SMR) (Figure 4.1). Since the model is in the prototype stage of development it is assumed (arbitrarily) that if a head office allocates more than 50 per cent of its spatially variable expenditures on one of the three elements then it will orientate itself towards the most economic and efficient location for that element. There are four types of orientation (Figure 4.1). There is an SMR orientation in which head offices will gravitate towards large cities with specialised labour pools or those which offer a high quality of life. Secondly, there is an ACS orientation and therefore greater externalisation of inputs which will encourage head offices to locate in major corporate complexes (Cohen, 1977) such as Paris, New York or Toronto. Corporate or producer service complexes will also be major points of orientation for the third group of head offices for which communication, including interaction at the international level is the key requirement. Finally, Figure 4.1 shows that the fourth type of orientation does not involve the dominant pull of any of the other factors and head offices therefore have locational flexibility.

These are interesting developments on the theoretical side of service industry location which should provide momentum for further research at the intra-urban level with reference to both the

Figure 4.1: A Typology of Head Office Location at the Inter-urban Scale (After Coffey and Polese, 1983)

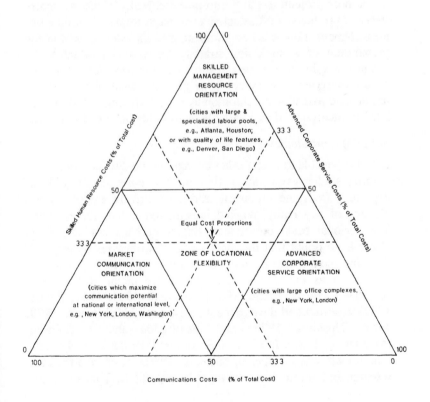

pattern and dynamics of location. Smith and Selwood (1983), for example, have used the negative exponential model to test four inter-related hypotheses concerning the relationship between distance, density and functional attributes of office dispersal within Columbus, Ohio. They show that distance from the centre of Columbus is becoming less important for discriminating between variations in the density of office floorspace (although it is still important), that absolute decentralisation has been dominant since 1970 for all except business service and government offices, and that distance decay effects in the geographical spread of dispersal are strongly developed and ensure the dominance of inner rather than outer suburban locations for the location of almost all types of service function. The value of this work is the scope which it provides for testing the conclusions suggested by the model in cities of different size, functional structure and position in the urban hierarchy.

It is of course easy enough to advocate more model building but much more difficult to put it into practice. Many of the raw materials and products of office activity present formidable problems of measurement; how is access to an item of knowledge used in the preparation of a marketing strategy for a new product to be assigned a value within an assessment of the total cost of a relocation exercise? The number, weight and availability of bolts required to assemble an automobile are clearly more easily calculated or incorporated as a variable in an industrial location model.

Sector-specific Studies

It is also possible to detect other changes in the direction of service industry studies even though they do not represent a significant departure from the empirical traditions already extant. In the absence of any really detailed information about, for example, inter-regional trade in services, this is perhaps not surprising. There is no doubt that the most useful contributions on issues of this kind have focused attention on some significant growth services such as business services which are mainly office-based activities (Daniels, 1983b, 1984a; Marshall, 1981, 1982; Polese, 1982), research and development (Howells, 1984; Malecki, 1979, 1982; Thwaites, 1978) and distribution and warehousing (McKinnon, 1983). In the British context the interest in the location, growth and linkages of business services or of investment in research and development arises, at least partially, from a continuing concern about the persistent underlying weaknesses in British urban and regional development and the belief that an improved understanding of the links between functions such as business services and other economic activities will help to isolate more effective policies for stimulating the contribution of mobile, as well as indigenous, service and office activities to more successful regional policy initiatives.

One of the most comprehensive studies of the regional demand for business services has been undertaken by Polese (1982) in the Eastern townships of Quebec, a compact region of 250,000 inhabitants 150km from Montreal. Data were collected from 408 establishments in the region: 31 per cent represented mining and manufacturing; 32 per cent retailers; 16 per cent wholesalers; and 21 per cent construction firms and business service establishments. The information obtained was used to examine the possibility that the way in which establishments obtain their service inputs will determine the direction and volume of inter-regional flows in the demand for services. The principal options available to establishments are to obtain services in-house, via intra-firm transfers, or by making purchases on the market from other firms. Intra-firm transfers will be controlled by head offices so that their location will also affect the level of inter-regional flows.

The propensity to use services (24 separate types are identified in the survey) increases with increasing size of establishment but some services are more likely to be internalised (or organisation oriented) than externalised (market oriented). The most organisation oriented services (i.e., they depend on intra-firm transfers) are insurance, legal services, long term debt factoring, accounting, publicity, and engineering and technical studies (research). Since most head offices are located outside the region, as they are in the provincial regions of Britain or France for example, the demand for these services will 'leak' to the other region(s) where the head offices are located. Services which are obtained mainly from the open market, and for which inter-regional flows will reflect the influence of distance for example, include construction services, real estate, repair, transportation services, equipment rental, management consultants and architects.

Polese (1982) also calculates the value of the expenditures on each service by the survey establishments and examines the regional distribution of purchases (Table 4.2). It emerges that over 50 per cent of regional service demand is fulfilled by imports, many of them in the form of intra-firm flows rather than market-oriented flows. Market-oriented transactions are heavily focused on the study region (95 per cent) and tend to be directed at a small number of services such as repairs, engineering services, construction and transport. By comparison, the structure of imported service flows is diverse and certain services for which intra-firm demand is significant, such as financial and business services, almost completely avoid the region. In view of changes in corporate structure and organisation, increased intra-firm transactions and their associated inter-regional flows of business service demand are likely. These will reinforce the comparative advantages of complexes comprising headquarters offices and dependent financial and business services which 'means that theories of service flows must necessarily be tied to theories of office location, especially head office location' (Polese, 1982, p. 162).

Marshall (1982) has collected information about the linkages between manufacturing establishments and business services in three British conurbations; Manchester, Leeds and Birmingham. In common with Polese (1982), he shows that the status of a manufacturing establishment and its size — whether, for example, it is a branch of a multi-site organisation or the sole production unit of a local manufacturer — affect the degree to which it seeks services from local suppliers. The type of industry represented by a manufacturing establishment is also important; those representing the chemicals industry in the North West purchased only 27 per cent of their service inputs from outside the company and a relatively high proportion of these purchases (almost 30 per cent) outside the local region. The prominent worsted and woollen industry companies in Yorkshire and Humberside, on the other hand, sought more than half of their service inputs from outside the company with less than 10 per cent supplied by service firms outside the local region.

There are spatial variations in the demand for service industries such as insurance, advertising, accountancy and banking both at the level of major cities and between regions (Daniels, 1984a). In the North West 61 per cent of the services required were supplied from within the companies surveyed whereas in the West Midlands the equivalent figure is almost 54 per cent; the fact that 66 per cent of the establishments surveyed in the former are branches and just 48.6 per cent in the latter goes some way towards explaining the difference (Marshall, 1982). Not only does this influence the

Table 4.2: Regional Distribution of Total and Intra-firm Service Expenditures (%) for Business Establishments, Eastern Townships of Quebec

Service[a]	Study region	Montreal	Rest of Quebec	Toronto	Rest of Canada	International	Total dollar value (000's)
Employment services	68.2[b]	28.1	3.8				58.1
		100.0[c]					121.1
Student training	98.2	0.5	0.9		0.4	5.1	1,993.9
	66.7	33.3	1.6				30.0
Factoring	5.2	86.2	0.8	7.9			3,949.7
		90.4	0.8	8.8			3,551.0
Insurance (premiums)	22.5	58.0	7.2	8.1	1.9	2.3	8,898.9
	1.6	81.1	0.6	11.9	2.8	2.0	5,288.0
Real estate	89.3		10.7				46.8
							0.0
Legal services	27.8	60.8	2.3	6.8	0.1	2.1	2,249.6
	0.2	85.8	1.1	11.0	2.1	2.1	1,404.1
Accounting	21.8	39.0	31.2	6.7	1.2	0.2	4,226.5
	2.2	38.6	46.1	10.8	1.9	0.4	2,617.1
Management consultants	24.7	45.7	7.2	4.3	6.4	11.6	498.5
	5.4	65.8	2.0	6.6	10.8	9.4	296.4
Marketing studies	2.9	68.3	0.6	3.9	3.9	20.3	560.9
	1.9	84.0	0.9	5.0	5.0	3.2	438.1
Computer services	3.0	86.5	3.6	4.1	2.8		5,239.1
	3.8	70.5	10.2	10.1	5.3		1,669.0
Trucking	50.1	15.2	28.2	2.0	2.0	2.6	34,951.9
	23.1	62.1	3.0	9.7	1.8	2.2	7,139.3
Total	44.3	34.7	12.2	3.9	1.9	3.0	100.0
	6.5	70.1	6.3	11.9	1.8	3.5	100.0

Notes: a. Selected services only. The full list comprises 24 services.
b. Proportion of total service expenditure. Row sums to 100.
c. Proportion of intra-firm expenditure on each service. Row sums to 100.

Source: Polese, M. (1982), compiled from Tables 5 and 6, pp. 159-60.

demand for services but also points to the difficulties confronting those that do exist in provincial locations when competing with London, where many of the headquarters of non-local manufacturing establishments are located and where any external business service inputs will most likely be purchased.

Spatial variations in the supply of services may also result from the way in which the service sector organises itself since this might also affect the demand from manufacturing. Services are just as much affected by organisational changes which may lead, for example, to greater centralisation of control in fewer organisations with a growing number of branches (Daniels, 1983b; Marshall, 1982). Alternatively, services such as the banks are reducing the number of local branches and bringing together many intermediate services to a more limited number of sub-regional locations, often in major service centres. It therefore seems that the 'relationship between the manufacturing and service sectors in provincial conurbations is likely to be two-way with changes in the composition of each affecting the other over time in historical rounds of investment' (Marshall, 1982, p. 1525).

It is of course too simplistic to view the place of service industries in the provincial conurbations as purely dependent upon the demand from manufacturing industry. Some services export their output to other regions and cities (Daniels, 1984a; Douglas, 1981) and as, in Britain at least, the manufacturing sector continues to contract there may, paradoxically, be increased demand for business services as companies which are no longer large enough decide to externalise rather than to internalise their requirements. In the context of regional policy it is therefore crucial to consider carefully possible ways of influencing the location behaviour and the growth of service industries as well as manufacturing.

Research and development (R and D) is a service which is not usually purchased externally but is undertaken internally by manufacturing industry or by government-supported research establishments and in universities and polytechnics (Malecki, 1982; Rothwell and Zegveld, 1981). It has been suggested that the level of R and D investment and activity in different regions of a nation leads to variations in the performance of their manufacturing industries. Hence, the Northern Region Strategy Team (1977) found a relatively small number of in-house and other R and D establishments in the Region and if this reduces the chances that manufacturing industry will apply new technology to production there may be implications for job growth and diversification (Thwaites, 1978). Studies of the spatial distribution of R and D activity have been surprisingly limited for an activity considered important for the relative performance of regions (Howells, 1983) or metropolitan areas (Malecki, 1982).

In a recent and comprehensive review of work on the location of R and D in Britain Howells (1983) finds that employment is heavily concentrated in the South East region and, furthermore, that this distribution has become stronger between 1971 and 1976. However, within regions private sector R and D establishments are increasingly located in less urbanised and rural counties where quality of life considerations are one important factor for the retention of highly skilled scientific and professional staff. The two most important location factors cited by pharmaceutical companies for the location of R and D, in Howells' survey, were proximity to the head or divisional office and proximity to the main production unit. While there may be detailed differences between industries, the concentration of corporate headquarters in London and the South East (Goddard and Smith, 1978) and the concentration of growth industries with a high research input in the same region (Keeble, 1980) ensures that R and D continues to flourish there, leaving peripheral regions to depend upon the expansion of indigenous R and D or the import of the activity from elsewhere (Oakey, 1983).

Warehousing is another service activity which incorporates a substantial intermediate function but which has also received limited attention until recent years (McKinnon, 1983; Vance, 1970; Watts, 1977). Improvements in national transport networks, legislation permitting the use of larger trucks or changes in the organisation and scale of retail companies and their outlets have encouraged firms to seek the benefits of economies of scale in large warehouses strategically located for efficient distribution. The location requirements for the new generation of warehouses are very different from their predecessors which were located near rail termini or port facilities in inner city areas. Consequently job losses and physical blight have been created in areas already disadvantaged by the almost universal decentralisation of population and manufacturing industry (see, for example, Hubbard and Nutter, 1982). The pressures of demand for warehousing adjacent to motorway intersections or more generally on the edges of the major conurbations has not only created a new land use problem for planners but has also encouraged a more positive attitude towards their contribution as an alternative source of employment to manufacturing. But McKinnon (1983, p. 397) draws attention to the limited knowledge available to planners and there 'is a need for similar geographical research to be done on warehousing as on manufacturing, examining factors influencing the choice of warehouse location, tracing the pattern of linkage between warehousing and other activities and measuring the employment potential of different types of warehousing'.

New Technology and Service Industries

There has been growing concern in Britain, but rather less so in North America, about the effects of new technology on service employment and its location (Coombs and Green, 1981; Goddard, 1980; Mandeville, 1983; Marshall and Bachter, 1984). The employment effects have received more attention but must ultimately lead to spatial consequences for the growth and spatial differentiation of the office function (Daniels, 1983a; Pritchard, 1982). It certainly cannot be assumed that the adoption of office technology will conform with intuitive notions, such as larger and more locationally centralised firms will be the first in the field. Evidence from a survey of more than 300 service firms in several British provincial cities (Daniels, 1983a) suggests that the location of organisational control or the functions performed by an office establishment are much more significant than size for the adoption of information processing and telecommunications equipment. The innovative establishments in provincial office centres are therefore most likely to be externally controlled but it remains uncertain whether this will lead to patterns of job losses, for example, which will vary according to the degree of external control in different centres.

Information technology may also be used as a mechanism for improving competitiveness so that smaller indigenous service firms in centres remote from the centre of gravity of a service-based economy will be more willing to adopt it than those firms located nearer to the principal markets. It remains the case, however, that it is extremely difficult to 'draw place-specific conclusions from existing research on technological change' (Marshall and Bachtler, 1984, p. 437). Edgington (1982) has also highlighted this limitation in his study of office activities in central Melbourne. In their study of the banking sector Marshall and Bachtler (1984) suggest that it has become more concentrated as a result of using information technology but that the prospects are for a more dispersed location pattern as the technology, such as electronic funds transfer, autobanking, customer-cashier terminals, automatic telling machines, and point of sale facilities, becomes even further advanced and more deeply embedded into the structure of bank organisations. During recent years a number of the major British banks have been rationalising the services directly available from branches which can be served from specialist staff located in local administrative offices electronically linked to the branches or even from regional headquarters. The diffusion of automatic cash dispensers outside bank premises has also reduced manpower requirements and caused banks to look closely at overheads such as the cost of premises at expensive city centre locations; this will probably lead to greater dispersal at branch level. It is interesting to note that the very limited evidence from the empirical studies so far undertaken lends support to Mandeville's (1983, p. 70) view that the effects of information technology are 'essentially paradoxical: the spatial consequences of information technologies are probably both centralising and decentralising. The determining factor is not the technology but how we choose to use the technology'.

Re-evaluating Established Assumptions

Finally, as research on office-based producer services has evolved during the 1970s a number of observers have re-evaluated some of the assumptions implicit in our interpretation of locational trends. Code (1983), for example, has questioned the merits of promoting decentralisation of office activities in Toronto. The argument against a policy which is an integral part of most strategic plans for large metropolitan areas in advanced economies is that the strong information linkages in certain parts of the central Toronto office complex cannot be adequately replaced in suburban office centres. Therefore 'summing the losses as well as the gains incumbent upon the progressive decentralisation of firms suggests that the net communication loss to the decentralised firms would be greater than the gain to the new suburban centres' (Code, 1983, p. 1379). The demand from firms in central Toronto for suburban offices as a proportion of all demand has declined during the last two decades and even those office functions which are theoretically most mobile (see also Gad, 1979) have also been reluctant to move.

Code suggests that the most important explanation may be the real or perceived variation in the quality of information between different parts of the metropolitan area and 'resistance on the part of most core firms to the suburban move may be a rational decision' (Code, 1983, p. 1380).

It may therefore be unwise to rely on conventional ideas about locational tendencies which largely reflect the influence of, for example, accessibility or land rents. It is necessary to take closer account of organisational and structural change as well as the effects of technology on the future of established concentrations of service activity. The core area of large cities is considered very vulnerable (see, for example, Sternlieb and Hughes, 1983) for reasons of cost as well as the pull to the suburbs as population has dispersed but while consumer services can reasonably be expected to respond, it is now far from axiomatic that producer services will follow. Therefore, Gottman (1983) suggests that the development of the transactional metropolis in which abstract transactions have replaced the production and handling of goods has re-invigorated central areas even though suburbanisation of residential population continues unabated (see also Cohen, 1979; Corey, 1982). Perhaps the key to the stability or even re-centralisation in large metropolitan office complexes is that cities and the services located there 'compete sharply between themselves. Each skyline has its own orbit. Each city belongs to a region and a nation, but also belongs to other circuits, increasingly of an international configuration ... *so that* ... the individual city's centrality is constantly being reborn' (Gottman, 1983 p. 15).

Service Industries in International Context

The international configuration of service industries is only just beginning to attract attention (Dunning and Norman, 1979, 1983; Heenan, 1977). The expansion of service firms has usually been confined to locations within their national boundaries; international operations become feasible when a service identifies a competitive or ownership advantage over similar firms in other countries, believes that these advantages are best exploited internally rather than by licensing or selling their specialism to other firms, and when internalisation of ownership advantages is best exploited by starting operations at locations outside the home country (Cowell, 1983; Dunning and Norman, 1983; McIver and Naylor 1980). North American business service firms opening branch or regional offices in Europe are able to draw upon a skilled pool of labour, specialist information reflecting more accurately the demands of the European market, or take advantage of flexible trading arrangements within the European Economic Community. By providing their service internally they can protect and exploit it to the full, ensure the highest level of control on the quality of their product, and exploit contacts which may already exist with clients in other countries and from this base develop completely new indigenous business contacts. The introduction of international operations may also reduce the cost of providing services formerly provided from the parent country; regular transatlantic travel by executives servicing client accounts in Paris or in New York is less cost effective (in time and monetary outlay) than retaining the same personnel at one strategically located office in Europe.

Assuming therefore that a market of adequate size has been identified the problem is where to locate a branch or regional office; factors such as access to clients or internal economies of scale through centralisation of operations at one location will be weighed against the benefits associated with external economies of scale. The empirical evidence accumulated by Dunning and Norman (1983) for the location of US-based business services in Europe suggests that major corporate complexes are a prime attraction, especially locations in CBDs and adjacent and easily accessible suburban centres; Brussels, Paris and London are by far the most prominent locations (Table 4.3). International airports also exert some locational pull (see also Bennett, 1980) for business services with extensive international connections. Advertising services, accountants, legal services, banking, insurance, management consultants, design engineers and property consultants are all represented and are helping to reinforce the comparative advantages of certain major cities which are well connected to both national and international telecommunications networks (Daniels, 1985). The emerging global service economy has implications for the status of major metropolitan areas as control points influencing development across a wide range of economic activities in other parts of the world as well as exaggerating the centralisation of producer services (both national and international) into a dominant city at the heart of a national urban system.

Table 4.3: Distribution of U.S.-based Business Service Offices in France (1977) and the UK (1976)

Business service	France Paris centre[a]	suburbs	Elsewhere	United Kingdom London centre[b]	suburbs	Elsewhere	Total
Management consultants/ executive search	19	9	*	40	9	3	80
Advertising	13	6	*	15	4	*	38
Accountancy	2	5	*	12	*	*	19
Insurance	6	6	*	16	4	1	33
Banking	32	7	*	73	1	2	115
Engineering design	9	7	1	8	8	2	35
Legal practices	*	*	*	24	3	*	27
Others	4	*	8	25	5	6	48
Totals	85	40	9	213	34	14	395

Note: a. 1st-9th arondissements.
b. EC, WC and W1 postal districts.
Source: Derived from Dunning, J.H. and Norman G. (1983), Table 2, p. 684.

Should Service Industries be Examined Separately?

There is at least one important question arising from the growing volume of recent research on aspects of an intrinsically diverse industry sector; is separate analysis of services a realistic way forward? The emergence of, for example, a more sector-specific approach together with a continuing recognition that non-production activities attached to manufacturing must also be incorporated in any analysis of service activities (Crum and Gudgin, 1978; Gershuny and Miles, 1983) has perhaps contributed to a devaluation of, in particular, office location research. In order to examine the location of offices within this sectoral framework it is, for example, necessary to take cognizance of organisational, operational, or business variables which may only have a tangential influence on office location choice. This causes the distinction between the office function and other functions within increasingly complex organisational structures to become blurred, creating undoubted difficulties for the effective analysis of office location and development as a separate phenomenon. Instead, Pickvance (1981) or Scott (1982) would argue that the office-based services are but one component of the capitalist mode of production and their contribution to the urbanisation process, for example, should be analysed in that context rather than as a distinctive entity.

It would seem unwise to accept this view until it can be convincingly shown that the analysis of service industry location is indeed subsumed by the larger problem of the relationship between urbanisation, planning and the socio-economic infrastructure within which it exists. In order to justify such a position, detailed efforts will continue to be necessary to see whether individual elements, such as business or financial services, conform to the general model. The brief and inevitably selective review offered here indicates that much remains to be done which is specific to the location of service industries and their role in urban or regional employment, development and change. It may well be, of course, that the location of services is determined by the larger scheme of things but this should not preclude attempts to understand it by approaching analysis from the direction of service firms, decision-makers, the office and commercial development industry (Barras, 1983; Fuchs, 1983) or the planners endeavouring to use service industries to achieve their goals for providing employment or changing the internal structure of metropolitan areas.

136   *Service Industries*

Conclusion

There are clear signs that the horizons of service industry studies have been greatly extended during the last decade. Furthermore, geographers on both sides of the Atlantic and in Australasia have contributed to this extension which conveniently coincides with a parallel trend towards the internationalisation of service industries. Prospects for more collective and comparative research on the location of producer services, in particular, and the consequences for metropolitan areas in spatially separate but increasingly inter-acting urban systems must therefore be considerable. This provides an opportunity for more wide-ranging analyses of the changing distribution of corporate headquarters or broad inter-regional studies of differentials in the growth of office functions or employ-ment. The now well advanced suburbanisation of office activities in low density office complexes seems to contradict our assump-tions about centrality, information linkages, ease of face-to-face contact, or access to external economies upon which the inter-pretation of office location is founded and suggests that systematic analysis of the function, establishment size, organisational status, client and input linkages and other facets of suburban, as well as regional, office development is long overdue. Corey (1982) has suggested a long list of measurements of the transactional bases of metropolitan areas which would certainly involve an examination of the relationship between central cities and suburbs. An assess-ment of the impact of office and science parks or more 'convent-ional' suburban commercial centres on transportation or the demand for consumer services such as retailing will also provide valuable input to more effective planning for suburban land use distribution. Extensive use of secondary data has characterised much of the research to date. Although there are clearly difficulties attached to applying generalisations from case studies to such an extensive and diverse phenomenon as the urban and regional system (see, for example, Goddard and Champion, 1983), more intensive efforts to generate primary data may be repaid with a more rewarding appreciation of both the pattern and the dynamics of service industry location and behaviour.

It is therefore axiomatic that service industries should continue to be the subject of separate examination. Their locational, physi-cal and transactional attributes, to name but a few, continue to give them a distinctive place in the internal organisation of metropolitan areas and the interdependence between cities and between regions. Combine this with the role of service industries as a major segment of the labour market and growing users of advanced telecommunications and related information technology, it soon becomes apparent that they will most likely exert a disproportionate influence on future development in advanced as well as less developed economies. The empiricist tradition and the emphasis on relating research questions to issues connected with suburbanisation or regional inequalities will probably remain to the fore while independent theoretical formulations will continue to advance along a relatively narrow front.

References

Alexander, I.J. (1979) *Office Location and Public Policy*, Longman, Harlow

Armstrong, R.B. (1972) *The Office Industry: Patterns of Growth and Location*, MIT Press, Cambridge, Mass.

Armstrong, R.B. (1979) 'National trends in office construction, employment and headquarters location in US metropolitan areas' in P.W. Daniels (ed.), *Spatial Patterns of Office Growth and Location*, Wiley, Chichester, 61-94

Attoe, W. (1981) *Skylines: Understanding and Modelling Urban Silhouettes*, Wiley, Chichester

Barras, R. (1983) 'A simple theoretical model of the office development cycle,' *Environment and Planning A, 15,* 1381-94

Bateman, M. and Burtenshaw, D. (1979) 'The social effects of office decentralization' in P.W. Daniels (ed.), *Spatial Patterns of Office Growth and Location*, Wiley, Chichester, 325-47

Bell, D. (1973) *The Coming of Post-Industrial Society*, Heinemann, London

Bennett, P.R. (1980) *The Impact of Toronto International Airport on the Location of Offices*, York University, Toronto

Bennett, R.J. (1980) *The Geography of Public Finance*, Methuen, London

Blackaby, F. (1979) (ed.) *Deindustrialization*, Heinemann, London

Burns, L.S. (1977) 'The location of the headquarters of industrial companies: a comment,' *Urban Studies, 14,* 211-14

Clapp, J.M. (1980) 'The intra-metropolitan location of office activities,' *Journal of Regional Science, 20,* 387-99

Code, W.R. (1983) 'The strength of the centre: downtown offices and metropolitan decentralization policy in Toronto,' *Environment and Planning A, 15,* 1361-80
80

Coffey, W.J. and Polese, M. (1983) 'Towards a theory of the inter-urban location of head office functions,' *Paper presented at the European Congress of the Regional Science Association*, Poitiers, France, September (mimeo)

Coombs, R.W. and Green, K. (1981) 'Microelectronics and the future of service employment,' *Service Industries Review, 1,* 4-21

Corey, K.E. (1982) 'Transactional forces and the metropolis,' *Ekistics, 297,* 416-22

Cowan, P. *et al.* (1969) *The Office: A Facet of Urban Growth*, Heinemann, London

Cowell, D.W. (1983) 'International marketing of services,' *The Service Industries Journal, 3,* 308-28

Crum, R. and Gudgin, G. (1978) *Non-Production Activities in UK Manufacturing Industry*, European Economic Commission, Brussels

Daniels, P.W. (1975) *Office Location: An Urban and Regional Study*, Bell, London

Daniels, P.W. (1979) (ed.) *Spatial Patterns of Office Growth and Location*, Wiley, Chichester

Daniels, P.W. (1980) *Office Location and the Journey to Work: A Comparative Study of Five Urban Areas*, Gower, Farnborough

Daniels, P.W. (1983a) 'Modern technology in provincial offices: some empirical evidence,' *The Service Industries Journal, 3*, 21-41

Daniels, P.W. (1983b) 'Business service offices in British provincial cities: location and control,' *Environment and Planning A, 15*, 1101-20

Daniels, P.W. (1984a) 'Business service offices in provincial cities: origins of input and destinations of output,' *Tijdschrift voor Economische en Sociale Geografie, 74*, 123-39

Daniels, P.W. (1985) 'Producer services and the post-industrial space economy' in R. Martin and R. Rowthorn (eds.), *Deindustrialization and the British Space Economy*, Macmillan, London

Davies, G. and Evans, J.W. (1983) 'Profitability and employment in UK financial services, 1971-1981,' *The Service Industries Journal, 3*, 241-59

Davies, R.L. (1972) 'The location of service activities' in M. Chisholm and B. Rodgers (eds.), *Studies in Human Geography*, Heinemann, London, 125-71

Davies, R.L. (1976) *Marketing Geography*, Methuen, London

Davies, R.L. (1979) (ed.) *Retail Planning in the European Community*, Saxon House, Farnborough

Dawson, J.A. (1980) (ed.) *Retail Geography*, Croom Helm, London

Dawson, J.A. (1983) *Shopping Centre Development*, Longman, Harlow

Dicken, P. and Lloyd, P. (1981) *Modern Western Society*, Harper and Row, London

Dornbusch, R. (1983) *Macroeconomic Prospects and Policies for the European Communities*, Centre for European Policy Studies, London

Douglas, S. (1981) Business Service Provision in Newcastle-upon-Tyne. *Unpublished M. Phil Thesis*, Newcastle-upon-Tyne Polytechnic, Department of Geography

Drury, P. (1983) 'Some spatial aspects of health service developments: the British experience,' *Progress in Human Geography, 7*, 60-77

Dunning, J.H. and Norman, G. (1979) Factors Influencing the Location of Offices of Multinational Enterprises, *Location of Offices Bureau, London, Research Paper 8*

Dunning, J.H. and Norman, G. (1983) 'The theory of the multinational enterprise: an application to multinational office location,' *Environment and Planning A, 15*, 675-92

Edgington, D.W. (1982) 'Organizational and technological change and the future of the central business district: an Australian example,' *Urban Studies, 19*, 281-92

Edwards, L.E. (1982) Intra-Urban Office Location: A Decision-Making Approach, *Unpublished PhD Thesis*, University of Liverpool, Department of Geography

Edwards, L.E. (1983) 'Towards a process model of office location decision making,' *Environment and Planning A, 15*, 1327-42

Evans, A.W. (1973) 'The location of the headquarters of industrial companies, *Urban Studies, 10*, 387-96

Foley, D.L. (1956) 'Factors in the location of administrative offices,' *Papers and Proceedings, Regional Science Association, 2*, 318-26

Fox, A. (1984) 'Employment trends in Britain and the USA: where will the new jobs come from?,' *Barclays Bank Review, 59*, 25-30

Fuchs, C. (1983) Developers and Users of Office Space: An Examination of the Location Decision Process in the Washington D.C. Area, 1981-83, *Unpublished MA Thesis*, University of Maryland, College Park

Gershuny, J. and Miles, I. (1983) *The New Service Economy: The Transformation of Employment in Industrial Societies*, Frances Pinter, London

Goddard, J.B. (1975) *Office Location in Urban and Regional Development*, Oxford University Press, London

Goddard, J.B. (1980) 'Technological change in a spatial context,' *Futures, 12*, 90-105

Goddard, J.B. and Champion, A.G. (1983) (eds.) *The Urban and Regional Transformation of Britain*, Methuen, London

Goddard, J.B. and Morris, D. (1976) *The Communications Factor in Office Decentralization*, Pergamon, Oxford

Goddard, J.B. and Smith, I.J. (1978) 'Changes in corporate control in the British urban system, 1972-77,' *Environment and Planning A, 10*, 1073-84

Gottman, J. (1983) *The Coming of the Transactional City*, University of Maryland, Institute of Urban Studies, College Park

Greenfield, H.I. (1966) *Manpower and the Growth of Producer Services*, Columbia University Press, New York

Guy, C. (1980) *Retail Location and Retail Planning in Britain*, Gower, Farnborough

Haig, R.M. (1927) *Major Economic Factors in Metropolitan Growth and Arrangement*, Committee on Regional Plan for New York and its Environs, New York

Hall, R.K. (1972) 'The movement of offices from London,' *Regional Studies, 6*, 385-92

Hartshorn, T.A. (1973) 'Industrial/office parks: a new look for the city,' *Journal of Geography, 72*, 33-45

Heenan, D.A. (1977) 'Global cities of tomorrow,' *Harvard Business Review, 55*, 79-92

Howells, J.R.L. (1984) 'The location of research and development: some observations and developments from Britain,' *Regional Studies, 18*, pp. 13-29

Hubbard, R.K.B. and Nutter, D.S. (1982) 'Service sector employment on Merseyside,' *Geoforum, 13*, 209-35

Keeble, D.E. (1980) 'Industrial decline, regional policy and urban-rural manufacturing shift in the United Kingdom,' *Environment and Planning A, 12*, 945-62

Kirby, A., Knox, P. and Pinch, S. (1984) (eds.) *Public Service Provision and Urban Development*, Croom Helm, London

Lea, A.C. (1979) 'Welfare theory, public goods and public facility location,' *Geographical Analysis, 11*, 218-49

McIver, C. and Naylor, G. (1980) *Marketing Financial Services*, Institute of Bankers, London

McKinnon, A.C. (1983) 'The development of warehousing in England,' *Geoforum, 14*, 389-99

Malecki, E.J. (1979) 'Locational trends in R & D by large US corporations, 1965-77,' *Economic Geography, 55*, 309-23

Malecki, E.J. (1982) 'Federal R & D spending in the United States of America: some impacts on metropolitan economies,' *Regional Studies, 16*, pp. 19-35

Mandeville, T. (1983) 'Spatial effects of information technology,' *Futures, 15*, 65-72

Marquand, J. (1979) *The Service Sector and Regional Policy in the United Kingdom*, Centre for Environmental Studies, London, Research Series 29

Marshall, J.N. (1981) *Business Service Activities in Provincial Conurbations: Implications for Regional Economic Development*, Centre for Urban and Regional Development Studies, Discussion Paper No. 37, Newcastle-upon-Tyne

Marshall, J.N. (1982) 'Linkages between manufacturing industry and business services,' *Environment and Planning A, 14*, 1523-40

140 *Service Industries*

Marshall, J.N. and Bachtler, J.F. (1984) 'Spatial perspectives on technological changes in the banking sector of the United Kingdom,' *Environment and Planning A, 16,* 437-50

Mathieson, A. and Wall, G. (1982) *Tourism: Economic, Physical and Social Impacts,* Longman, Harlow

Northern Region Strategy Team (1977) *Strategic Plan for the Northern Region: Economic Development Policies, Vol. 2,* HMSO, London

Oakey, R.P. (1983) 'New technology, government policy and regional manufacturing employment,' *Area, 15,* 61-5

Oakey, R.P., Thwaites, A.J. and Nash, P.A. (1980) 'The regional distribution of innovative manufacturing establishments in Britain,' *Regional Studies, 14,* 235-53

O'Hara, D.J. (1977) 'Location of firms within a square central business district,' *Journal of Political Economy, 85,* pp. 1189-207

Perry, D.C. and Watkins, A.J. (1977) (eds.) *The Rise of the Sunbelt Cities,* Sage, Beverley Hills

Phillips, D. and Joseph, A. (1984) *Accessibility and Utilization: Geographical Perspectives on Health Care Delivery,* Harper and Row, London

Pickvance, C.G. (1981) 'Policies as chameleons: an interpretation of regional policy and office policy in Britain' in M. Dear and A.J. Scott (eds.), *Urbanization and Urban Planning in Capitalist Society,* Methuen, London, 231-66

Polese, M. (1982) 'Regional demand for business services and inter-regional service flows in a small Canadian region,' *Papers of the Regional Science Association, 50,* 151-63

Pred, A.R. (1977) *City Systems in Advanced Economies,* Hutchinson, London

Pritchard, G. (1975) 'A model of professional office location,' *Geografiska Annaler, 57B,* 100-108

Pritchard, M.J. (1982) *The Spatial Implications of Technological Innovation in the Office Sector,* University of Liverpool, Department of Geography Working Paper No. 4

Rhodes, J. and Kan, A. (1971) *Office Dispersal and Regional Policy,* Cambridge University Press, London

Robinson, O. and Wallace, J. (1983) 'Employment trends in the hotel and catering industry in Great Britain,' *The Service Industries Journal, 3,* 260-78

Rosenberg, M.W. (1983) 'Accessibility of health care: a North American perspective,' *Progress in Human Geography, 7,* 78-87

Rothwell, R. and Zegweld, W. (1981) *Industrial Innovation and Public Policy,* Frances Pinter, London

Scott, A.J. (1982) 'Locational patterns and dynamics of industrial activity in the modern metropolis,' *Urban Studies, 19,* 111-41

Semple, R.K. and Green, M.B. (1983) 'Interurban corporate headquarters relocation in Canada,' *Cahiers de Geographie du Quebec, 27,* 389-406

Shannon, G.W. and Dever, G.E.A. (1974) *Health Care Delivery: Spatial Perspectives,* McGraw Hill, New York

Singelmann, J. (1979) *From Agriculture to Services,* Sage, Beverley Hills

Smith, A.D. (1972) *The Measurement and Interpretation of Service Output Changes,* National Economic Development Office, London

Smith, D.M. (1977) *Human Geography: A Welfare Approach,* Wiley, Chichester

Smith, W.R. and Selwood, D. (1983) 'Office location and the distance decay relationship,' *Urban Geography, 4,* 302-16

Stanback, T.M. (1979) *Understanding the Service Economy: Employment, Productivity, Location,* Johns Hopkins University Press, Baltimore

Stanback, T.M. and Noyelle, T.J. (1982) *Cities in Transition: Changing Job Structure in Atlanta, Denver, Buffalo, Phoenix, Columbus (Ohio), Nashville and Charlotte,* Allenheld, Osmun, Totowa, N.J.

Sternlieb, G. and Hughes, J.W. (1981) (eds.) *Shopping Centres: USA*, Centre for
Urban Policy Research, Rutgers University, N.J.

Tauchen, H. and Witte, A.D. (1983) 'An equilibrium model of office location and
contact patterns,' *Environment and Planning A, 15,* 1311-26

Tauchen, H. and Witte, A.D. (1984) 'Socially optimum and equilibrium distribution
of office activities: models with endogenous and exogenous contacts,' *Journal of
Urban Economics, 15,* 66-86

Thwaites, A.T. (1978) *The Future Development of R & D Activity in the Northern
Region: A Comment,* Centre for Urban and Regional Development Studies,
Newcastle-upon-Tyne, Discussion Paper 12

Vance, J.E. (1970) *The Merchants' World: The Geography of Wholesaling,* Prentice
Hall, Englewood Cliffs, N.J.

Walls, D. (1977) 'The impact of warehouse growth,' *The Planner, 63,* 105-7

5 FOREIGN DIRECT INVESTMENT AND DIVESTMENT TRENDS IN INDUSTRIALISED COUNTRIES

I.J. SMITH

Introduction

The interest of industrial geographers in the phenomenon of the multinational enterprise is of comparatively recent date. This is perhaps somewhat surprising in view of the rapid growth of overseas direct investment during the past two decades and the increasingly important role which multinationals have assumed in the processes of national and regional economic change. The reluctance of geographers to come to grips with the process of internationalisation may stem in part from an over-concern with the regional as opposed to the national spatial scale. One problem in this respect has been the strong research tradition of economists in this field, which may have deterred some geographers from entering into it. Nevertheless, the increasing integration of regional and national economies brought about by the emergence of the multinational enterprise, implies that geographers, in seeking explanations for industrial change at any spatial scale, must pay some attention to the international operations of these firms. For example, explanations of employment change which ignore the possibility of investment being diverted overseas or 'indigenous' firms supplying the domestic market through imports, must necessarily be partial. The fact that these issues are sensitive and therefore difficult to research should not prevent us from attempting some assessment of their impact.

The recent upsurge of interest amongst industrial geographers in multinational investment strategies can be attributed first and foremost to the onset of the current recession. In the United Kingdom for example, whilst regional disparities have persisted, all regions have experienced major employment losses, particularly in the manufacturing sector. Since the mid-1970s, the major disparities have been between the performances of nation states rather than between regions within these states. The employment performance of the United States, where the manufacturing sector expanded by over two and a half million jobs between 1975 and 1979, for example, stands in stark contrast to that of the United Kingdom where manufacturing employment contracted by over half a million jobs during the same period. Of course, multinational enterprises are only one element in the generation of international growth disparities; the relative performance of national small to medium sized enterprises as well as the role of state intervention must also be taken into account. For example, in the case of the United States protectionist policies are likely to have played a significant part in generating employment through limiting imports and encouraging direct inward investment. Clearly the locational strategies of multinational enterprises still need to be considered within a broad framework of political intervention particularly in so far as this relates to market access through the medium of tariff barriers.

Although a great deal of research has been done in this field by economists, much of it has been handicapped by data deficiencies and inadequate conceptualisation. Even where official statistics relating to foreign direct investment are reasonably comprehensive, as in the United States and United Kingdom, the different definitions adopted make international comparisons extremely hazardous. Also arising from the way in which data are provided, is the conceptual problem of equating foreign owned enterprises with multinational enterprises in general. For example, comparisons are more often made between the performance of foreign-owned and 'indigenous' enterprises than between multinational and national enterprises. In the former case location of control is assumed to have some explanatory power which is rarely made explicit, whereas in the latter case, although medium sized firms are increasingly investing abroad and the operations of some large, mainly state-owned enterprises are confined to one country, it is the absolute size of the enterprise which is the main differentiating characteristic. Although there may still be some justification for the belief that multinationals will differentiate between their country of origin and their overseas operations with respect to their locational decisions, with the development of truly global corporations and the need to integrate production on a supra-national basis, home country interests may increasingly receive less priority than in the past. Thus, just as the theoretical basis of regional studies which compare the performance of 'indigenous' and 'externally controlled' enterprises has recently been seriously challenged, so too may the distinction between foreign and nationally owned enterprises become an increasingly fine one.

The main purpose of this essay is to fill a gap in the literature of the multinational enterprise by assembling and analysing the rather limited information on international trends in foreign direct investment (FDI) within the major industrialised countries during the last 20 years. The mid-1960s marks the start of a major phase of internationalisation, the most obvious manifestation of which was the international merger wave of the late 1960s and early 1970s; it thus provides a convenient starting point for an analysis of the role of FDI in the development of multinational corporations. It must be admitted at the outset however that FDI, although by far the most important means of expansion overseas, is by no means the only route open to multinational enterprises. For example, a recent United Nations report (UN, 1978) has suggested the increasing importance of non-equity forms of overseas involvement such as licensed technology, franchise agreements, and subcontracting arrangements. These have been particularly important not only in parts of the world where restrictions are placed on majority ownership, such as in Japan and some newly industrialising countries (NICs) in South East Asia, but also in the socialist countries of Eastern Europe where private ownership is not permitted. Where political pressures are less in evidence, however, the preference for *direct* investment which implies some kind of equity stake is marked. This has been particularly true of United States based multinationals, which have shown a much greater preference for majority owned foreign affiliates than European-based multinationals (Vaupel and Curhan, 1973). The advantages of majority ownership are probably most apparent when the need arises to rationalise integrated global operations; in such circumstances minority holdings are likely to be increased and joint ventures abandoned.

A major problem is that published data on FDI flows is subject to considerable time lags; the most recent readily available data for most industrialised countries is for the mid 1970s (OECD, 1981). This is particularly unfortunate in that it is not possible as yet to determine how the international recession has affected the locational investment and divestment behaviour of multinational enterprises, although it is likely that some of the trends which became apparent during the early 1970s will have intensified as the recession has deepened. To partially overcome this difficulty, the analysis focuses upon United Kingdom evidence for the late 1970s in the belief that this provides some insight into what is likely to have been happening elsewhere in the developed world.

In the final section of the paper, the evidence is synthesised in an attempt to isolate the part played by FDI in growth differences between the major industrialised nations. It is argued that previous analyses of the costs and benefits of FDI have been partial in not taking into account the links with the trade balance, technological innovativeness and market structure of individual countries. It is concluded that when this more comprehensive view is taken of its likely impact, FDI will tend to exaggerate the growth differences between more buoyant and stagnant national economies.

Data problems

Data deficiencies are the root cause of many of the uncertainties surrounding the international activities of multinational enterprises and so merit some discussion. A recent report (UN, 1978) suggests that direct investment data are subject to three inherent limitations; time lags which means that the latest available data is a minimum of five years old; non-comparability, resulting from the use of varying definitions from country to country; and, in the case of value data, distortions produced by varying rates of inflation from country to country. The sources of direct investment data are also somewhat limited; only the US Department of Commerce and UK Department of Industry have monitored direct investment by means of direct surveys for any length of time; in other developed countries capital flow data are the sole means of gauging changes in the level of direct investment over time. Apart from these official sources, multinational data banks compiled at the Harvard Business School provide useful evidence on the international activities of the world's largest US and non-US manufacturing enterprises, (Curhan *et al.*, 1977; Vaupel and Curhan, 1973) but in the latter case only for an extremely limited time period.

Only four OECD countries at present monitor overseas direct investment by direct surveys: The Netherlands, United States, United Kingdom and Federal Republic of Germany. These surveys, which are based upon the book value of foreign owned assets at particular points in time, are the most satisfactory approximation of overseas fixed capital formation at present available, although book values tend to underestimate current net asset values particularly during inflationary periods. Also, except in the case of the most recent United Kingdom survey (the *Census of Overseas Assets*, 1978), participation is voluntary and the figures are usually based upon the returns of a sample of reporting companies.

For the majority of OECD countries, therefore, the only available indices of direct investment are the capital flow data collected on a balance of payments basis through the banking system. These data, upon which the OECD have been forced to make their international comparisons, are much less satisfactory and tend to substantially underestimate direct investment flows (OECD, 1981). Two particular problems arise with the use of these data to measure international direct investment trends. Firstly, the data are defined and collected on a different basis by various OECD member countries. The data for the United States and United Kingdom, for example, collected under the IMF/OECD *Common Reporting System on Balance of Payments Statistics* are much more comprehensive than those of other member states. Reinvested overseas earnings, an important source of direct investment finance, are included only in the US and UK data, so that the OECD have had to exclude these to make the flows more internationally comparable. To this extent the level of direct investment is considerably understated in the OECD figures. Secondly, the 'control' threshold adopted by various countries in their definitions of direct investment varies widely. For most countries it lies between 20 and 25 per cent of the shareholdings of individual companies, but in the case of the Netherlands it is as high as 80 per cent and in the case of the United States as low as 10 per cent. This implies that in comparison with the majority of countries, financial flows into and out of the Netherlands and US are likely to be considerably under- and overstated respectively.

To compare the relative values of cash flows between the major developed countries, the OECD have converted all values to current US dollars. This permits an assessment of the relative *level* of direct investment at any point in time, but it is problematical to assess *changes* in the *real* value of direct investment over time because of the difficulty of finding consistent and relevant price deflators (OECD, 1981). The higher rate of inflation during the late 1970s thus gives an exaggerated picture of the rate of increase during this period. This should be borne in mind in interpreting the tables in the following section which show current rather than real values.

Aggregate Trends Since the Mid-1950s

Although there is some divergence of opinion as to causes, there is general agreement that the importance of foreign direct investment (FDI) increased substantially during the 1960s and early 1970s both in absolute terms and relative to domestic investment, visible trade and gross domestic production (GDP) in all 13 OECD countries. During the period 1960-73 the growth rate of FDI from the major industrialised countries was equal to that of their international trade and one and a half times that of their GDP (OECD, 1981). Growth appears to have been particularly rapid during the later part of this period when the sales of foreign affiliates of the largest global corporations (with sales of more than one billion dollars) increased 25 per cent faster than the total consolidated sales of these companies (UN, 1978).

In attempting to explain this explosive growth of FDI, the OECD report emphasises the importance of the gradual reduction of some of the barriers to international capital flows during the 1950s, such as the increasing convertibility of the currencies of OECD member countries. More often, however, emphasis is given to the growing importance of protectionist policies during the early part of the 1960s when market saturation and over-capacity became a major problem in many industries for the first time since the Second World War (Cowling, 1982). Faced with rising tariff barriers, a new generation of multinational enterprises emerged as national firms increasingly found FDI a more profitable proposition than exporting. FDI flows are likely to have been further stimulated during the late 1960s by the increased level of government assistance in the form of investment and export subsidies, offered in both developed and developing countries, as international competition for potentially mobile investment intensified. As a result many smaller corporations may have been forced to internationalise their operations, the alternative being extinction in the face of highly subsidised imports.

The OECD report claims that the mid-1970s were something of a turning point for international foreign direct investment. The report suggests that the onset of the current international recession saw a marked deceleration in the rate of increase of the value of direct investment flows from the major industrialised countries when the effects of higher levels of inflation during the late 1970s are taken into account. Although FDI remained buoyant in comparison with domestic investment, the rate of increase of the value of outward flows in current terms between 1974 and 1979 was marginally below the rate of increase between 1960 and 1973, suggesting a deceleration in *real* terms.

This conclusion must however be accepted with some caution in view of the inability of capital flow data to monitor direct investment trends adequately. It must be stressed once more that these data do *not* include some important sources of overseas finance such as re-invested earnings, local borrowing or borrowing in third countries. The increasing tendency for US and UK enterprises in particular to draw on local sources of finance in the host country suggests that capital flow data may increasingly understate FDI over time. In the case of the United Kingdom, for example, Dicken (1983) shows that the book value of overseas assets during the 1970s (1971-78) increased at almost three times the rate of the 1960s (1962-71). Given a greater tendency for book values to understate market values in times of inflation, this does *not* suggest any pronounced deceleration of outward investment from the United Kingdom.

Further confirmation of accelerated outward investment during the late 1970s is provided by Table 5.1 which compares the annual rate of increase of overseas assets in the UK and US over three time periods, the late 1960s, the early 1970s and late 1970s. It can be seen that in both cases the highest rate of increase of outward investment occurs after 1974, when it is some 3 per cent per annum higher than during the early 1970s and, in the case of the United Kingdom, over twice as high as during the late 1960s. The United States figures do, however, show evidence of reduced levels of outward investment in the *manufacturing* and *commercial* sectors after 1974 but this was more than made up for by increased levels in the oil and financial sectors. The United Kingdom figures display an exactly opposite trend with a marked acceleration of the level of outward manufacturing investment after 1974, and a reduced level of 'non-manufacturing' investment. Explaining these apparently contradictory trends is difficult because of the large number of possible influences at work. It is possible however that

Table 5.1: Average Annual Percentage Increase in Book Value of Direct Outward and Inward Investment by Industrial Sector

a. United States

	1966-70		1970-74		1974-79	
	Out	In	Out	In	Out	In
Manufacturing	12.4	15.5	16.2	17.3	12.7	18.6
Trade	10.8	8.6	20.7	85.3	16.6	30.9
Insurance & Finance	14.6	2.2	18.8	5.2	23.6	32.6
Petroleum	10.5	18.0	2.3	21.9	18.6	18.8
All Sectors	11.4	11.6	11.5	22.4	15.0	21.6

Source: OECD (1979).

b. United Kingdom (excluding oil, banking & insurance)

	1965-71		1971-74		1974-78	
	Out	In	Out	In	Out	In
Manufacturing	14.5	15.6	18.4	16.6	24.7	17.6
Non-manufacturing	5.0	13.1	19.4	61.1	15.8	14.2
Total	9.7	15.1	18.8	24.0	21.0	16.7

Source: Census of Overseas Assets (1979), Tables 4 and 16.

increased protectionist policies in the US may have discouraged some outward manufacturing investment, particularly where the investment is in the form of component manufacture or sub-assembly for re-importation into the United States. It is apparent also that a high level of UK outward and inward direct investment in the 'non-manufacturing' sector characterises the period of entry into the EEC (1971-74). Much of this may represent cross invest-ment in distributive trades by UK and EEC based multinationals to take advantage of actual or proposed tariff reductions; the reduced level of 'non-manufacturing' investment after 1974 may therefore represent a return to more 'normal' conditions after the major firms had secured their market outlets.

In the case of the United States, an alternative time series for outward investment is provided by the Harvard Business School multinational data bank (Curhan *et al.*, 1977). Unfortunately, published data from this source does not yet go beyond 1975; nevertheless it provides a detailed breakdown of the overseas investment of the largest 180 US manufacturing enterprises covering a 25-year time period, 1951-75. In Table 5.2 annual average entry and exit rates are shown for both the manufacturing and non-manufacturing sectors for each five-year period after 1951.

Table 5.2: Annual Average Entry and Exit Rates of Overseas Affiliates of 180 Large US Manufacturing Corporations by Five-year Time Periods

Time period	MANUFACTURING					NON-MANUFACTURING				
	Overseas subsidiaries in base year N	Entries N	%	Exits N	%	Overseas subsidiaries in base year N	Entries N	%	Exits N	%
1951-55	947	419	8.8	42	0.9	1,249	570	9.1	74	0.8
1956-60	1,291	960	14.9	67	1.0	1,719	997	11.6	140	1.6
1961-65	2,106	1,612	15.3	127	1.2	2,474	1,613	13.0	189	1.5
1966-70	3,452	2,213	12.8	499	2.9	3,828	2,172	11.3	655	3.4
1971-75	4,915	1,675	6.8	638	2.6	5,050	1,564	6.2	721	2.9
1951-75	947	6,879	29.1	1,373	5.8	1,249	6,916	22.1	1,779	5.7

Notes: Exits include both liquidations and sell-offs, but not exits through mergers with other US firms. Entries include both acquisitions and new subsidiaries.

Source: Curhan *et al.* (1977).

It can be seen that although the manufacturing entry rate is generally higher than that for non-manufacturing, as might be expected in view of the manufacturing origins of the investing firms, both follow a similar pattern over time with a maximum rate of entry in the early 1960s and the lowest rate in the early 1970s. In both cases also the maximum number of entries occurred in the late 1960s so that there was an absolute as well as relative fall in *numbers* of entrants after 1970. We can safely conclude, therefore, that in terms of numbers of new subsidiaries established or acquired, there was a fall in the overseas investment rate of the largest US manufacturing enterprises. This clearly, however, does not take into account changes in the growth rate of existing subsidiaries, nor the relative size of new entrants; as Table 5.1 shows, in terms of US assets owned overseas there was a relative increase in all sectors during the early 1970s, although the rate of increase of the value of *manufacturing* assets did diminish after 1974.

Geographical Trends since the Mid-1960s

Three major geographical trends in FDI characterise the period since 1965:

1. In spite of the increasing value of capital flows both in current and real terms from developed to developing countries (OECD, 1981), there was a fall in the actual share of developed country assets in developing countries as a result of greatly increased FDI within the developed countries themselves.
2. Within the developed countries there was a major re-direction of FDI flows towards high income markets such as the United States and West Germany.
3. Whereas inward flows tended to become geographically more concentrated, the sources of FDI became more diversified as enterprises from the majority of OECD countries increasingly internationalised their operations. Thus the dominance of the United States and the United Kingdom as source nations, which characterised the period up to the mid-1960s, was gradually reduced.

A 1978 UN report maintains that FDI has always been and remains mainly a phenomenon of developed country markets because 'transnational corporations seek out and flourish most in foreign markets that most closely resemble the home markets for which they first developed their products and processes' (UN, 1978).

It could be argued however that transnational corporations are often looking for very *different* markets from those at home, particularly if the domestic economy is not particularly dynamic. This may explain why, during a period of increasing economic recession, outward FDI flows have become increasingly directed towards more dynamic national economies in the developed world. The increasing concentration of FDI in a small number of developed market economies is suggested by Table 5.3 which shows changes in the share of overseas assets located in major host countries between 1967 and 1975. During this period the share of developed countries increased by 5 per cent to almost three-quarters of the total stock of FDI. In the developing world, only the tax havens increased their share of overseas assets, although increases are also likely to have occurred in some of the newly industrialising countries (NICs) particularly in South East Asia. Table 5.3 clearly demonstrates the increasing attractiveness of the high income economies of West Germany and the United States, whilst the drop in Canada's high share may be indicative of a swing away from semiperipheral developed market economies. More disaggregated capital flow data for the same period suggest that the Netherlands, Belgium and France also attracted a high share of FDI from other developed countries whilst there was a reduced flow into Australia.

In Table 5.4 an attempt has been made to summarise changes in international FDI flows into three major developed regions and the developing countries, using the latest data available. Unfortunately, except in the case of the United States and United Kingdom, recourse has had to be made to capital flow data and often the time periods and regional aggregates to which the data refer do not exactly correspond. Nevertheless, the figures are as close an approximation as can be obtained of trends during the 1970s given existing data deficiencies.

With respect to investment in developing countries, it can be seen that the experience of individual OECD countries was extremely varied. Most of the increased investment to non-OECD countries during the decade originated in Japan and represents, in the main, a switch from Western Europe. Most other important

Table 5.3: Stock of Direct Investment Abroad of Developed Market Economies, by Host Country, 1967-1975

Host and country group	1967	1971	1975
Total value of stock ($ billion) —	105	158	259
Distribution of stock (percentage) —			
Developed market economies —	69	72	74
of which:			
Canada	18	17	15
United States ·	9	9	11
United Kingdom	8	9	9
Federal Republic of Germany	3	5	6
Other	30	32	33
Developing countries —	31	28	26
of which:			
OPEC countries[a]	9	7	6
Tax havens[b]	2	3	3
Other	20	17	17
Total	100	100	100

Notes: a. Algeria, Ecuador, Gabon, Indonesia, Iran, Iraq, Kuwait, Libyan Arab Jamahiriya, Nigeria, Qatar, Saudi Arabia, United Arab Emirates and Venezuela.
b. Bahamas, Barbados, Bermuda, Cayman Islands, Netherlands, Antilles and Panama.
Source: UN (1978).

Table 5.4: Changes in the Share of Outward Capital Flows from Major OECD Sources to Major Developed Regions and the Developing Countries During the 1970s

	Destination regions			
	Western Europe %	United States %	Other OECD countries %	Developing countries %
France[a]	−1.0 (e)	2.3	11.6	−12.9
West Germany[b]	−2.1 (e)	8.9	−0.4	−6.4
Japan[b]	−27.2	7.6	0.0	19.6
Netherlands[c]	−15.0 (e)	12.0	0.5	2.5
United Kingdom[d]	9.1	7.7	−10.3	−6.5
United States[d]	8.8	n.a.	−8.2	−0.6
Canada[a]	−2.6[e]	−9.3	4.2	7.7

Notes: a. 1973-78.
b. 1970-79.
c. Change in three-year cumulative totals 1968-70 to 1977-9.
d. Book value data (UK 1971-78; US 1970-79).
e. EEC countries only (Other European investment in Column 3).
Sources: OECD (1981); UK Census of Overseas Assets (1978).

capital exporting countries in fact switched investment away from developing countries during the 1970s, although the share of investment originating in the United States declined only marginally. It is also obvious from the table that the main beneficiary of this diverted investment was the United States itself; with the exception of Canada all the capital exporting countries listed increased the proportion of investment flowing into the world's largest and richest market. Direct investment flows from the United Kingdom, in particular, became markedly more concentrated in the US and Western Europe, mainly as a result of the diversion of capital from commonwealth OECD countries.

Table 5.4 also suggests that the more mature OECD economies have continued to be the most important destinations for outward investment; just as investment from Western Europe has become increasingly directed towards the United States, US investment has become increasingly concentrated in Western Europe. It would seem on this evidence that multinationals have shown an increasing preference for market oriented investment as the world economic recession has deepened. Panic (1982) has suggested that much of the *internal* flow of capital within the OECD countries represents movement from slower to faster growing economies, as multinationals attempt to weather the recession by investing in markets with the best growth prospects. On this basis one would expect substantial UK investment not only in the United States but also in the Federal Republic of Germany and Switzerland. An analysis of changes in the UK's stock of overseas manufacturing assets during the 1970s by Dicken (1983) provides some support for this thesis, particularly for the period between 1971 and 1978 (Table 5.5). During this period OECD countries with the largest percentage increase in the book value of UK manufacturing assets were, in order of importance, Switzerland, Japan, Belgium/ Luxembourg, United States and Sweden.

Unfortunately, time series book value data for West Germany and the Netherlands are too limited to provide any evidence on this issue. Although United States book value data show an increasing concentration of US assets in Europe, and to a more limited extent in Japan, there is little evidence of a redirection of US investment towards faster growth economies *within* Europe. In fact, as Table 5.6 shows the United Kingdom increased its share of US assets throughout the period 1966-79. On the other hand US Department of Commerce data show a continuing fall in the UK's

Table 5.5: Rank Order of Developed Host Countries by Increases in the Stock Value of United Kingdom Manufacturing Assets 1971-78

Host nations	Average annual percentage increase in value of UK manufacturing assets		
	1971-4	1974-8	1971-8
Switzerland	21.0	95.8	98.3
Japan	22.0	58.6	64.9
Belgium/Luxembourg	25.2	50.9	61.8
United States	13.2	22.5	50.7
Sweden	43.9	22.5	48.6
West Germany	29.8	31.2	46.6
Denmark	18.9	37.6	41.7
Italy	33.4	15.0	31.4
France	20.3	18.2	25.4
Netherlands	12.5	20.2	21.3
South Africa	20.8	12.1	20.1
Australia	20.0	12.0	19.6
Canada	9.3	13.4	18.5

Source: Dicken (1983).

Table 5.6: Changes in the Share of Year End Stock Values of US Outward Direct Investment by Region and Selected Countries of Destination, 1970-79

Host regions/nations	1966 %	1970 %	1974 %	1979 %
Developed Countries	68.1	68.7	75.4	71.6
of which:				
Canada	30.3	27.8	25.8	21.3
Japan	1.4	2.0	3.0	3.0
Australia/New Zealand	3.8	4.4	4.6	4.0
Europe	21.6	33.5	40.6	42.3
Of which:				
United Kingdom	10.5	10.6	11.4	12.6
West Germany	5.4	5.7	7.2	6.5
France	3.5	3.5	4.4	4.0
Belgium/Luxembourg	1.5	2.0	2.7	2.9
Netherlands	3.8	4.4	4.6	4.0
Developing Countries	26.8	25.4	18.0	24.8

Source: OECD (1981).

share of all US *manufacturing* assets in Europe during the past two decades.

The Harvard data provide additional evidence on the overseas investment behaviour of the largest US manufacturing corporations. Table 5.7 shows entry and exit rates in six of the most important locations for US overseas investment and highlights the relative attractiveness of the faster growing developed economies; Japan, which experienced the highest entry rates during the 1950s, and West Germany which had relatively high entry rates during the 1960s. The increasing attractiveness of investment in some East Asian NICs, particularly Taiwan, the Philippines and South Korea is also suggested; since 1966 the highest entry rates of all have been in this part of the developing world. Compared to the other host countries shown, US investment in Brazil appears to have been at a relatively low level throughout, although holding up better during the early 1970s. The reduced level of entry after 1970 thus appears to have been accompanied by some redirection of investment by the largest US manufacturing corporations away from traditional developed country markets. As the share of the stock of total US investment in developing countries declined in aggregate between 1970 and 1974 (Table 5.6), three reasonably firm conclusions can be drawn:

1. Large firm investment increasingly focused upon selected countries within the developing world, in particular the NICs.
2. The increasing participation of medium-sized US enterprises in FDI was directed mainly at developed country markets.
3. A higher proportion of investment by large US non-manufacturing firms was directed at developed country markets.

Whereas inward flows of FDI have tended to become increasingly concentrated in particular markets of the developed and developing world, the sources of FDI have tended to become somewhat more diverse as enterprises from both high income developed economies and the NICs have increasingly internationalised their operations. With the exception of Italy, Belgium/Luxembourg and France, other OECD countries increased their stock of overseas assets at a faster rate than the two traditionally dominant overseas investors, the United States and United Kingdom between 1967 and 1976. The main reason for the

Table 5.7: *Percentage Annual Average Entry and Exit Rates of Overseas Affiliates of 180 Large US Manufacturing Corporations in Selected OECD and Developing Countries*

	1951-55		1956-60		1961-65		1966-70		1971-75	
	Entry	Exit	Entry	Exit	Entry	Exit	Entry	Exit	Entry	Exit
United Kingdom	5.2	2.0	11.1	1.0	13.3	2.1	14.0	3.6	7.5	2.9
West Germany	10.9	0.9	17.8	0.9	17.7	2.0	15.3	3.8	7.1	2.6
Japan	46.7	3.3	21.1	0.5	34.5	0.8	12.5	1.5	9.6	2.1
Australia	13.8	0.5	17.2	0.6	13.8	1.1	12.8	2.3	5.1	3.0
East Asia[a]	11.4	0.8	13.6	0.8	17.9	1.7	20.8	3.0	10.7	1.9
Brazil	9.9	0.0	12.5	0.6	7.2	0.8	9.5	3.3	9.4	3.2
World	9.0	1.1	13.0	1.4	14.1	1.4	12.0	3.2	6.5	2.7

a. Includes Hong Kong, Indonesia, Malaysia, Philippines, Singapore, South Korea, Thailand, Taiwan.
Notes: Exits include both liquidations and sell-offs, but not exits through mergers with other US firms. Entries include both acquisitions and new subsidiaries.
Source: Curhan *et al.* (1977).

declining share of overseas assets held by US and UK multinationals, however, as Table 5.8 shows, was an exceptionally high
rate of increase of West German and Japanese interests overseas;
both countries had a relatively low share in 1967 but had become
the third and fourth most important capital exporting countries
respectively by 1976. Japanese and West German firms appear to
have preferred servicing their overseas markets through exports
rather than direct investment, but the gradual increase in, for
example, US protectionist policies, may have caused a switch to
overseas production. Strong balance of payments positions resulting in strong currencies may also have been important in making
domestic production for export a less profitable alternative. In the
Japanese case, of course, direct investment in Western Europe has
also been stimulated by the introduction of import quotas on a
wide range of manufactured goods.

Although the relative dominance of the US and UK as source
nations for FDI has been somewhat reduced, it has clearly been
maintained. The reasons for this dominance are very different in
each case. In the US case, the size of the domestic market was
clearly of crucial importance, permitting the growth of large
national enterprises with the organisational and financial ability to
expand overseas at an early date. In particular, the early adoption
by US enterprises of the product divisional structure seems to have
been of major significance in easing the internal co-ordination
problems associated with the establishment of an overseas division
(Stopford and Wells, 1972). Additionally, the ability to maintain
large R and D budgets gave US enterprises an early technological
lead which encouraged overseas production once the product
became mature in the US. Other factors in the early flow of US
investment abroad may have been a relatively strong national
currency and relatively high domestic labour costs. The former was
probably of greater significance during the period before 1960
when a much higher proportion of US overseas investment was
funded from domestic as opposed to host country sources.

Technological advantage explanations of FDI seem to have
rather less relevance in the case of the UK's high level of involvement overseas. Historically, of course, UK overseas investment
was orientated towards primary production activities in commonwealth countries and this is one reason for a relatively high level of
outward FDI in food and mineral processing industries. That this
sectoral specialisation has persisted is suggested by Dunning's

Table 5.8: Share of the Stock of Direct Investment of Developed Market Economies in billions of US Dollars, by Major Country of Origin, 1967-76

Country of origin	1967	1971	Percentage distribution 1973	1975	1976	Percentage average annual increase 1967-76
United States	53.8	52.3	51.0	47.8	47.6	14.2
United Kingdom	16.6	15.0	13.5	11.9	11.2	8.3
Federal Republic of Germany	2.8	4.6	6.0	6.2	6.9	56.3
Japan	1.4	2.8	5.2	6.1	6.7	119.3
Switzerland	4.8	6.0	5.6	6.5	6.5	27.2
France	5.7	4.6	4.4	4.3	4.1	9.8
Canada	3.5	4.1	3.9	4.1	3.9	20.0
Netherlands	2.1	2.5	2.8	3.2	3.4	34.5
Sweden	1.6	1.5	1.5	1.7	1.7	19.4
Belgium/Luxembourg	1.9	1.5	1.4	1.2	1.2	8.0
Italy	2.0	1.9	1.6	1.3	1.0	3.8
Total above	96.2	96.8	96.9	94.3	94.2	16.7
All other (estimate)	3.8	3.2	3.1	5.7	5.8	32.0
Grand total	100.0	100.0	100.0	100.0	100.0	17.3

Source: United Nations (1978).

(1979) comparison of inward and outward FDI flows; the latter he maintains are more biased towards less technology intensive industries in which less than 2 per cent of the value of net output is spent on R and D. An alternative explanation of a relatively high rate of FDI by UK companies, however, has recently become more fashionable: this relates the high level of industrial concentration in the United Kingdom to the existence of a larger proportion of enterprises with both the financial and managerial resources to invest overseas. In addition, the relative slow growth of the UK economy provides the motivation for overseas investment on the part of these companies (Panic, 1982). Finally, Britain's exclusion from the EEC until 1973 must have been responsible for a relatively high level of FDI in Western Europe during the 1960s when tariff barriers were in operation. In fact, the highest rate of increase of UK manufacturing investment in the EEC occurred in the period 1965-71 before the UK became a member country (Table 5.1).

Although the UK and US were responsible for a diminishing share of overseas assets between 1967 and 1976, it must be emphasised that this does not imply any reduction in the rate of growth of FDI from either country. In fact the total book value of both US and UK overseas assets increased at a higher rate during the late 1970s than during the early 1970s (Dicken, 1983). This in itself casts doubt on the validity of the argument that the higher rate of investment by European companies in the US during the 1970s was a kind of reverse 'product cycle' resulting from the erosion of US technological leadership. Rather, there seems to have been an increased level of investment flow in both directions following the rapid growth in concentration sponsored by many European governments in the face of the American 'challenge' during the late 1960s. The theory of FDI which appears to best account for this situation was first advanced by Hymer (1960) and later refined by Kindleberger (1968) and Vernon (1979). In essence FDI is seen as a form of oligopolistic reaction in which multinationals, operating in highly concentrated international markets, react to entry into their home market by investing in the overseas market of the foreign firm. The level of outward flow is further increased by the 'follow the leader' behaviour of rival domestic firms (Knickerbocker, 1973) so that eventually each multinational is represented in both markets. Evidence that the overseas investments of multinationals operating in the same industry are typically 'bunched' in a relatively short time period supports this thesis (Dubin, 1976).

Sectoral Trends since the Mid-1960s

In many respects data availability in this area is the most unsatisfactory of all. Even where official statistics provide an industrial breakdown, the low degree of industrial disaggregation involved makes for extremely difficult interpretation (Hymer, 1960). Hence attempts to show that FDI is associated with high technology industries (Dunning, 1979) or with international oligopoly (Hymer and Rowthorn, 1970) are forced to rely on extremely crude measures of research intensity or market concentration respectively. This more than any other factor explains the continuing absence of a unified, generally accepted theory of FDI.

The latest available figures on the industrial structure of FDI are for 1976 and are limited to the few main investing nations in that year. Table 5.9 (column A) shows that the sectoral distribution of FDI varies greatly according to source nation both in industrialised and developing countries. Similarly except in the case of the US and UK, there is very little tendency for the share of investment in each sector to move in the same direction over time. The most extreme positions are occupied by West Germany with a high but decreasing share of investment in manufacturing and Japan with a high but decreasing share of investment in service activities in developed countries. As multinationals from both nations are relative newcomers to FDI, it may be that the industrial structures of their overseas investments are moving closer to those of the US and UK which have the closest similarity. In the West German case, service sector investment abroad may have been delayed by the relatively late expansion of manufacturing activities; in the Japanese case government restrictions on overseas manufacturing investment in operation before 1969 (Dicken, 1980) are likely to have been responsible for a relatively high proportion of investment in distribution and trade activities in the industrialised countries.

In the case of the US and UK the structure of overseas investment is broadly similar except that a high level of US activity in petroleum extraction results in a lower share of FDI in manufacturing and services. The overall sector growth rates of US and

Table 5.9: Changes in the Industrial Structure of Foreign Owned Assets of Four Major Overseas Investors in Developed and Developing Nations 1971-76

Investment source	United States A %	United States B %	United Kingdom A %	United Kingdom B %	West Germany A %	West Germany B %	Japan A %	Japan B %
Developed countries	68.7	15.5	72.1	15.4	71.9	18.4	50.9	61.1
Extractive	19.3	15.3	6.4	10.0	5.4	10.8	10.7	60.0
Manufacturing	34.1	15.1	47.5	13.1	55.3	16.2	9.1	73.3
Services	15.1	16.8	18.2	21.7	11.2	31.9	31.2	58.2
Developing countries	25.3	7.7	27.9	8.4	28.0	32.4	49.1	70.0
Extractive	11.5	6.4	2.0	0.0	1.5	40.0	20.7	51.4
Manufacturing	7.2	18.0	11.5	12.5	20.4	15.5	17.7	64.0
Services	6.5	26.3	14.4	6.0	6.2	40.0	10.7	70.0
Total	100.0	13.1	100.0	13.4	100.0	19.5	100.0	68.3

Column A = share of investment in sector in 1971.
B = average annual increase 1971-76 (US$ billion).
Notes: Amounts referring to industrialised and developing countries do not always add to the total as investments per business establishment are not disaggregated on a regular basis. United Kingdom figures are for 1971-5 and exclude petroleum.
Source: OECD (1981).

UK FDI (column B of Table 5.9) are also similar except that UK service sector investment expanded at a faster rate in the industrialised countries whereas US service sector investment expanded faster in the developing countries. The rate of growth of US manufacturing investment in developing countries was slightly higher than in the industrialised countries but this was not so for the other three source nations. This suggests that US multinationals may have made relatively more use of third world free trade zones than UK or West German multinationals; similarly, relatively high growth of US service sector investment in developing countries could indicate greater use of tax havens for the establishment of holding, finance and insurance companies (OECD, 1981).

Table 5.9 shows that the rate of increase of FDI from Japan has been consistently high across all industrial sectors. Although manufacturing investment represented a low share of total Japanese investment in industrialised countries, the rate of increase in this sector was in fact highest of all between 1971 and 1976 suggesting that the structure of Japanese FDI may soon be similar to that of other developed countries. Similarly, the highest rate of expansion of West German FDI was in the service sector which suggests that the over-representation of manufacturing investment may be a short-lived phenomenon. A relatively high rate of increase of West German investment in developing countries during this five-year period was attributable mainly to non-manufacturing activities.

Within the manufacturing sector, the structure of FDI also appears to vary considerably between source nations, although again there is some evidence that these differences may be disappearing over time. Using an extremely crude level of sectoral disaggregation, Buckley and Casson (1976) attempt to show that outward FDI from the United Kingdom, Japan and France had a high representation in non-research-intensive industries defined as wood, metal and food processing, textiles, clothing and 'miscellaneous' manufacturing. In each case, however, the over-representation was due to only one industry; food processing in the case of the UK, textiles in the case of Japan, and 'miscellaneous' manufacturing in the case of France. It is particularly difficult to understand how the latter sector can be classified at all in view of its heterogeneity. Also, much of the explanation for these specialisms may be put down to historical factors such as the high level of Japanese investment in labour intensive industries in developing countries and the UK's involvement in primary pro-cessing activities in Commonwealth countries, both of which may be expected to diminish as investment is increasingly oriented towards the United States and Western Europe. Both Panic (1982) and Dicken (1983), for example, have found evidence of a major increase in UK outward investment in 'high technology' industries during the 1970s, particularly chemicals and engineering, so that the structure of outward investment has come to resemble more closely that of inward investment in the UK.

The tendency for FDI in the manufacturing sector to be markedly concentrated in specific industries characterised by high entry barriers resulting from a high intensity of research and development, extensive product differentiation and high market concentration was first pointed out by Hymer (1960), who main-tained that: 'international operations occur in some industries throughout the world rather than in all industries in some coun-tries'. The basis for this theory is that high entry barriers are necessary to overcome some of the disadvantages associated with overseas production such as unfamiliarity with the host nation's business environment and conditions of employment. To secure adequate returns for the high level of investment involved, some guarantee of protection from encroachment by indigenous competitors is essential. Much empirical evidence has since accumulated to support Hymer's hypothesis and contemporary theories of FDI such as those of Graham (1978), Dunning (1982) and Rugman (1981) lay heavy emphasis on the significance of market inter-nalisation in direct investment; where there is less need to protect assets (both tangible and intangible), overseas investment is more likely to take non-equity forms such as licensing or franchising arrangements.

International Disinvestment Trends in the Late 1960s and Early 1970s

The paucity of information on multinational world-wide rational-isation strategies is nothing short of extreme; only the Harvard data provide a consistent time series of liquidations and sell-offs by US manufacturing corporations for the period up to 1975. One of the reasons for data deficiencies in this area is the definitional problem as to what actually constitutes a disinvestment. Fortunately, the Harvard definitions are very precise in this matter; liquidations represent not only the end of a subsidiary as a legal entity but also the termination of its activities, hence subsidiaries disappearing as a result of internal reorganisation are excluded. Published data on disinvestment by non-US corporations are even more restricted being limited to the period before 1971. The absence of comparable data for the late 1970s is particularly unfortunate, in view of the escalating rate of disinvestment as the international recession has deepened.

Exit rates for US manufacturing and non-manufacturing subsidiaries are shown in Table 5.2. Although non-manufacturing subsidiaries have been divested at a higher rate than manufacturing affiliates since 1956, their exit rates display a similar time trend, rising to a peak in the late 1960s and declining slightly during the early 1970s. However, in both cases the maximum *number* of exits occurred after 1970 suggesting a steadily upward trend. The data also show that whereas liquidations were the most common form of exit in the 1960s, sell-offs to non-US corporations became increasingly important after 1970. The explanation for this may be related to the rapid expansion of these corporations through acquisition during the international merger wave of the late 1960s and early 1970s.

The Harvard data show an increased level of entry through takeover of both manufacturing and non-manufacturing affiliates after 1966. After 1972 the proportion of entries through acquisition fell to roughly pre-1967 levels once more. At the height of the merger wave, acquisitions accounted for almost two-thirds of manufacturing entries and approximately four-fifths of non-manufacturing entries. The majority of acquired affiliates are likely to have been operating in the same market as the US parent, and in so far as geographical extension (first time entry) was not involved, liquidations may subsequently have occurred in response to rising excess capacity. A substantial minority of acquired entries however, would represent some form of diversification into either related or unrelated product markets. A common strategy adopted by many multinationals in response to falling profitability during the recession of the early 1970s was divestment of many peripheral activities acquired during the late 1960s, either because an inadequate market share had been acquired or because post-merger integration problems had developed (Kitching, 1974). This would therefore provide an explanation of the increasing importance of US divestment through sell-offs after 1970.

The five-year average annual exit rates in Table 5.7 show some remarkable variations between individual host nations. Although they exhibit a general tendency to rise after 1960 only in the United Kingdom has the level of divestment been consistently above the average for all US foreign affiliates. Relatively high rates of US divestment in West Germany during the 1960s gave way to a more moderate rate during the 1970s and above average rates of exit did not arise in Brazil and Australia until the late 1960s and early 1970s respectively. US divestment rates in Japan, except during the early 1950s, and East Asia, except during the early 1960s, have been at a relatively low level suggesting that these have been the most stable locations for FDI.

The comparatively high rates of US divestment in the UK and West Germany during the 1960s may be related to the early development of overcapacity in the most industrialised countries as the post-war growth of demand slackened. One indication of this is the increasing use of acquisition as a means of entry into both countries during the late 1960s. In contrast to entry through new investment, takeovers have the advantage of not adding to excess capacity in industries where demand is already saturated. An additional explanation, however, presents itself in the case of the UK where US divestment continued at a relatively high rate into the 1970s. This was the period of UK entry into the EEC when the removal of tariff barriers caused many UK-based American companies to re-orientate their operations towards the enlarged EEC market, often resulting in sub-optimal plant sizes in the UK (Hood and Young, 1982a). The relatively high exit rate for the period 1971-75 may thus be an early indication of rationalised integrated production by US manufacturing enterprises, a trend which was to assume much greater importance during the later part of the decade.

The relatively high rate of US divestment in Brazil and Australia after 1970 suggests that problems of overcapacity may have arisen somewhat later in these countries possibly as a result of declining demand for their exports from the major industrialised countries. This explanation cannot however apply to the East Asian NICs where exit rates were at a low level after 1970. This implies that the export orientated investment of the free trade zones was relatively less affected by the development of overcapacity in industrialised markets, which in turn suggests that the increased level of US divestment in Brazil and Australia after 1970 was primarily the result of increased overcapacity in local markets. This may have arisen as a result of over-investment by transnational corporations during the 1960s in an attempt to secure their market position behind tariff walls.

Disinvestment in the UK during the Late 1970s

The absence of comparative international data on the more recent locational divestment behaviour of transnational corporations forces us at this point to focus upon UK evidence for the late 1970s in order to determine to what extent the trends which emerged during the early 1970s have continued during the current recession. The case of the United Kingdom also serves to illustrate in more detail how the internationalisation process has contributed to deindustrialisation in a relatively slow growing industrialised country. At this spatial scale, of course, much of the emerging evidence refers to manufacturing establishments and employment rather than enterprises and often to specific regions rather than the UK as a whole. Recent detailed evidence from North West England (Lloyd and Shutt, 1983), and the West Midlands (Gaffikin and Nickson, 1983) has revealed the scale and significance of multinational divestment during the recent recession.

Lloyd and Shutt (1983), describe recent corporate restructuring in the North West as being characterised by wholesale rationalisation. Using Factory Inspectorate records, the authors found that the 54 largest manufacturing firms in the region in 1975 had shed more than one-fifth of their manual employees by 1980 so that their share of total manual employment in the region declined by 5 per cent. Although locally controlled firms contracted employment more slowly, there was little difference between the rate of contraction in foreign and UK externally owned multinationals, both of which reduced their blue collar employment by over one-quarter during this period. The authors cast doubt on the significance of local ownership in employment generation in view of the very similar internationalisation strategies employed by 'indigenous' companies such as Tootal and Renold, both of which expanded their overseas interests at the same time as embarking upon extensive rationalisation in the North West.

Similar evidence has been produced by Gaffikin and Nickson (1983) for the West Midlands but in this case for both employment and output during the deep recession years 1978 to 1981. Using both primary survey and secondary source data, the authors found the ten largest manufacturing employers in the region reduced their UK employment by 25 per cent during these four years, whilst at the same time increasing their overseas work force by 9 per cent in spite of the world recession. That this represented a shift in the productive base of these companies abroad and not merely the introduction of more capital intensive processes in the UK, is confirmed by the output figures; the value of overseas production of these firms increased at five times the rate of UK production and in nine of the ten companies there was a marked decrease in the British share of global output. The authors consider that the productive shift abroad is understated owing to the ability of multinationals to conceal the value of overseas production through transfer pricing and the exclusion of the production of associated companies overseas. Finally, they provide evidence that FDI by these companies did not have a beneficial effect upon UK exports as is often claimed; in fact the contribution of UK exports to overseas sales fell by 6 per cent during this period, as a higher proportion of overseas sales was accounted for by overseas production.

It is important to set this high level of divestment by UK manufacturing multinationals in the context of recent aggregate UK trends in FDI. Recent *Bank of England* figures indicate that the value of overseas assets increased at much the same rate between 1979 and 1982 as between 1974 and 1978 (Table 5.1) which suggests that the abolition of exchange controls in 1979 did not have a marked effect on outward FDI. This is perhaps not very surprising in view of the large contribution of overseas borrowing and unremitted profits to overseas FDI (Dicken, 1983). Although in many respects misleading, recent capital flow data (*Business Monitor MA4*, 1983) show that the average value of outward FDI between 1977 and 1981 was approximately double that of inward FDI, a situation which has existed since 1973, but a deterioration on the net investment situation of the late 1960s. A marked deterioration in the UK's net direct investment position seems to have occurred in 1981, when for the first time, the value of outward capital flows exceeded inward flows by a wide margin. This was mainly attributable to a doubling of the value of outward manu-

facturing flows and an almost total drying up of inward manufacturing flows between 1980 and 1981, so that inward flows were
a mere 4 per cent of the value of outward manufacturing flows in
1981.

Conclusion: FDI and Growth Differences between Industrialised Countries

The reasons for this sudden deterioration in the UK's net manufacturing direct investment situation may have much to do with
government policy, and in particular the high interest rates and
strong currency situation which have made export oriented production increasingly unattractive. The sudden upturn in the value
of outward manufacturing investment in 1981 also corresponds
with a marked deterioration in the growth of manufacturing output
in the UK as shown by the *Index of Industrial Production*.
Michalet (1983) suggests the recent recession may have caused an
acceleration in the rate of internationalisation as multinationals
increasingly look for overseas investment opportunities to compensate for slow growth at home. If such is the case, a reinforce-
ment of the trends which increasingly became apparent during the
early 1970s is likely to have occurred, with the highest rates of outflow from slow growth economies such as the United Kingdom
and the highest rate of inflow to more buoyant industrialised
countries such as the United States and West Germany. Indeed the
most recent capital flow figures do show a marked increase in the
share of UK investment in the United States.

The extent to which these developments will exacerbate differences in the relative economic performance of the major industrialised countries depends largely on the extent to which FDI
flows represent *diversion* of investment from the source to the host
nation. As a high proportion of UK outward investment to the
United States is through acquisition, it is unlikely to represent
diverted investments if the objective is to secure a market foothold
in the US. Nevertheless, there is still the possibility of supplying
the UK market from acquired plants abroad. Cowling (1983), for
example, has argued that, faced with declining demand, multinationals will prefer to rationalise production in lower income,
slower growing markets which they will then service externally
from higher income, faster growing markets. Although there has

been a big increase in import penetration across a wide range of manufactured goods in the UK information on the origin of these imports is extremely scanty.

In considering the relationship between FDI and deindustrialisation in the UK therefore, account must also be taken of the links between FDI and import penetration. Another important link to be taken into account is that between FDI and export replacement. For example Holland (1979) has argued that as FDI normally follows exports, there will be a marked tendency for substitution to occur. He quotes evidence produced by the *Labour Research Department* that larger UK multinationals have a very low share of exports in national production compared to their smaller counterparts; if the latter have gone abroad more recently, as seems likely, increasing experience abroad could lead to export replacement. The evidence of Gaffikin and Nickson (1983) mentioned earlier in this essay, tends to support this view.

It is important also to consider the *type* as well as the quantity of FDI flowing into and out of the UK. Dunning (1979) suggests that the UK has benefited from a high proportion of inward investment in high technology sectors in comparison to a high proportion of outward investment in low technology sectors. We have already pointed out that this difference may have been disappearing during the 1970s and in fact more recent evidence suggests that the situation may now be reversed. Panic (1982) for example suggests that relatively low unit labour costs, and low incomes may increasingly attract low value-added production to the UK, whilst UK multinationals produce a higher proportion of their sophisticated products overseas in higher income markets. Hood and Young (1982b) provide indirect support for this view by pointing out that the share of R and D employment in UK foreign affiliates fell between 1975 and 1978 whereas their share of total employment continued to rise. The same authors have noted the high propensity for UK multinationals to invest through acquisition in the US between 1974 and 1978 and suggest that access to high technology was a major motive (Young and Hood, 1980). In this case, the possibility of supplying the UK market with high technology products seems very real. In fact, several recent reports by the *Monopolies and Mergers Commission* bewail the increasing level of imports of high technology goods into the UK, and the inability of domestic producers to compete with these imports (e.g. Monopolies and Mergers Commission, 1980). The similarity to the situation of external technological dependence which has given rise to increasing concern in Australia and Canada is striking; in so far as the competitiveness of domestic manufacturing is reduced, FDI in high technology industries is thus likely to reinforce the growth differences between industrialised nations.

Finally, it is important to realise that there are significant links between FDI, market structure and monopolistic behaviour which may tend to reinforce growth differences between industrialised countries. For example, the high level of market concentration in the United Kingdom is likely to have encouraged a relatively high level of outward FDI owing to the financial and organisational advantages possessed by large companies for investing overseas. Conversely, the dominance of these companies across a wide range of product markets within the UK may have deterred potential manufacturing investment in the UK. For example, Lall and Siddarthan (1982) have shown how UK firms investing in the US have avoided product markets in which US firms have been traditionally dominant. As UK multinationals exhibit a high degree of market dominance in less technology intensive industries, the low level of inward investment in these sectors (Dunning, 1979) may have been influenced by this dominance. For example Cowling (1982) suggests that the level of competition in the UK was not substantially raised through entry into the EEC as might have been expected owing to the lowering of trade barriers. This he attributes mainly to the control which established corporations are able to exert over market outlets through both ownership (vertical integration) and agency and franchise agreements. Another major deterrent to inward investment in concentrated markets is the threat of retaliation by established oligopolists in the home market of the potential investor. Courtaulds for example was able to use this threat to prevent potential European competitors from entering the UK cellulosic fibre market following the creation of EFTA (Monopolies and Mergers Commission, 1968).

What this discussion implies is that in industrialised countries with concentrated market structures such as the United Kingdom, the net balance of foreign direct investment may become increasingly negative over time. On the other hand, in countries like the United States where anti-trust legislation has kept markets more competitive, the net balance of FDI may become increasingly favourable because potential investors are faced with a wider choice of industries not dominated by established firms.

Acknowledgements

I would like to thank Mr. Ash Amin for his many helpful comments on this paper and Mrs. Joan Cassell for the typescript and preparation of the tables.

References

Buckley, P.J. and Casson, M. (1976) *The future of multinational enterprise* Macmillan, London
Cowling, K. (1982) *Monopoly capitalism*, Macmillan, London
Cowling, K. (1983) 'Excess capacity and the degree of collusion: oligopoly behaviour in the slump,' *The Manchester School*, 4, 341-59
Curhan, J.P., Davidson, W. and Suri, R. (1977) *Tracing the Multinationals*, Ballinger, Cambridge, Mass.
Dicken, P. (1980) *Recent trends in international direct investment with particular reference to the United States and United Kingdom*, paper presented at Anglo American workshop, Chapel Hill, North Carolina, USA
Dicken, P. (1983) *Overseas investment by U.K. manufacturing firms: some trends and issues*, Discussion paper 12, North West Industry Research Unit, University of Manchester
Dubin, M. (1976) *Foreign acquisitions and the spread of multinational firms*, Unpublished doctoral Thesis, Harvard Business School, Boston, Mass.
Dunning, J.H. (1979) 'The U.K.'s international direct investment position in the mid-1970s,' *Lloyds Bank Review, 132*, 2, 1-21
Dunning, J.H. (1982) 'Explaining the international direct investment position of countries: towards a dynamic or developmental approach' in J.Black and J.H. Dunning (eds.), *International Capital Movements*, Macmillan, London
Gaffikin, F. and Nickson, A. (1983) *Job crisis and the multinationals: deindustrialisation in the West Midlands*, West Midlands County Council, Birmingham
Graham, E.M. (1978) 'Transatlantic investment by muitinational firms: a rivalistic phenomenon?,' *Journal of Post-Keynesian Economics 1*, No. 1, 82-99
Holland, S. (1979) Comment on A.D. Morgan 'Foreign manufacturing by UK firms' in F. Blackaby (ed.), *Deindustrialisation*, Heinemann, London
Hood, N. and Young, S. (1982b) 'US multinational R & D: corporate strategies and policy implications for the UK,' *Multinational Business*, 6(2), 10-23
Hood, N. and Young, S. (1982b) US multinational R & D: corporate strategies and policy implications for the UK, *Multinational Business*, 2, pp. 10-23
Hymer, S. (1960) *The International Operations of National Firms: a Study of Direct Foreign Investment*, MIT Press, Cambridge, Mass.
Hymer, S and Rowthorn, R. (1970) 'Multinational corporations and international oligopoly: the non-American challenge' in C.P. Kindleberger (ed.), *The International Corporation*, MIT Press, Cambridge, Mass.
Kindleberger, C.P. (1968) *American Business Abroad*, Yale University Press, New Haven, Conn.
Kitching, J. (1974) 'Why acquisitions are abortive,' *Management Today, 11*, 82-7
Knickerbocker, F.T. (1973) *Oligopolistic Reaction and Multinational Enterprise*, Harvard University Press, Cambridge, Mass.

Lall, S. and Siddarthan, N.S. (1982) 'The monopolistic advantages of multinationals: lessons from foreign investment in the US,' *The Economic Journal*, 92, 668-83

Lloyd, P.E. and Shutt, J. *Recession and restructuring in the North West region: the policy implications of recent events*, Discussion Paper 13, North West Industry Research Unit, University of Manchester

Michalet, C.A. (1983) 'Multinationals: change of strategy in the face of crisis,' *Multinational Business*, 7(1), 1-10

Monopolies and Mergers Commission, (1968) *Report on the sup)ply of cellulosic fibres*, HMSO, London

Monopolies and Mergers Commission, (1980) *Domestic gas appliances: a report on the supply of certain domestic gas appliances in the United Kingdom*, HC 703, HMSO, London

OECD, (1981) *International investment and multinational enterprises: recent international direct investment trends*, OECD, Paris

Panic, M. (1982) 'International direct investment in conditions of structural disequilibrium: UK experience since the 1960s' in J. Black and J.H. Dunning (eds.), *International Capital Movements*, Macmillan, London

Rugman, A.M. (1981) *Inside the Multinationals*, Croom Helm, London

Stopford, J.M. and Wells, L.T. (1972) *Managing the Multinational Enterprise*, Basic Books, New York

United Nations, (1978) *Transnational Corporations in World Development: a Re-examination*, United Nations, New York

Vaupel, J.W. and Curhan, J.P. (1973) *The World's Multinational Enterprises*, Harvard Business School Research Division, Boston, Mass.

Vernon, R. (1979) 'The product cycle hypothesis in a new international environment,' *Oxford Bulletin of Economics and Statistics*, 41, 225-68

Young, S. and Hood, N. (1980) 'Recent patterns of foreign direct investment by British multinational enterprises in the United States,' *National Westminster Bank Review*, 2, 20-32

6 THE GEOGRAPHY OF MASS-REDUNDANCY IN NAMED CORPORATIONS

A.R. TOWNSEND AND F.W. PECK

Introduction

In Western capitalist economies during the 1980s, major employers have commonly reacted to world recession by shedding labour on a large scale. In most years since the depression of the early 1930s, job losses in these proportions were largely unknown except perhaps in the coal-mining industry. Mass-redundancy was viewed by many European governments as one aspect of the 'unacceptable face of capitalism' which should be avoided if at all possible. This is not the prevailing ideology in the 1980s. Mass-redundancy programmes became so numerous that one could almost regard them as the accepted political fashion of the day. Indeed, such programmes came to be viewed by many national governments as an appropriate and justifiable response to recession conditions, action which in the long term, it is hoped, will increase national industrial competitiveness and speed the transition towards an ideal 'post-industrial' society.

The realities of the situation, at least in the short- to medium-term, were somewhat different. Of course, closures and compulsory redundancies have always formed a part of the process of industrial change and therefore of geographical change. What is different about the 1980s, however, is the widespread occurrence and huge scale of redundancies, which, in many cases, form part of a programme of disinvestment and labour-shedding dictated by the head offices of major corporations. In no other national economy have such programmes had such a devastating effect upon employment as in the UK, where official figures record 2,708,152 redundancies across all industries and services in the five years between 1977 and 1981. Table 6.1, derived from reports in the *Financial Times*, demonstrates the key role played by 20 of the larger public and private corporations in generating job losses in general. The list is headed by two major nationalised corporations, British Steel Corporation with 76,800 job losses, and British Leyland with 36,400. Of the private corporations, the leading

174

national textiles group, Courtaulds, has by far the greatest number of losses (23,200), whilst the list also includes several notable foreign-owned companies in the manufacture of vehicles (Peugeot-Citroën, General Motors), agricultural equipment (Massey Ferguson), sewing machines (Singer) and domestic appliances (Hoover). In total, the 20 corporations amassed 264,200 job losses which represented 22.8 per cent of all manufacturing redundancies in the official series, ES955, and 49.7 per cent of the FT total on our records.

This evidence alone shows the indisputably central role played by large corporations in generating employment decline in the UK since 1976. Naturally, the first effect of worsening conditions in the employment market lay in a reduction in the rate of labour turnover in the factory workforce at large (Townsend, 1983a, p.47), which continued at a significant but reduced level even after industry was forced to announce redundancy, generally as a last resort, after 1979. Despite the numerical significance of mass-redundancies, geographers' work on industrial change has rarely focused on corporations as such. 'Enterprise geography' has begun to analyse the comprehensive decision-making of the large multi-plant corporation (Hayter, 1976; Healey, 1982; Watts, 1980), especially within traditional and clearly-defined industries such as textiles, brewing, coal, steel or shipbuilding. It is put forward here that comprehensive use of the financial press does provide an approach to the geographer's study of modern decision-making units such as Courtaulds, GKN or Peugeot-Citroën, as well as many other leading private corporations, as shown in Table 6.1. Some methods of analysing the spatial allocation of job losses within the individual corporation have been outlined elsewhere in Townsend and Peck (1985) and Massey and Meegan (1982). Such studies may take the form of the individual case studies already cited, or of comparative case studies, such as Peck and Townsend (1984) which deals with British Shipbuilders (Rank 4), Plessey (Rank 8) and Metal Box (Rank 20), or of work on the interaction or interplay between corporations in making rationalisation plans, as in Peck and Townsend (1985).

The aim of this chapter is to deal with the collective spatial behaviour of all the corporations which were reported as having job losses. It represents the first use of the FT data-base demonstrated in Table 6.1. Using ownership codes, it is possible to extract all job losses announced by each corporation. Figure 6.1,

Table 6.1: The Leading 20 Job Losers in the UK: Losses Reported at Known Locations, October 1976—September 1981

Rank	Corporation	Main product	Reported losses	Numbers of affected			
				Reports	Locations	Counties	Regions
1 N	BSC (British Steel Corporation)	Steel	76,800	86	48	22	8
2 N	BL (British Leyland)	Vehicles	36,400	42	21	11	7
3	Courtaulds	Textiles	23,200	77	49	18	10
4 N	British Shipbuilders	Ships	15,600	37	23	12	6
5	GKN (Guest, Keen & Nettlefolds)	Vehicle parts	13,100	41	20	11	5
6 F	Peugeot-Citroën	Vehicles	10,700	12	5	3	3
7	ICI (Imperial Chemical Industries)	Chemicals	9,300	17	16	9	5
8	Plessey	Telecommunications	9,200	12	5	3	3
9 F	General Motors (Vauxhall)	Vehicles	7,900	11	5	4	2
10	Burton	Clothing	7,400	17	9	5	3
11	Lonrho	Varied holdings	6,300	11	4	3	3
12	GEC (General Electric Co.)	Electrical goods	6,200	18	14	13	8
13	Dunlop	Rubber goods	6,100	8	6	6	5
14 F	Massey Ferguson	Agricultural machines	5,800	9	4	4	4
15 F	Singer	Sewing machines	5,700	5	1	1	1
16	Imperial	Food and drink	5,300	14	13	11	8
17 F	Hoover	Domestic appliances	5,100	14	5	3	3
18	Thorn-EMI	Electrical goods	5,000	11	9	7	4
19	Tootal	Textiles	4,700	28	19	5	5
20	Metal Box	Metal containers	4,400	26	21	16	9
	Total		264,200				

Notes: N = nationalised group owned by British Government.
F = foreign-owned corporation.

'Counties' = include Northern Ireland, and regions of Scotland, as single units.

Source: Monitoring and classification of *Financial Times* reports, October 1976—September 1981.

Figure 6.1: British Steel Corporation (BSC) Job Losses Reported in the *Financial Times*, 1977-81

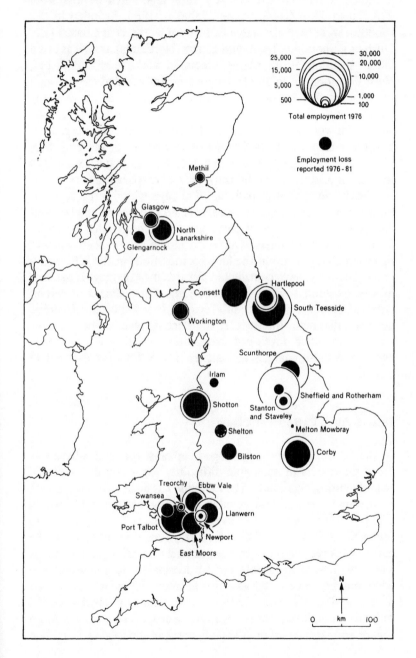

for example, shows the pattern of job loss in the British Steel Corporation, a nationalised industry with high rates of loss from 228,000 in 1976 falling below 75,000 in 1984. Included in this rundown were several notable closures of works as at Consett (Co. Durham), Shotton (Clwyd) and Corby (Northants) as well as rapid labour shedding at other large integrated works (e.g. Port Talbot, West Glamorgan). In 1983, the government avoided the question of whether five major works could remain — at Ravenscraig (Strathclyde), South Teesside (Cleveland), Scunthorpe (Humberside), Llanwern (Gwent) and Port Talbot (West Glamorgan) — but it was feared in 1984 that the closure of one or more of these must come up again. This was only a major and public example of the sort of problem faced by many private corporations.

Clearly, geographical patterns of change within large corporations can vary enormously. Yet aggregate patterns of employment change indicate that overall, some places have been much harder hit by recession than others. Our main aim is to establish whether recorded changes within the large corporations in the UK, singly and collectively, have contributed towards these aggregate patterns in any substantial way by concentrating disinvestment in certain types of places, regions or sub-regions. It is important to stress, however, that many industrial changes taking place in the UK have parallels in other developed economies, and that the processes generating these changes are largely international or national in origin.

International Patterns of Change

In varying degrees, most developed capitalist economies have suffered the effects of economic difficulties especially in traditional manufacturing heartlands. The outcome has been a steady increase in unemployment in these economies throughout the 1970s, with a slight recovery after 1975 (Townsend, 1983a, p.29), but leading to intensified crises after 1979 (Margirier, 1983). In many ways, the early 1980s recession can be seen as part of continuous difficulties since 1973, with the whole period dominated by a slowdown in economic growth as well as a rise in unemployment (Cripps and Ward, 1983). By early 1983, official figures totalled over 16 million unemployed across Western Europe as a whole. More recent estimates based on official figures put the total at 19 million

(Kaletsky, 1984). Despite some uniformity of experience across Europe, the intensity and timing of the current crisis vary from nation to nation. Output decline among the leading industrial nations has been most severe in the UK, which suffered an overall decline of 5.2 per cent during the financial year 1980/1 alone. Germany and France mostly continued to experience output increases, but at a much reduced level compared with figures at or above 2 per cent per year in the mid 1970s. So too, unemployment rose most sharply in the UK, from 3.9 per cent in 1975 to 8 per cent in 1980 and 13.1 per cent for 1984 (annual averages on current basis, Department of Employment, 1985, p.S20). Neither has North America been immune from these influences. The United States has experienced greater cyclical variation in manufacturing employment than in the past, with reductions of 9 per cent during the 1973-5 recession and (after a full recovery between 1975 and 1979) a further decline of 10.7 per cent between 1979 and 1982. None the less, between October, 1982 and December, 1984 the recovery of employment was enough to reduce seasonally-adjusted unemployment from 10.4 per cent to 7 per cent. This strong recovery occurred principally, but not exclusively, in service employment rather than manufacturing. It left higher than average unemployment rates, over 10 per cent, in the industrial areas of the 'manufacturing belt' and Appalachia, and was not considered a reliable precedent for Europe (Kaletsky, 1984).

Setting 'mass-redundancy' in an international context is a fairly complex task, as the concept of redundancy varies quite widely between nations (Yemin, 1982, p.4). In North America, for example, contracts of employment are deemed to be from day to day, while in Japan some corporations adopt 'life-time employment' systems. Variations in workpeople's terms of employment thus have consequences for the ways in which employment can be increased or decreased, ranging from total severance through to temporary lay-offs with part-pay. In nations where employees are protected by legislation, as in the UK, official figures are collected and can be used for research purposes (Townsend, 1983b). In other nations systematic information is more difficult to obtain. In consequence, there are conceptual and empirical problems when making international comparisons.

International Perspectives on Recession

Early empirical evidence nonetheless suggests that recession in the 1980s has intensified some spatial patterns of industrial change while interrupting others. Within the UK and the USA the urban-rural shift in manufacturing employment has dominated trends since the 1960s (Fothergill and Gudgin, 1979, 1982; Keeble, 1976; Norton and Rees, 1979; Lonsdale and Seyler, 1979). In the UK these trends appear to have been partially, if not completely, overtaken by the effects of recession, working under international financial influences, which threw manufacturing industry into a spiralling decline from 1979 at least until 1983. In turn the place of British manufacturing, and the performance of industry in different industrialised nations, relative to that of the newly-emerging industrial nations, has become sharply defined.

Recent downward trends in levels of profitability and return on investment have been interpreted by some Marxist commentators as a crisis of capital accumulation (Frank, 1980; Mandel, 1980; Margirier, 1983) which has led to significant alterations in the geographical orientation of capital flows in search of more productive outlets. This tendency toward a restructuring of capital on a global scale has become a major theme in industrial geography in the 1980s (Castells, 1980; Grahl, 1983; Harvey, 1982; Peet, 1983). These fairly radical changes, though possibly slowed down by recession (Fitzgerald, 1980), have qualified the supremacy of many of the advanced capitalist economies and enabled several newly-industrialised countries to emerge (Balassa, 1981; Edwards, 1979).

All the above writers agree on a single 'radical' interpretation of world change, which is certainly relevant to this chapter. This view dominates what little writing is available from the USA. The interpretation particularly stresses the relative shift in investment to industrialising countries within individual multinational corporations. It needs to be stressed that divestment from developed countries is only one international influence upon mounting unemployment; others comprise trade competition (as in the effects of Japanese car-production on the UK West Midlands), the effects of competition and changing terms of trade between developed countries (particularly the pound's high exchange rate as a petro-currency in 1980) and the inter-penetration of multinationals' manufacturing facilities between developed countries.

The multinational corporation (such as General Motors or ICI in Table 6.1) has been viewed as an important instrument whereby capital movements are controlled and directed (Bluestone and Harrison, 1980; Cohen, 1983; Taylor and Thrift, 1982). Various permissive factors have made possible the concentration of economic power into fewer and fewer global (mainly American) 'giants'. Standardisation of production methods, high levels of output per unit, the transportability of products in modern industry and technical advances in world communications have all played some part in the growth of multinational power (Brooke and Beusekom, 1979; Brooke and Remmers, 1978). A major driving force behind these shifts, however, has been the need for large corporations to compete and capture markets which guarantee returns on high investment, and this was a major factor in the expansion of US firms in the UK in the 1950s and 1960s. However, in order to capture markets, corporations are bound by cost constraints, and in recession conditions, the pressures to disinvest in high cost locations in favour of often existing plants in low cost locations becomes intense. Once market leaders have established such patterns of behaviour, it becomes extremely difficult for other corporations not to follow suit, although Bluestone and Harrison (1980) argue that corporations in the USA have artificially engineered the closure of profitable plants. Peet (1983, p.129) argues, from the perspective of state patterns of unionisation of workers in the USA, that 'capitals which move to regions of low-intensity class struggle are then able to out-compete capitals which remain in regions of high-intensity struggle, which are coerced into drastic adjustment'. Peet extends this argument to an international level where capital has dispersed from traditional core manufacturing nations in search of savings in wage costs as a means of restoring levels of profitability.

The end result of these changes, first in Europe then in parts of the Third World, has been the emergence of corporation production systems which span the world in some sectors of manufacturing activity. Functional separation of different activities within multinational corporations has also created a new international division of labour (Froebel, Heinrichs and Kreye, 1980) which has intensified manufacturing decline in many advanced industrialised nations. This provides one vital perspective from which to view the effects of the current recessionary period upon the UK.

Geographical Perspectives on Recession in the UK

The persistence of high unemployment in the peripheral regions of
the UK has been the subject of considerable debate over the past
20 years or so. It has become popular to view such inequalities as
inevitable under capitalist systems (Holland, 1976; Massey, 1983;
Massey and Meegan, 1978). The control of capital within the
'meso-economic sector' has been given prominence by Holland
(1976, pp.28-33) as a major catalyst to imbalanced growth. Large
corporations create internal divisions of labour which, in aggregate, imprint themselves upon regional structures. However,
regional structures themselves have for many years featured a shift
in employment from manufacturing to service activities, a pattern
generally linked with the process of 'de-industrialisation'
(Blackaby, 1979; Goddard, 1983; Singh, 1977; Thirlwall, 1982).
The prominent studies of job loss and employment decline have
concentrated on manufacturing decline (Fothergill and Gudgin,
1979, 1982; Keeble, 1980; Massey and Meegan, 1978, 1982).
Others have researched manufacturing decline in particular inner
city areas (Evans and Eversley, 1980; Gripaios, 1977; Lloyd and
Mason, 1978), and in particular industries and regions (Dunnett,
1980; Healey, 1982; Law, 1982; Lloyd and Reeve, 1982).

However, what is significant about events in the 1980s is that
decline in manufacturing has been so general, affecting traditional
declining industries and regions, as well as formerly prosperous
ones (Martin, 1982; Townsend, 1982, 1983a). Large corporations
within the 'meso-economy' have played an influential part in this
decline. The Scottish economy, for example, has been badly hit by
closures of foreign owned establishments (Grunberg, 1983; Hood
and Young, 1982). Other UK regions have suffered badly at the
hands of indigenous private and public corporations (Lloyd and
Shutt, 1984; Peck and Townsend, 1984; Townsend, 1983a, p.74)
generating absolute decline in some localities which had traditionally escaped the worst effects of cyclical down-turns in the
national economy (Healey and Clarke, 1984). Recession so severe
and widespread is no doubt a factor which contributes to the new
impotence of organised campaigns to resist large closures (Baldry
et al., 1983; Hudson and Sadler, 1982, 1983).

On the other side of the coin, direct foreign investments by UK
corporations, in Europe and elsewhere, has proceeded and
increased in the 1980s (*Barclays Review*, August 1982). Despite

some claims to the contrary (Morgan, 1979) it is difficult not to blame part of the manufacturing decline in the UK on investments being directed overseas and into the British service sector. Patterns of foreign investment from the UK have been the subject of some study (Taylor and Thrift, 1981; Watts, 1982); this is however a notoriously difficult area of empirical work. To a large extent, those international difficulties are common to any research which aims at documenting the activities of individual corporations. The rest of this chapter deals with British and foreign corporations in the UK using a unique source which covers the whole UK, but which can extend no further.

Corporate Data Sources

The absence of any reliable, consistent and publicly-available source of company information remains a major obstacle to research that seeks to bridge the gulf between individual corporate case studies and wider economic trends (Grunberg, 1981, p.23). Fortunately, it has become standard practice in the UK for major employers to announce redundancy programmes to unions and the press from their central headquarters, as a means of 'setting the record straight' with all parties concerned. In the manufacturing sector, these announcements are often geographically specific, so that the location of intended redundancies at one site or across various sites can be established. Naturally, there are problems of coverage and accuracy when using this source, but at least it provides the vital facility of being able to identify locatable job losses under known ownership.

The present analysis makes first published use in computerised form of a data-set derived from reports in the *Financial Times* (FT) between October 1976 and September 1981. All references to any form of job loss at a known location, including many individual cases which do not merit the word 'programme', have been coded systematically throughout this period, along with details of ownership and a number of locational characteristics of the place affected by job loss. These data have proved an effective basis upon which to build case studies of individual corporations (see, for example, Peck and Townsend, 1984). The purpose here, however, is to describe and analyse the overall shape of the whole data-set with principal reference to the spatial (and temporal) patterns contained within it.

The *Financial Times* reported 1,633 cases of job loss under identifiable locations and ownership. Vigorous cross-checking of reports, as well as correspondence with some corporations, was intended to ensure the accuracy of redundancy figures. Out of a total of 563,600 reported job losses in 1,555 cases, 94.3 per cent (531,400) were in the manufacturing sector, with only 0.7 per cent and 5 per cent in the primary and service sectors respectively. This strong weighting towards manufacturing industry was as expected. Firstly, only 24 per cent of *all* redundancies in this period (as known in the best official source — see below) were in the service sector (or 35.5 per cent including construction). Secondly, redundancies announced by large employers in the service sector less often provided precise geographical details of job losses, which were commonly spread across a large number of relatively small establishments. In manufacturing, on the contrary, employment (and hence redundancies) is more highly concentrated at particular sites, although increasingly there are certain corporations whose patterns of employment and rationalisation (notably in food, drink and catering) may involve the manufacturing, service and/or extractive sectors.

Testing the coverage of the FT data has formed an integral part of the analyses performed. The most relevant official redundancy series is that collected by the Department of Employment, ES955, which has been tabulated, described and evaluated as a source elsewhere (Department of Employment, 1983, pp. 245-59; Townsend, 1983b). Some useful results have already emerged from analyses of these data which have used shift-share techniques (Martin, 1983; Townsend, 1982). The impact of recession through redundancy has been heaviest in those regions which are more dependent on manufacturing industries in general, reflected in high levels of redundancies in the traditionally depressed peripheral regions, as well as an unprecedented rise in levels of redundancies in the West Midlands. ES955 itself is not a fully comprehensive source of redundancy statistics. Nevertheless, this series is the best available and it provides a useful yardstick against which to assess the coverage of the FT data. Overall, the FT recorded 496,100 redundancies in GB manufacturing industries over this period, which comprised 42.8 per cent of the official ES955 figure of 1,159,200.

Table 6.2: Regional Coverage of Reported Redundancies in Manufacturing: Financial Times in Relation to Official Series ES955, 1977-81

	Financial Times	ES955	Coverage (%)
Scotland	57,100	146,819	38.9
Wales	54,100	89,840	60.2
North	47,300	92,409	51.2
North West	93,400	220,522	42.3
Yorkshire and Humberside	41,100	132,736	31.0
East Midlands	27,000	77,946	34.7
West Midlands	85,000	141,910	59.9
South West	13,300	56,453	23.6
East Anglia	11,300	23,741	47.5
South East	66,500	176,856	37.6
Total	496,100	1,159,232	42.8

Sources: *Financial Times* data-set; *Employment Gazette*, 1983, p. 254.

This study seeks to establish patterns within large corporations (singly and collectively) which are strongly represented in the data-set. Aggregate coverage, at 42.8 per cent, is therefore perhaps less of a concern to this study than are variations in coverage between different regions, years and industries. Table 6.2 shows substantial variations in coverage between the Regions of the UK (excluding Northern Ireland which is not covered by ES955). Figures range from 60 per cent in Wales and the West Midlands down to only 24 per cent in the South West. Communications with the *Financial Times* suggest that lower coverage in the South West and South East is partly related to their lower proportionate share of FT regional correspondents. This suggested relationship is not entirely consistent in the Northern Region, however, which was also listed as having few local correspondents, yet whose coverage was fairly high (51 per cent). The more convincing evidence is for under-reporting in some regions due to small size of establishment (and hence small average size of redundancies). It seems likely, for example, that good coverage in Wales reflects the above average size of redundancies in that country, which receive greater press coverage. Despite having only ten data points (as in Table 6.2), a high positive association (a product moment correlation co-efficient of 0.56) was established between the percentage regional coverage and the proportion of large plants in the factory size structure of different regions.

There are also variations in the coverage of job losses from year to year. Dates of announcement in the press rarely coincide with dates of implementation of redundancies. In compiling Table 6.3, normal announcements of redundancy are set back by 90 days (the standard period of notice for redundancies greater than 100) and other adjustments were made to equate the data with calendar years. Inevitably, this introduces an element of approximation in the precise allocation of job losses between years. The pattern of coverage over time rose from a low level of 23.6 per cent in 1977 up to a peak of 53.8 per cent in 1979, thereafter falling back to 43 per cent by 1981. This fits well with a possible model of public consciousness over these years, with somewhat higher coverage coinciding with the initial phases of a new recession in the winter of 1979/80 when mass-redundancies were still a relatively new phenomenon attracting press attention. High coverage in 1979 could also reflect the large size of redundancy programmes announced in this year, particularly within BSC (British Steel Corporation), British Shipbuilders and BL (British Leyland).

There are also differences in coverage between industries, which ranges from over 90 per cent in Shipbuilding down to a mere 8 per cent in Instrument Engineering. Significantly, the three industry groups with highest coverage are dominated by nationalised corporations which have implemented large scale redundancies at relatively few sites. Press coverage of the events in these corporations (BL, BSC, British Shipbuilders) has consequently been fairly

Table 6.3: Annual Coverage of Reported Redundancies in Manufacturing: Financial Times in relation to Official Series ES955, 1977-81

	Financial Times	ES955	Coverage (%)
1977	23,400	99,076	23.6
1978	50,600	119,315	42.4
1979	75,700	140,809	53.8
1980	175,400	402,021	43.6
1981	171,100	398,011	43.0
Total	496,200	1,159,232	42.8

Sources: *Financial Times* data-set; *Employment Gazette*, 1983, p. 254.

intense. Indeed, higher levels of reporting in these industries will largely explain the high coverage during the year of 1979 and in regions such as Wales, and the West Midlands in the data-set as a whole. Excluding these nationalised industries, coverage of the remaining orders lies at fairly modest levels between 20 and 40 per cent. Variations are associated with those in the national average level of 'firm concentration'; the *Census of Production* for 1976 shows the percentage of employment in each order belonging to the leading 100 private companies. These data produced a product moment correlation of +0.5 in comparative analysis with industry coverage.

In essence, these various checks on the level of coverage across regions, years and industries indicate that variations between regions and years are largely a function of the industrial and size structure of industrial plants. They are consistent with the view that the FT data represent major changes in major companies and public corporations, and that individual financial groups may be expected to be represented with reasonable consistency between regions: the record is disproportionately successful with large-scale redundancies announced centrally by major UK employers.

Some Alternative Spatial Patterns of Decline within Corporations in the UK, 1977-1981

In approaching more detailed analysis of geographical patterns in the FT data it is useful to reflect on changes which were taking place during the 1970s and speculate on patterns which might emerge during the 1980s. Since 1979, much discussion has surrounded the urban-rural shift in manufacturing employment which occurred between the 1960s and the recessions centred on 1971 and 1975. National economic performance has altered dramatically since the mid-1970s. It is essential therefore to inquire whether this urban-rural trend has continued through the recession, whether previous differences between 'core' and 'peripheral' regions (Keeble, 1976) have been re-asserted or whether both features have been superseded by other patterns of change evident in the behaviour of our dominant corporations.

Despite general agreement over the existence of urban-rural shift before 1977, there is still much debate surrounding the causes of these changes (Fothergill and Gudgin, 1979, 1982; Fothergill, Kitson and Monk, 1983; Massey and Meegan, 1978). The main explanations imply that manufacturing *expansion* underlies part of the urban-rural shift. This view is supported by studies of industrial movement up to 1971 (Keeble, 1976; Sant, 1975) which established clear association between migration out of conurbations and the need to accommodate expansion of output. Similarly, there are some indications that the urban-rural shift became less marked during the mid-1970s in response to a general slow-down in manufacturing output growth (Regional Studies Association, 1983). This leads one to speculate whether these trends have been halted by the effects of recession after 1977. It should be noted, however, that the urban-rural shift might continue in terms of '*relative decentralisation*' in recession conditions; for instance, a corporation might have no expansions after 1979, but more job losses in urban than in rural areas.

There is some evidence which suggests a weakening in the urban-rural shift in the late 1970s. Owen, Coombes and Gillespie (1983, p.15) concluded on the basis of employment estimates between 1978 and 1982 that regional location in the UK is an increasingly important factor modifying the urban-rural dichotomy, and that recession appears to have led to the re-emergence of a stronger north-south divide in terms of employment change. Analyses of regional patterns of redundancies support this conclusion (Martin, 1982; Townsend, 1982, p.1401). In terms too of the large additions to unemployment rates, from 1979 to 1981, there appear to be only small average differences between urban and rural areas (Townsend, 1983a, p.153).

This partial evidence suggests that whereas urban-rural shift was primarily growth induced, and therefore investment-led, the spatial patterns of change in manufacturing employment leading into recession after 1977 were more closely associated with differential patterns of *dis*investment, particularly within major public and private corporations. One obvious possibility is that the recession may have disproportionately affected branch plants in the peripheral regions over and above any differences in industrial composition. It seems plausible, for example, that many of the initial regional policy factories set up in the 1960s and before were reaching obsolescence together when the onset of severe recession precipitated closure.

What, then, has been the pattern of employment decline in large corporations, individually and collectively, over the years 1977 to 1981? Has it had a differential impact on urban and rural areas, or has decision-making generated regional divisions, perhaps on a north versus south basis? These are the types of questions which have governed the selection of variables and the descriptive analyses which follow. Compared with aggregate figures of *net* employment change by sex, revealed by the 1981 Census of Employment (Department of Employment, 1983, pp. 61-5), the particular merit of our data is to identify large components of job loss by date and by name of company (usually undifferentiated as regards sex and occupations). The approach was designed to allow the assessment of the decisions of individual named corporations over five years in the allocation of job losses between their differently-located plants. The data base has the facility to dis-aggregate job loss totals in ways which are not a feature of official data:

(a) The data base can distinguish between cases of closure (or part-closure) as opposed to redundancies in general.

(b) Analyses can be performed either on the number of cases reported (say in a particular year or company), or on the associated total figures of the loss of jobs.

(c) Each case is classified according to 'parent ownership' as indicated in the relevant year of *Who-Owns-Whom* (Dun and Bradstreet). It is thus possible to analyse patterns of job loss within selected groups of corporations or individual ones.

(d) The coding includes the date of announcement in the FT as well as some control over retrospective and deferred announcements which can be distinguished from those which are imminent.

(e) Also, the data base includes codes for the type of settlement (details below) and 'assisted area status', under regional policy, of each place involved in job loss announcements. These two codes are particularly important as a means of investigating the alternative patterns of job loss described above, and these form respectively the basis of the two sections which follow.

UK Corporate Job Loss and the Urban-Rural Dimension

'Settlement type' has become a key variable in aggregate studies of employment change. Classifications have varied from fairly generalised categories which detect broad urban-rural contrasts (e.g. Keeble, 1980), to more complex forms (e.g. Fothergill and Gudgin, 1979). Massey and Meegan (1978) have argued that the 'degree of rurality' measured is, in fact, a crude surrogate for the different investment histories experienced by urban and rural areas of various types, such that in the early 1970s, capital restructuring coincidentally had its most severe effects on the conurbations rather than rural areas. This view has influenced the settlement classifications, or 'codes', employed in the present study, but they also introduce some new features to reflect more closely the investment histories of different parts of the UK.

Six settlement types can be distinguished in this study (Table 6.4). Two of these can be described as 'traditional' locations of manufacturing industry; 'industrial towns' and 'coalfield settlements'. The industrial towns, numbering 87, are based in England and Wales on Moser and Scott (1961, p.17) who used a cluster

Table 6.4: Classification of Settlement Type used in Locating Reports of Job Loss

Code	Description	Definition
N	New and expanded towns	as designated at December 1976 (with certain exclusions)
I	Industrial towns	commercial and industrial towns as identified by Moser and Scott (1961), plus Scottish Burghs over 50,000 and Belfast
O	Larger overspill areas	Boroughs and Urban Districts with overspill agreements and factory space over 400,000 sq ft completed or under construction at 1971 (Evans, 1972, p. 184)
L	Coalfield settlements	settlements on, or within 10 km of, exposed coalfield areas
S	Coastal settlement	locations within Employment Office Areas of towns with borders on tidal water
X	Other	not allocated above, mostly inland small towns and rural areas

Note: Where locations qualify for more than category, the higher one is taken; i.e. Warrington is coded as a New Town (N) despite being listed as an 'industrial town' (I) by Moser and Scott.

analysis to group towns (population 50,000+) of different social and economic character. Here we select their 'industrial' towns, together with commercial towns with some industry, as representing the denser main historical concentrations (at 1951) of manufacturing industry and traditional engineering skills. Scottish cities and burghs with over 50,000 inhabitants and Belfast in Northern Ireland were added to this list. It was expected that the age of factory investment in some 'coalfield' areas (but not its diversity) would be similar to the industrial towns, although some contrasts emerge in response to post-war diversification in most coalfields.

In contrast, the remaining four codes represent various types of location which have not been traditional areas of manufacturing activity; hence investment is in various forms more recent on average. New and expanded towns form one category largely by definition (*Town and Country Planning*, February 1977, p.98). Larger areas of overspill from the conurbations form a second category, including dispersal areas around Birmingham (Daventry, Droitwich), Liverpool (Widnes, Winsford) and Manchester (Macclesfield) as well as areas fed by Greater London (e.g. Banbury, Kings Lynn) (Evans, 1972, p.184). Industry in coastal settlements commonly includes post-war developments (characteristically in engineering consumer goods and clothing) in resorts such as Weymouth and Great Yarmouth as well as in smaller ports like Falmouth and Harwich. Finally, all remaining locations, most of which involved the Home Counties and rural areas, adopted by industry over only the last 50 years, were placed in one category of 'other settlement'.

Table 6.5 shows the distribution of the FT job losses across these settlement types. A large proportion of all cases (45.2 per cent) and of all job losses (44.8 per cent) occurred in the 'industrial towns'. We must, however, see these volumes as percentages of the much larger total number of all manufacturing jobs (use of 1971 base-data from the Census of Population ensures that estimates for County Boroughs exclude surrounding areas). In the 'industrial towns', with an estimated total of 2,672,300 jobs, the FT data recorded 230,400 job losses, an apparent decline between 1977 and 1981 of approximately 9 per cent. The proportional incidence of employment loss in most other rows of Table 6.5 is similar. In marked contrast, the 67,700 jobs lost in 'other settlement', i.e. the suburban and rural areas, represent only a 3 per cent

Table 6.5: Distribution of Reported Job Losses in Manufacturing by Settlement Type, 1977-81

		Announcements (1) No.	(2) %	Job Losses (3) No.	(4) %	(5) Estimated manufacturing employment 1976 (approx)	Col. (3)/Col. (5) (%)[a]
Industrial towns	(I)	660	45.2	230,400	44.8	2,672,300	8.6
Coalfield	(L)	319	21.9	118,500	23.1	1,370,400	8.6
New Towns	(N)	95	6.5	31,800	6.2	445,900	7.1
Overspill areas	(O)	36	2.5	14,500	2.8	170,200	8.5
Coastal	(S)	121	8.3	51,100	9.9	523,700	9.8
Other	(X)	228	15.6	67,700	13.2	2,063,400	3.3
Total		1,459	100.0	514,000	100.0	7,245,800	7.1

Note: a. Col. provides a first approximation of the ratio of FT job losses to total manufacturing employment at start of period, and ignores other components of change.

Sources: 1) FT data.
2) 1976 (unpublished county version) *Census of Employment.*
3) *1971 Census of England and Wales,* OPCS, 1975.
4) *Town and Country Planning,* February 1977, p. 98.
5) *Department of Manpower Services, Northern Ireland DMS Gazette,* No. 3, 1979.

reduction over the four-year period. There is a need for some caution in interpreting these figures, chiefly due to incomplete coverage discussed in a previous section. Nevertheless, the contrast is substantial and it suggests that the recession from 1977 up to the end of 1981 had its worst effects upon industrial, coalfield, coastal and overspill settlements and least effects upon 'other settlement' which comprises medium and small size towns, predominantly in the South East, East Anglia and the South West. If one accepts the general direction of these figures, it appears that job losses within the corporate sector displayed an urban-rural dichotomy in 1977-81, apparently reflecting general trends of the early 1970s.

This conclusion *does not stand* for the years of heaviest recession, 1980 and 1981. Analyses of changes over time in the FT data indicate that the proportion of job losses in different settlement types was not uniform from year to year. This type of analysis using FT data assumes that patterns of reporting did not change from year to year; it is, however, invaluable in the absence of a Census of Employment between 1978 and 1981. Table 6.6 shows in its first two columns the number of cases and volume of job loss reported in traditional manufacturing locations for each of the years between 1977 and 1981 (grouping the two settlement types 'I' and 'L'). In the three years 1977 to 1979 over three-quarters of all job loss announcements affected traditional locations, but the figure fell to less than two-thirds of all cases in 1980 and 1981. The proportion of cases affecting non-traditional locations is available by subtraction and rose from a low point of 19.7 per cent in 1978 up to 37.5 per cent in 1981, with a fairly distinct discontinuity between 1979 and 1980. Analysis of closures alone brings out this general pattern even more sharply. In 1977, 86.4 per cent of all closures occurred in traditional locations. This high percentage is certainly in keeping with evidence from other studies of closure in earlier years. Marquand (1980, p.71), for example, used Scottish data for 1964 to 1975 to show that closures were disproportionately an urban phenomenon. By 1981, however, only 54.4 per cent of all closures in the FT data were in industrial towns, suggesting that closures by large corporations became much more geographically widespread after 1979. This supports the views of Fothergill and Gudgin (1982, p.172) and the Regional Studies Association (1983, p.44) that the urban-rural shift declined in the later 1970s, perhaps through closures becoming spatially more even in their effects. Any continued urban-rural

Table 6.6: Reported Job Loss: Traditional Locations, and Conurbations, by Year, 1977-81

		Traditional locations (l, L)[a]		Conurbations[b]		Total
		No.	Per cent of row	No.	Per cent of row	
1977	Cases	37	75.5	28	57.1	49
	Job losses	23,100	75.7	13,800	45.0	30,500
1978	Cases	110	80.3	88	63.8	137
	Job losses	46,300	90.6	36,400	70.0	51,100
1979	Cases	151	74.7	113	55.9	202
	Job losses	60,900	77.1	46,900	58.7	79,000
1980	Cases	325	64.9	209	41.1	501
	Job losses	125,300	69.5	86,000	47.7	180,400
1981	Cases	356	62.5	219	38.4	570
	Job losses	93,300	54.0	66,300	38.3	172,900
Total	Cases	979	67.1	657	45.0	1,459
	Job losses	348,900	67.9	249,400	48.5	513,900

Notes: a. 'Non-traditional locations' (N, O, S, X) may as a group be found by subtraction from final column.
b. 'Conurbations' are introduced as a different and alternative measure.

Source: FT data.

shift therefore depended more heavily on preferential investment into rural areas after 1977.

Within these general trends, there were some significant shifts in the loss of employment between individual settlement types. In 1977, 55.7 per cent (17,000) of all reported job losses occurred in 'industrial towns', and 20 per cent (6,100) in 'coalfield settlement' compared with 10 per cent or less in 'coastal' and 'other settlement' respectively. By 1981, however, job loss in 'industrial towns', though rising to 67,900, claimed a lower (39.2) percentage of all job losses in the year. Perhaps more significantly still, 'other settlement', covering many South-East towns and rural areas, was the second largest contributor with 35,100 job losses, higher even than the 25,500 job losses announced in 'coalfield' settlements. Even 'coastal' job losses amounted to 24,900, close behind losses in the coalfields. These details seem to suggest that while job losses within large corporations in traditional manufacturing locations increased rapidly after 1977, the rate of increase was even greater in coastal and rural settlements, particularly after 1979. In 1981, the peak year of recession, the geography of job loss was entirely different from any period of the 1970s. 'Non-traditional' locations were involved in an unprecedented way, although their rate of loss per thousand jobs was still lower than the continuing rate of 'traditional' areas.

As some verification of our broad results, the same direction of change emerges when one applies another group of categories based upon types of county (Keeble, 1980, p.962). Using the same classification, the numbers of cases in the conurbations were cross-tabulated by year and added to Table 6.6. Again, a divide occurs between 1977-79 and 1980-1 in the pattern of change. In the earlier period, the number of announcements in the conurbations was consistently above the number in non-conurbation locations. After 1979, this situation was reversed, such that in 1981, a large proportion of all job loss announcements (61.6 per cent) affected settlements outside the conurbations, including 34.1 per cent alone in 'less-urbanised counties'. Again, this indicates that as recession deepened, job loss, redundancy and closure became phenomena affecting a wide range of manufacturing locations.

How one interprets these overall trends from a corporate perspective is not at first clear. It is tempting to suggest that individual corporations with plants in many types of settlement concentrated their job losses in traditional locations up to 1979, and thereafter shifted the weight of losses towards non-traditional locations. However, these aggregate trends could equally well represent *inter*-corporate contrasts. In the earlier period (1977-79), for instance, recession may have been more severe for corporations with a large proportion of plants in traditional locations, while the deeper recessionary years (1980-1) began to hit a larger proportion of other corporations which were geographically more concentrated in other locations.

The intra-corporation hypothesis has been given prominence by Massey and Meegan (1978) who detected a trend in the period 1968-73 for many large electrical engineering firms to transfer production out of conurbation areas, particularly into assisted areas. Dennis (1978), however, was clear that the massive decline in manufacturing in Greater London was largely due to 'deaths' rather than transfers to new openings. Even so, Keeble (1978) questioned whether there was some reorganisation within large corporations working to the detriment of the cities in the early 1970s. The key point in the period 1977 to 1981 is whether *individual corporations* concentrated disinvestment in 'traditional locations' up to 1979 and preserved jobs in 'non-traditional locations' until deeper recession in 1980 and 1981. Analyses were undertaken for all 'traditional locations' (codes I and L), and for 'industrial towns' alone (code I). The work presented here is for 'industrial towns' alone, in order to concentrate attention on mainly older cities and towns, and to exclude the post-war investment of many corporations in coalfield areas.

When we tabulate results from our 'top 20' job losers, first seen in Table 6.1, there is no strong common pattern of job loss over time (Table 6.7). The last column is concerned with each corporation's total number of cases of job loss in two periods and considers, within each of these totals, what proportion of cases fell in 'industrial towns'. Nine of the corporations, marked (1), had a higher proportion of all cases in 'industrial towns' in the earlier period, but seven others had proportionally more in the period after 1979. In several corporations (GEC, Massey Ferguson, Tootal, Metal Box) it is possible to see the announcement of job loss in 'industrial towns' concentrated in the earlier period, with more miscellaneous locations following. Some of these industrial towns, however, are in assisted areas (Sunderland, Liverpool, Kilmarnock) rather than historic locations of craft skill, hence the pattern does not easily conform with a stylised de-skilling process.

Table 6.7: The Leading 20 Job Losers: Cases of Reported Losses in Industrial Towns (I) in Two Time Periods, 1977-79/1980-81

| Rank | Corporation | Cases in 'Industrial Towns' | | | | Period of highest proportional incidence |
| | | (1) 1977-79 | | (2) 1980-81 | | |
		No.	% of all cases	No.	% of all cases	
1.	BSC (British Steel Corporation)	24	54.5	10	25.6	(1)
2.	BL (British Leyland)	9	60.0	11	42.3	(1)
3.	Courtaulds	7	43.8	27	45.8	(2)
4.	British Shipbuilders	15	68.2	11	91.7	(2)
5.	GKN (Guest, Keen & Nettlefolds)	2	22.2	12	37.5	(2)
6.	Peugeot-Citroën	0	0.0	7	58.3	VOID
7.	ICI (Imperial Chemical Industries)	1	25.0	7	23.1	(1)
8.	Plessey	9	90.0	2	100.0	(2)
9.	General Motors (Vauxhall)	0	0.0	1	11.1	(2)
10.	Burton	10	76.9	2	66.7	(1)
11.	Lonrho	6	75.0	2	66.7	(1)
12.	GEC (General Electric Co.)	2	66.7	8	53.3	(1)
13.	Dunlop	2	50.0	4	100.0	(2)
14.	Massey Ferguson	2	66.7	2	33.3	(1)
15.	Singer	0	0.0	0	0.0	VOID
16.	Imperial	1	33.3	5	45.5	(2)
17.	Hoover	4	80.0	4	57.1	(1)
18.	Thorn-EMI	3	37.5	1	33.3	(1)
19.	Tootal	2	100.0	14	70.0	(1)
20.	Metal Box	2	66.7	12	52.2	(1)
	Total (inc. void cases)	94	56.3	136	45.8	(1)

Indeed in electrical engineering, previously analysed by Massey and Meegan (1978), the earlier period's job losses tend to be 'replacement industries' of 'industrial towns' in assisted areas, for example Sunderland, Hartlepool and Merthyr Tydfil. There is some tendency in British Steel (see Figure 6.1 above) for the earlier *closures* to be in Victorian industrial towns such as Motherwell, Hartlepool, Glasgow and Bilston in the West Midlands and later job loss to hit former 'greenfield' sites as at Llanwern, Corby and lower Teesside. In BL (British Leyland), the earlier period tended to involve closures with heavy losses on Merseyside (Speke, 3,000, 1978), in Greater London (Southall, 2,500, 1978), Birmingham (Castle Bromwich, 6,600, 1979) and Glasgow (Prestcold, 900, 1979) but spreading to more dispersed locations after 1979 (e.g. Swindon, Abingdon, Grantham, Solihull).

There were many other corporations, however, which had proportionally more job losses in traditional locations after 1979 (see Table 6.7; British Shipbuilders, General Motors, Dunlop, Imperial). It appears that at least for the 20 corporations, there is no systematic corporate behaviour discriminating between settlements of different kinds, suggesting that aggregate patterns of change result from the *varied* experience of different corporations over these years. This *inter-corporation hypothesis* was further examined by taking all corporations with more than one case, and in turn selecting those with a clear arithmetical balance of cases in one period as the other. Of 197 eligible corporations, about 40 had a majority of cases before 1980, while 100 others had *all* their cases in 1980 and 1981. This implies strongly that any temporal changes in the data set as a whole may be dominated by inter-corporation variations in behaviour and experience of recession. In fact, further inspection of the data indicates that the latter 100 included a proportion of two-thirds with the majority of their cases in areas other than 'industrial towns'.

To summarise, it is clear from the FT data as a whole that the collective effect of large corporations upon settlements of different types has been to concentrate job losses in industrial towns and coalfield areas up to 1979, but to shift losses more towards coastal, overspill and rural locations in 1980 and 1981. Examination of patterns of change *within* individual corporations has shown no obvious consistency in behaviour, at least among the 'top 20' job losers. This suggests that aggregate patterns of change as regards settlement types were due to differences between corporations. It seems likely that one type of corporation represented particular elements of weakness in the 1977-79 period — shipbuilding, steel, vehicles, electrical engineering — often with particular features of labour intensity, while after 1979, general conditions of manufacturing recession affected many other corporations in less traditional industries and in less traditional locations outside the conurbations.

The Impact of Corporate Job Loss on Government 'Assisted Areas'

So far, our analysis has shown that corporate job losses in 1980 and 1981 affected many non-traditional manufacturing locations as well as traditional ones, suggesting, in the absence of significant employment gains, a weakening urban-rural dichotomy in employment performance in these years. To what extent, then, has this led to a re-emergence of regional, or more simply north-south divisions? Most previous work on industrial change in peripheral regions of the UK has centred around the influence of area financial assistance upon rates of industrial migration into these regions (e.g. Keeble, 1976; Sant, 1975) and the impact of regional policies upon employment totals (e.g. Marquand, 1980; Moore, Rhodes and Tyler, 1977). As the supply of mobile factories has dwindled in the recession conditions (with only 60 inter-regional moves per year, 1976-80; Killick, 1983) these regions have experienced a serious erosion of employment, not only in traditional declining industries like shipbuilding and steel, but also in some of those industries which have experienced high rates of growth and mobility in the post-war period (e.g. Electrical Engineering, Vehicles). Taking the three main 'assisted Regions' together, Scotland, Wales and the Northern Region, manufacturing employment as a whole declined by 22 per cent between 1977 and 1981. Of the total decline of 300,000 jobs, 84,000 were in iron, steel and shipbuilding. With regional policy under review at the time of writing (Secretary of State for Trade and Industry, 1983), the assessment of job losses and mass-redundancies in peripheral regions has considerable importance.

Our FT data record many significant closures of large plants whose foundation in former years represented strategic victories for regional policy (Townsend, 1983, p.92). Between November

1979 and February 1981, for example, over 7,700 jobs were lost at Peugeot-Citroën's factory at Linwood in Scotland (formerly owned by Chrysler USA). Other examples include closures by Massey Ferguson at Kilmarnock (1,400 job losses), by GEC at Hartlepool (5,000 job losses) and by Dunlop at Speke on Merseyside (2,400 job losses) as well as a series of smaller cases in these and many other corporations. A simple compilation of FT reports has already indicated a pronounced withdrawal of large and small plants from assisted areas (Townsend, 1983a, p. 193). This can now be verified and analysed in greater detail with the aid of the computerised data base, with particular reference to the spatial incidence of job losses within corporations.

The distribution of reported job losses in assisted and non-assisted areas is shown in Table 6.8. Over the five years as a whole, 55 per cent (813) of all announcements and 63 per cent of all job losses (322,800) affected plants located in 'assisted areas' as defined at the beginning of our study, 1976, and including the large Intermediate Areas of that date. These figures indicate that, on average, job losses in assisted areas were individually larger than those reported in non-assisted areas, as might be expected given the above-average size of employment in the old established factories, and branch factories in assisted areas (Sant, 1975, p.41). To assess the apparent relative reductions in assisted and non-assisted areas, these totals can be related in Table 6.8 to manufacturing employment figures at the start of our study period. Ratios vary quite widely around an average apparent proportional incidence of job loss of 7 per cent. Non-assisted areas were slightly less badly affected than the average. These ratios are only estimates and must necessarily understate the true position, but are sufficient to demonstrate a clear difference within assisted areas, from a 3 per cent incidence in DAs up to an astonishing 15 per cent in all SDAs. Thus there are much greater variations in this record for different types of assisted area, than between assisted and non-assisted areas.

There are reasons to expect that reporting levels in SDAs might be inflated relative to other areas. Job losses in SDAs tend to be of large size. The plants themselves tend to be large employers and owned by well-known corporations like BSC, Lucas, BL and Dunlop. All these features, together with the greater employment problems of areas chosen as SDAs, will tend to result in high publicity. Nevertheless, if we check the coverage of redundancies

Table 6.8: Distribution of Reported Job Losses in Manufacturing by Assisted Area Status, 1977-81

Assisted Area Status 1976		Announcements		Job Losses		(5) Manufacturing Employment 1976	Col (3)/Col (5) (%)[a]
	(N)	(1) No.	(2) %	(3) No.	(4) %		
Non-assisted		655	44.6	192,900	37.4	2,927,200	6.6
Intermediate	(IA)	332	22.6	115,700	22.5	1,647,100	7.0
Development Area	(DA)	131	8.9	52,800	10.2	1,575,700	3.4
Special Development Area	(SDA)	301	20.5	138,800	26.9	948,600	14.6
Northern Ireland	(U)	49	3.3	15,500	3.0	147,200	10.5
All assisted areas		813	55.4	322,800	62.6	4,318,630	7.5
Total UK		1,468	100.0	515,700	100.0	7,245,800	7.1

Note: a. Apparent proportional incidence of reported job losses, ignoring other components of change.

Sources: 1) FT data.
2) *DMS Gassette*, 1978, 1.
3) Department of Trade and Industry.

announced in those regions containing SDAs (Scotland, Wales, North, North-West), we find that the FT reports cover 45.8 per cent of ES955 figures, only marginally above a national average of 42.9 per cent (see above). It seems from our FT data that the slightly poorer performance of assisted areas as a whole is largely due to massive loss of jobs in SDAs rather than other assisted areas. This result tends to imply some continuity in the industrial history of the UK in two ways. Firstly, the SDAs of Clydeside, Cumbria and the North-East coast had been designated as such partly because of inherent problems in heavy industry, which continued in our study period in steel and shipbuilding. Secondly, higher levels of job losses within newer 'replacement industries' in these areas as well as in SDAs on Merseyside and in South Wales partly reflect their greater numbers in these areas; these areas had, with few exceptions, been priority areas for the government attraction of such industries since 1934, whereas the DAs of 1976 dated as assisted areas mainly from 1966, and the IAs in the main only from 1972.

The patterns of change in assisted areas 1977-81, however, have not been consistent from year to year. They provide a clear direction of change even when one allows for the selective coverage of FT data reported earlier in this Chapter. Table 6.9 compares the number of job loss reports in assisted and non-assisted areas by year from 1977 to 1981. As in our analysis of settlement types, there is a noticeable change in the geographical distribution of reported job losses between 1979 and 1981. Up to 1979, in each year at least 69 per cent of all announcements and over 74 per cent of all job losses occurred in the assisted areas as a whole. In 1980, however, the majority of cases (52 per cent) affected the *non*-assisted areas, although above average size of job losses in assisted areas still meant 55 per cent of losses in these areas. These trends are even more marked for job losses involving plant closures. In 1977, a mere 6 per cent of *reported* job losses through plant closure occurred in non-assisted areas. This figure rose year by year up to 47 per cent in 1981. The same is true of the *number* of closures in assisted and non-assisted areas. The proportion of closures within DAs and SDAs together fell from 77 per cent of all cases in 1977 down to only 24 per cent in 1980 and 27 per cent in 1981.

As indicated above, however, the reports for SDAs are much worse than other assisted areas over the five years. These areas are

Table 6.9: Reported Job Loss: Assisted Area Status by Year, 1977-81

		SDA		Other Assisted Areas (DA, Interm., N. Ireland)		Non-assisted Areas		Total
		No.	% of row	No.	% of row	No.	% of row	
1977	Cases	25	51.0	16	32.7	8	16.3	49
	Losses	19,200	62.7	8,000	26.2	3,400	11.1	30,600
1978	Cases	41	29.7	55	39.9	42	30.4	138
	Losses	23,600	45.2	15,800	30.3	12,800	24.5	52,200
1979	Cases	68	33.3	67	32.8	69	33.8	204
	Losses	31,900	40.3	26,900	33.9	20,400	25.8	79,200
1980	Cases	78	15.4	164	32.3	265	52.3	507
	Losses	32,100	17.7	67,900	37.5	81,000	44.8	181,000
1981	Cases	89	15.6	210	36.8	271	47.5	570
	Losses	32,000	18.5	65,400	37.8	75,400	43.6	172,800
Total	Cases	301	20.5	512	34.9	655	44.6	1,468
	Losses	138,800	26.9	184,000	35.7	193,000	37.4	515,800

Source: FT data.

again quite distinctly different in their experience of reported job loss from year to year. Other assisted areas are affected by just under one third of all FT job losses before 1979, *rising* to 38 per cent in 1980 and 1981. In contrast, 63 per cent of all reported job losses in 1977 occurred in the SDAs *falling* dramatically year by year to only 18 per cent in 1980 and 1981. This indicates that the poorer record of SDAs in relation to other areas was a consequence of disproportionate loss of jobs in the years 1977 to 1979. The aggregate picture is verified in unemployment trends (*Employment Gazette*, monthly), in employment data at least up to the 1978 Census, and in certain macro-economic and redundancy data for Scotland, Wales and the Northern Region. Our data here enable us to concentrate on the contributory decisions of the meso-economic sector.

As with our analysis of job loss in different settlement types, the FT data enable us to observe how the overall trends apply in particular corporations or groups of corporations. Disproportionate job loss in assisted areas in the early period (1977-79) could be the result of corporations closing or reducing employment in branch plants in peripheral regions in the particular economic environment of 1977-79, while sheltering jobs in the 'core' regions until after 1979 (*intra-corporate hypothesis*). Table 6.10 suggests that this may be the case. The majority of these corporations (12) allocated a greater proportion of their decisions for job losses to assisted areas in 1977-79 than in 1980-81. This change was particularly marked in the electrical engineering industry involving the closure of large branch plants typically employing semi-skilled workers as in Plessey, GEC, Hoover and Thorn-EMI. In fact, this industry can be regarded as the decisive one affecting the outcome of analysis in Table 6.10, as corporations in other industries do not exhibit such strong regularity. Six of these other corporations, for example, are involved in the vehicles industry, historically located in the South East and West Midlands but with many branches established in the 'assisted areas' during the 1960s expansion. Withdrawal of investment and jobs in assisted areas in the early period was a feature of Massey Ferguson (tractors, etc.) and Dunlop (tyres), but in BL, GKN (components, etc.) and General Motors there was a higher proportion of announcements in assisted areas in the *second* period.

The varied experience of SDAs relative to other assisted areas in the total data set prompted an analysis of intra-corporate

Table 6.10: The Leading 20 Job Losers: Cases of Reported Losses in Assisted Areas in Two Time Periods, 1977-79/1980-81

Rank	Corporation	Cases in 'Assisted Areas'				Period of highest proportional incidence
		(1) 1977-79		(2) 1980-81		
		No.	% of all cases	No.	% of all cases	
1.	BSC (British Steel Corporation)	37	84.1	37	94.9	(2)
2.	BL (British Leyland)	6	40.0	11	42.3	(2)
3.	Courtaulds	13	81.3	39	66.1	(1)
4.	British Shipbuilders	22	88.0	8	66.7	(1)
5.	GKN (Guest, Keen & Nettlefolds)	1	11.1	10	31.3	(2)
6.	Peugeot-Citroën	0	0.0	3	25.0	VOID
7.	ICI (Imperial Chemical Industries)	3	75.0	10	76.9	(2)
8.	Plessey	8	80.0	0	0.0	(1)
9.	General Motors (Vauxhall)	0	0.0	3	33.3	(2)
10.	Burton	13	100.0	3	100.0	VOID
11.	Lonrho	8	100.0	3	100.0	VOID
12.	GEC (General Electric Co.)	3	100.0	4	26.7	(1)
13.	Dunlop	2	50.0	1	25.0	(1)
14.	Massey Ferguson	1	33.3	1	16.7	(1)
15.	Singer	4	100.0	1	100.0	VOID
16.	Imperial	2	66.7	3	27.3	(1)
17.	Hoover	5	100.0	6	85.7	(1)
18.	Thorn-EMI	2	25.0	0	0.0	(1)
19.	Tootal	2	100.0	16	64.0	(1)
20.	Metal Box	2	66.7	13	56.5	(1)
	Total (inc. void cases)	124	72.9	169	56.0	(1)

Source: FT data.

behaviour in relation to SDAs alone. Table 6.11 shows cases of reported job losses in SDAs in two time periods. Again, there is strong support for the *intra-corporate hypothesis* as 13 corporations announced proportionally more job losses in SDAs in the earlier period (1977-79) compared with the later one (1980-81); only six had their worst reported effects on SDAs after 1979. Earlier announcements affecting SDAs were again a strong feature in electrical engineering. More interestingly, BL and Peugeot-Citroën now emerge in support of the intra-corporate hypothesis, implying that, in the earlier period, jobs in SDAs alone were disproportionately affected, spreading to other assisted areas and non-assisted areas after 1979.

While this evidence seems to suggest that the years preceding deep recession (1977-79) were marked by the withdrawal of jobs from assisted areas by major corporations, some further corroboration is necessary. How typical, for example, was the experience of our top 20 job losers compared with the corporate sector as a whole? Several different analyses suggest that the top 20 were typical in this respect. The top 20 as a whole announced 73 per cent of their job losses in assisted areas in 1977-79; if we combine all the *other* corporations in our record, the equivalent figure was 72 per cent. This compares with the later period (1980-81), in which 44 per cent of all announcements in the top 20 were in assisted areas and 50 per cent of those in the remaining corporations. There appears, therefore, to be a fairly uniform experience over time comparing the top 20 job losers with all the remaining corporations in the data-set.

As a separate point, however, the top 20 were very different from the rest in the balance of total job losses in different parts of the UK. The most noticeable feature was that SDAs and DAs were more heavily involved in the top 20 (69 per cent of all job losses) compared with remaining corporations (56 per cent); a major finding, but an understandable difference given the predominance of 'large firm' branch plants in SDAs in particular, and the way in which expanding labour-intensive companies were attracted and, at times, coerced into development in Britain's problem regions in the 1940s and 1960s.

It is difficult in turn to escape the conclusion that there was a strong element of withdrawal of jobs from SDAs and assisted areas within corporations in general between 1977 and 1979. This is supported by other evidence (Townsend, 1983a, p.81) which

Table 6.11: The Leading 20 Job Losers: Cases of Reported Losses in Special Development Areas in Two Time Periods, 1977-79/1980-81

Rank	Corporation	Cases in SDAs				Period of highest proportional incidence
		(1) 1977-79		(2) 1980-81		
		No.	% of all cases	No.	% of all cases	
1.	BSC (British Steel Corporation)	17	38.6	14	35.9	(1)
2.	BL (British Leyland)	4	26.7	1	3.8	(1)
3.	Courtaulds	7	43.8	3	5.1	(1)
4.	British Shipbuilders	15	60.0	4	33.3	(1)
5.	GKN (Guest, Keen & Nettlefolds)	0	0.0	0	0.0	VOID
6.	Peugeot-Citroën	2	100.0	1	10.0	(1)
7.	ICI (Imperial Chemical Industries)	0	0.0	3	23.1	(2)
8.	Plessey	8	80.0	0	0.0	(1)
9.	General Motors (Vauxhall)	0	0.0	3	33.3	(2)
10.	Burton	4	30.8	0	0.0	(1)
11.	Lonrho	2	25.0	1	33.3	(2)
12.	GEC (General Electric Co.)	3	100.0	2	13.3	(1)
13.	Dunlop	2	50.0	0	0.0	(1)
14.	Massey Ferguson	0	0.0	1	16.7	(2)
15.	Singer	4	100.0	1	100.0	VOID
16.	Imperial	0	0.0	2	18.2	(2)
17.	Hoover	5	100.0	6	85.7	(1)
18.	Thorn-EMI	1	12.5	0	0.0	(1)
19.	Tootal	0	0.0	1	4.0	(2)
20.	Metal Box	2	66.7	4	17.4	(1)
	Total (inc. void cases)	70	41.2	49	16.2	(1)

Source: FT data.

established that the majority of the leading 20 corporations in terms of *total employment* announced their 'first' job losses in 'assisted areas'. If one goes on to consider the profile of these announcements over time, the 'intra-corporate shift' is, on average, clear.

These results encouraged a closer inspection of *closures* in the main assisted areas. The analysis can also be refined by concentrating on closures within industries (fairly narrowly defined by minimum list headings — mlh) associated with higher than average rates of geographical movement (Howard, 1968). Through narrowing in this way the analysis is designed to focus to a high degree on closures of 'regional policy factories' set up in earlier decades in (then) assisted areas. The data-set contains 100 cases of closures in these industries (such as electrical engineering, artificial fibres, etc.) within the main assisted areas (SDAs, DAs, Northern Ireland), defined again as at 1976. These closures involved 57 private companies; the 42 which were ranked in *The Times 1000, 1981-2* are shown in Table 6.12, together with the earliest announcement of closure in this period in these assisted areas. The table, however, would be little different if we had listed closures *anywhere in the UK*, as only the groups marked by asterisk (*) had an 'earlier' closure announced in other parts of the UK.

Inspection of all closure cases in all these companies revealed that on 24 occasions (57 per cent of total) the first (and sometimes only) closure after 1976 was in a SDA. For all assisted areas together, this count rose to 35 or 83 per cent of all closures. Even allowing for the possibility of reporting omissions and for those companies with no equivalent plants in non-assisted areas, this figure is remarkably high, suggesting that these companies commonly closed plants 'first' in this period in assisted areas rather than others in non-assisted areas. The data-set does not include systematic records of all non-closing plants. However, surviving plants in the same mlh category in non-assisted areas (26 per (incomplete) records it was established that at least ten of the companies announcing their first closure in an assisted area retained plants in the same m1h category in non-assisted areas (26 per cent). This figure is probably an underestimation. Use of *Key British Enterprises 1982* demonstrated indeed that 41 of the 42 companies had surviving sites in non-assisted areas (though not necessarily in the same mlh as the plant involved in the closure). Also in these corporations as a whole 27 per cent of all closures

Table 6.12: Closures within Post-war Mobile Industries in Assisted Areas: First Announcement by Private Companies after October 1976

Company (ranked by turnover, Times 1000 1981-82)	Location	Assisted area status (1976)	Date of announcement
1 BP	Baglan Bay	SDA	Sept. '80
* 4 ICI	Carrickfergus	N. Ireland	Oct. '80
9 GEC	Liverpool	SDA	March '78
19 Weston	Windermere	DA	Sept. '79
20 Lonrho	Felling	SDA	May '78
27 Courtaulds	Skelmersdale	SDA	Nov. '76
29 Thorn-EMI	Bradford	Intermed.	April '78
45 BICC	Newtonabbey	N. Ireland	Oct. '78
50 Lucas	Liverpool	SDA	March '78
66 IBM	Peterlee	SDA	Nov. '78
82 Plessey	Sunderland	SDA	
	Speke	SDA	March '77
	Kirkby	SDA	
* 88 Coats Patons	Irvine	SDA	Oct. '78
* 101 Pilkingtons	St. Helens	SDA	June '81
* 108 Rank	Redruth	DA	Oct. '80
114 Massey Ferguson	Knowsley	SDA	Feb. '80
115 ITT	Enniskillen	N. Ireland	March '81
* 117 Delta	Washington	SDA	July '81
134 U.D.S.	Peterlee	SDA	Feb. '78
141 Albright & Wilson	Kirkby	SDA	Dec. '76
* 144 Fisons	Plymouth	DA	Jan. '81
147 Hoechst	Limavady	N. Ireland	Oct. '80
149 Tootal	Bolton	Intermed.	April '78
169 Clark	New Tredegar	SDA	Aug. '80
179 Smiths Industries	Ystradgynlais	SDA	Feb. '80
210 Monsanto	Crook	SDA	March '79
	Peterlee	SDA	
229 Du Pont	Maydown	N. ireland	Sept. '80
250 Hoover	Hamilton	SDA	Sept. '78
258 Burton	Sunderland	SDA	May '77
277 United Glass	Alloa	DA	Aug. '80
307 Low & Bonar	Dundee	DA	Dec. '77
321 BSR	East Kilbride	SDA	Nov. '79
332 Burroughs	Cumbernauld	SDA	Nov. '80
336 Peugeot-Citroën	Linwood	SDA	Feb. '81
339 Dawson	Coleraine	N. Ireland	Sept. '78
350 Honeywell	Uddingston	SDA	Sept. '80
481 Ryland Vehicles	Liverpool	SDA	Feb. '81
618 Black & Edgington	Denny	DA	May '80
* 627 Hepworth	Hetton-le-Hole	SDA	July '80
655 Clayton Dewandre	Aberdare	SDA	Sept. '80
771 RCA	Washington	SDA	March '81
794 Alfred Booth	Liverpool	SDA	March '78
879 Akzo	Kirkby	SDA	March '79

Note: In all corporations except those marked (*), this was the first closure in the same industry anywhere in the UK.

were in non-assisted areas, compared with only 7 per cent of first closures, suggesting again some discrimination against peripheral assisted area plants in early decisions.

It is not necessarily difficult for the individual researcher to relate reports of redundancies to the overall UK geographical distribution of plants at a particular year in a given corporation (as lists can be obtained in many cases from directories, correspondence, etc.). Use of such information on Courtaulds, our leading private corporation for job losses (see Table 6.1), has shown that this corporation had nearly 300 plants in 1976 spread across all categories of government assisted areas. This stock of plants, according to FT reports, fell by about 14 per cent nationally, but this rate varied from 20 per cent in assisted areas down to only 5 per cent in non-assisted areas. This pattern is partly a consequence of the geographical spread of products and different technologies in different regions of the UK (e.g. artificial fibres in Northern Ireland, spinning of cotton in the North West, hosiery in the East Midlands). What is more difficult is to establish the relationship of findings like those of Table 6.12 to longer-term trends. Although there have been periods when closures have appeared to affect branch rather than parent plants, the record none the less indicates that the failure of branch factories is quite common, and can be more common in peripheral areas than elsewhere (Henderson, 1979). Among 4,000 plants established under inter-regional moves from 1945 to 1965, one-quarter had failed to survive to 1966: among 2,000 such moves made between 1965 and 1975, 362 had already closed by 1975, before our study period began (Pounce, 1981). Our evidence states that the 'mobile' mlhs analysed above contributed 47,000 job losses from closures alone in Northern Ireland, SDAs and DAs in 1977-81. This is certainly unprecedented but may only represent an acceleration of an already established trend. It indicates that the balance of job gains and losses from industrial movement swung into a negative net position at some point in the mid-1970s. This pattern of change had also been implied by new methodology reported by the Department of Trade and Industry (1984) using unpublished work of Moore, Rhodes and Tyler. This methodology suggests a decline from the plateau of employment in migrant plants in assisted areas in the 1970s (though precise figures are not yet available).

High levels of job loss in assisted areas in the years 1977-79 have one important corollary for patterns of corporate job loss.

There has been some debate concerning the view that plants at a greater distance from their corporate headquarters are more vulnerable to redundancy or closure than plants in the headquarters region, especially during cyclical downturns in the economy (Massey, 1979; Watts, 1981). An initial view of the pattern of job losses in this respect is provided in Figure 6.2, by reference to physical distance (in kilometres) simply to the UK 'parent headquarters'. The outer ring of each regionally-located circle indicates the distribution of job losses in the region by location of the parent group's headquarters other than London. Comparatively few of the sites of job loss were themselves head office locations; indeed closures or part-closures of such sites were minimal before 1980. The feature of overwhelming importance is the dominance of the circle-centres, reflecting the importance of London as the UK headquarters for a large proportion of corporations; while this is naturally a strong feature in the South East, it has little less importance in, say, Scotland or Northern Ireland. Throughout our study period, the majority of closures involved plants over 250 kilometres from headquarters.

In the recession conditions of 1980 and 1981 well over half of all reported job losses were at locations within 250 km of the UK headquarters, compared with a clear majority at more than 250 km at the start of the period. It would be too crude to jump to the conclusion that 'firms close their most distant plants first': the data are compatible with this view, but we prefer rather to regard this variable as a surrogate for particular types and ages of investment in assisted area given that *most* assisted areas are 'peripheral' in national location, relative to the dominant headquarters centre in London. Like many of our results these data naturally mirror the arrival of significant volumes of redundancy in the South East, East Anglia and the South West only in 1980 and 1981 (Department of Employment, 1983).

One significant feature of the FT data, so far not discussed, is the role played by multinational corporations with *foreign headquarters* in creating job losses in the UK, particularly in peripheral assisted areas. In total our record covers 100,400 job losses at known locations in the United Kingdom within foreign corporations. As a whole, foreign cases of job loss accentuate the contrasting experience of 'peripheral' and 'core' areas. Where foreign-owned corporations have created serious unemployment it has arisen from their concentration of investment in large sites.

Figure 6.2: Reported Job Losses by Location of UK Corporate Headquarters

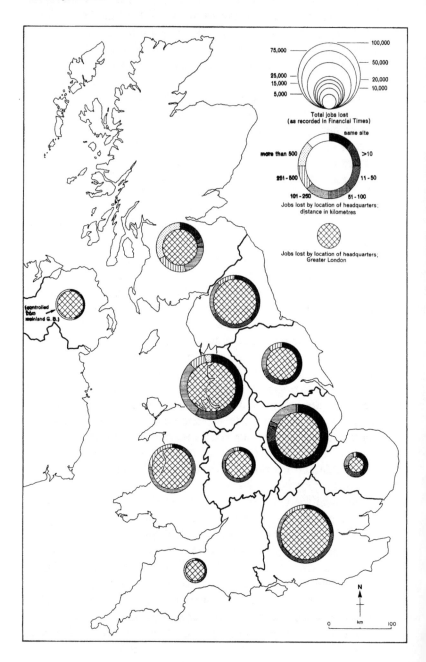

Indeed, disproportionate job losses in Strathclyde and the West Midlands result partly from the location there of particular vehicle plants of Peugeot-Citroën and Massey-Ferguson (both in our 'top 20' job losers). By contrast, Merseyside had comparatively few job losses in its important post-war foreign plants (Dicken and Lloyd, 1980), and this is attributable to the relatively good redundancy record of the USA car plants of Ford and, to a lesser extent, General Motors. Of course, these events must be seen in the general European pattern of planning and investment. However, the monitoring of our overall data on 1,633 occasions of job loss reveals relatively few in which withdrawals from the UK, whether by British or foreign corporations, are *directly* attributable to openings in the Third World or in the EEC.

Conclusions

For the first time in UK history, foreign corporations have played a significant part in a manufacturing recession. Contrary to many impressions, however, these 'multinational' corporations did not play a disproportionate part in the incidence of job losses in the UK between 1977 and 1981. UK-owned corporations had on average a greater incidence of job losses and shared some clear spatial trends of disinvestment with that of international capital in the UK. At least within the corporate sector, as embodied in the FT data, all the evidence suggests that in company with the weakening urban-rural dimension (characterised by urban decline and rural expansion), there was a re-emergence of a more traditional north-south division in terms of relative employment decline, prior to general manufacturing decline in 1980-81.

Our study period is thus divided into two by the arrival of 'mass-redundancy' in 1980. Trends between 1977 and 1981 show a noticeable break after 1979; in the early period the 'assisted areas' in general, and the SDAs in particular, were worst hit by job losses, whereas in 1980-81 there was a marked relative decline in corporate job losses in assisted areas (especially SDAs) and relative increases in losses in non-assisted areas. Whereas we found that the urban-rural contrasts in patterns of job loss over time (i.e. the reduced share met in conurbations) were largely, if not totally, a consequence of *different* corporations shedding labour at different times and in different places (*inter-corporate hypothesis*), these north-south contrasts reflect some regularity in the behaviour of major corporations (*intra-corporate hypothesis*), including several significant foreign-owned examples. This corporate behaviour can be characterised by their concentration of reports of job losses in assisted areas (especially the then SDAs) in the period 1977-79, followed by more widespread job losses in assisted and non-assisted areas of the country in 1980 and 1981. In this respect the pattern of change is substantially different from that of the two previous recessions contained in the period 1970-76 (Keeble, 1980). In that period industrial decline was concentrated in the conurbations, in whatever Region they were located: regional policy had already ceased to have any significant positive effect (according to Keeble), but the factories it created were not observed to be closing much more rapidly than before or than factories elsewhere. By contrast, FT reports indicate that the later 1970s were years of heavier redundancy for older and newer factories in SDAs, sufficient to register a preponderance of job losses at a long distance from headquarters (which were predominantly in the South-East), and to influence a trend of 'divergence' in the relative aggregate performance of assisted Regions, and their leading sub-regions such as Clydeside, Tyneside and Merseyside.

To make such connections betwen the 'meso-economy' and aggregate trends is to claim a useful step in the progress of industrial geography. On balance, it appears that there is most to be gained from work on corporations in the 'meso-economy' because they provide an opportunity to relate overall trends to events on the ground in local geographical areas. It may be, however, that the UK is unique in the range of corporations that are engaged in disinvestment in their home country, alongside the now common 'inter-penetration' of national corporations' investment between developed countries. In western European countries and the USA, the pattern of redundancy most readily indicates weakness in iron and steel, shipbuilding and motor vehicles, rather than in the general mass of modern corporations equivalent to the UK's Metal Box, Tootal or Thorn-EMI. Our study omits many gradual reductions through natural wastage of staff. Even so, it must remain a matter of doubt whether a study in any other European country could demonstrate job loss in such a wide range of modern corporations and industries. In the USA there is clearly a continued absolute loss of jobs in the 'manufacturing belt', but these are accompanied by only slow improvements in productivity in industry at large, and by absolute gains of employment in the 'periphery' of the country. In the UK, however, there is no sign of the national trend to a 'leaner, fitter' economy benefiting 'assisted areas'.

The overall picture challenges many assumptions of past growth planning. It would seem that 'peripheral' areas of the UK are less likely to receive multinational corporations' investment in the future, compared with the EEC area, the Mediterranean and the Third World. This experience does not argue for a reduction of regional policy in 'assisted areas'. Indeed, the renewed attraction of foreign investment appears to be one of the main reasons for a Conservative government's re-dedication to a modified regional policy.

Acknowledgements

Prepared under an ESRC grant entitled 'Sub-regional employment decline and the corporate sector, 1976-1981'. Thanks are due to the late G. Brown who produced the maps and to D.A. Michie who prepared the typescript.

References

Balassa, B. (1981) *The Newly Industrialising Countries in the World Economy*, Pergamon, London
Baldry, C. *et al* (1983) 'Fighting multinational power: possibilities, limitations, contradictions', *Capital and Class, 20*, 157-66
Blackaby, F. (1979) (ed.), *De-industrialisation*, Heinemann, London
Bluestone, B. and Harrison, B. (1980) 'Why corporations close profitable plants,' *Working Papers for a New Society*, May/June, 15-23
Brooke, M.Z. and Remmers, H.L. (1978) *The Strategy of Multinational Enterprise*, Pitman, London
Brooke, M.Z. and Van Beusekom, M. (1979) *International Corporate Planning*, Pitman, London
Castells, M. (1980) *The Economic Crisis and American Society*, Princeton University Press, Princeton, N.J.
Cohen, R.B. (1983) 'The new spatial organisation of the European and American automotive industries' in F. Moulaert and P. Salinas (eds.), *Regional Analysis of the New International Division of Labour*, Kluwer Nijhoff, London
Cripps, F. and Ward, T. (1983) 'Government policies, European recession and problems of recovery,' *Cambridge Journal of Economics, 7*, 85-99
Dennis, R. (1978) 'The decline of manufacturing employment in Greater London, 1966-74', *Urban Studies, 15*, 63-73
Department of Employment (1983) 'Statistics of redundancies and recent trends,' *Employment Gazette*, 245-59

Department of Trade and Industry (1984) *Regional Industrial Policy: Some Economic Issues*, London

Dicken, P. and Lloyd, P.E. (1980) 'Patterns and processes of change in the spatial distribution of foreign-controlled manufacturing employment in the United Kingdom, 1963 to 1975,' *Environment and Planning A, 12*, 1405-27

Dunnett, P.J. (1980) *The Decline of the British Motor Industry*, Croom Helm, London

Edwards, A. (1979) *The New Industrial Countries and their Impact on Western Manufacturing*, Economic Intelligence Unit Special Report No. 73 (2 vols.), London

Evans, A. and Eversley, D. (1980) (eds.) *The Inner City*, Heinemann, London

Evans, H. (1972) (ed.) *New Towns: The British Experience*, Charles Knight and Co. Ltd., London

Fitzgerald, E. (1980) 'The new international division of labour and the relative autonomy of the state: notes for a reappraisal of classical dependency,' *Bulletin of Latin American Research, 10*, (1), 7

Fothergill, S. and Gudgin, G. (1979) 'Regional employment change: a sub-regional explanation,' *Progress in Planning, 12*, 155-219

Fothergill, S. and Gudgin, G. (1982) *Unequal Growth*, Heinemann Educational Books, London

Fothergill, S., Kitson, M. and Monk, S. (1983) 'Changes in industrial floorspace and employment in cities, towns and rural areas,' *Working Paper 4*, Industrial Location Research Project, Department of Land Economy, University of Cambridge

Frank, A.G. (1980) *Crisis: in the World Economy*, Heinemann, London

Froebel, F., Heinrichs, J. and Kreye, O. (1980) *The New International Division of Labour*, Cambridge University Press, Cambridge

Goddard, J. (1983) 'Structural change in the British space economy' in J. Goddard, and A. Champion (eds.), *The Urban and Regional Transformation of Britain*, Methuen, London

Grahl, J. (1983) 'Restructuring in West European industry,' *Capital and Class, 19*, 118-42

Gripaios, P. (1977) 'The closure of firms in the Inner City: the South-East London case 1970-75,' *Regional Studies, 11*, 1-6

Grunberg, L. (1981) *Failed Multinational Ventures*, Lexington Books, Lexington, Mass.

Harvey, D. (1982) *The Limits to Capital*, Blackwell, London

Hayter, R. (1976) 'Corporate strategies in industrial change in the Canadian forest product industries,' *Geographical Review, 66*, 209-28

Healey, M.J. (1982) 'Plant closures in multi-plant enterprises — the case of a declining industrial sector,' *Regional Studies, 16*, 37-51

Healey, M.J. and Clark, D. (1984) 'Industrial decline and government response in the West Midlands — the case of Coventry,' *Regional Studies, 18*, 303-18

Henderson, R.A. (1979) 'An analysis of closures amongst Scottish manufacturing plants,' *ESU Discussion Paper* No. 3, Edinburgh

Holland, S. (1976) *Capital versus the Regions*, Macmillan, London

Hood, N. and Young, S. (1982) *Multinationals in Retreat. The Scottish Experience*, Edinburgh University Press, Edinburgh

Howard, R.S. (1968) *The Movement of Manufacturing Industry in the United Kingdom, 1945-65*, HMSO, London

Hudson, R. and Sadler, D. (1982) 'Anatomy of a disaster: the closure of Consett steelworks,' *Northern Economic Review, 6*, 2-18

Hudson, R. and Sadler, D. (1983) 'Region, class and the politics of steel closures in the European Community,' *Society and Space, 1*(4), 405-28

Kaletsky, A. (1984) 'Jobs: what Europe can learn from America,' *Financial Times*, 13 February, p.18

Keeble, D. (1976) *Industrial Location and Planning in the United Kingdom*, Methuen, London

Keeble, D. (1980) 'Industrial decline, regional policy and the urban-rural manufacturing shift in the United Kingdom,' *Environment and Planning A*, *12*, 945-62

Key British Enterprises (various editions) 2 vols., Dun and Bradstreet, London

Killick, T. (1983) 'Manufacturing plant openings, 1976-80,' *British Business*, *11*, 466-8

Law, C.M. (1982) 'The geography of industrial rationalization — the British motor car assembly industry, 1972-82,' *Discussion Papers*, No. 22, Department of Geography, University of Salford

Lloyd, P.E. and Mason, C.M. (1978) 'Manufacturing industry and the inner city. A case study of Greater Manchester,' *Transactions, Institute of British Geographers*, *3*, 101-14

Lloyd, P.E. and Reeve, D.E. (1982) 'North West England 1971-77: a study in industrial decline and economic re-structuring,' *Regional Studies*, *16*, 345-60

Lloyd, P.E. and Shutt, J. (1985) 'Recession and restructuring in the North West region: some preliminary thoughts on the employment implications of recent events,' in D. Massey, and R. Meegan, (eds.), *The Politics of Method: Contrasting Studies in Industrial Geography*, Methuen, London

Lonsdale, R. and Seyler, H. (1979) *Non-metropolitan Industrialisation*, Wiley, London

Mandel, E. (1978) *The Second Slump*, New Left Books, London

Margirier, G. (1983) 'The Eighties: a second phase of the crisis?' *Capital and Class*, *21*, 61-86

Marquand, J. (1980) 'Measuring the effects and costs of regional incentives,' *Government Economic Service Working Paper* No. 32, Department of Industry, London

Martin, R. (1982) 'Job loss and the regional incidence of redundancies in the current recession', *Cambridge Journal of Economics 6*, 275-396

Massey, D. (1979) 'In what sense a regional problem?', *Regional Studies*, *13*, 233-44

Massey, D. (1983) 'Industrial restructuring as class restructuring: production decentralisation and local uniqueness,' *Regional Studies*, *17*, 73-90

Massey, D. and Meegan, R. (1978) 'Industrial restructuring versus the cities,' *Urban Studies*, *15*, 273-88

Massey, D. and Meegan, R. (1982) *The Anatomy of Job Loss*, Methuen, London

Moore, B., Rhodes, J. and Tyler, P. (1980) 'The impact of Regional Policy in the 1970s,' *CES Review*, *1*, 67-77

Morgan, A. (1979) 'Foreign manufacturing by UK firms' in F. Blackaby, (ed.), *Deindustrialisation*, Heinemann, London

Moser, C. and Scott, W. (1961) *British Towns: A Statistical Study of their Social and Economic Differences*, Oliver and Boyd, London

Norton, R.D. and Rees, J. (1979) 'The product cycle and the spatial decentralisation of American manufacturing,' *Regional Studies*, *13*, 141-52

Owen, D., Coombes, M. and Gillespie, A. (1983) 'The differential performance of urban and rural areas in the recession,' Paper presented to the SSRC Urban and Regional Economics Study Group, University of Reading

Peck, F.W. and Townsend, A.R. (1984) 'Contrasting experience of recession and spatial restructuring in different British corporations: British Shipbuilders, Plessey and Metal Box,' *Regional Studies*, *18*, 319-38

Peck, F.W. and Townsend, A.R. (1985) 'Corporate interaction in oligopolistic markets; the role of case studies of employment decline,' forthcoming in M.

Danson, (ed.), *Redundancy and Recession: Restructuring the Regions*, Geo Books, Norwich

Peet, R. (1983) 'Relations of production and the relocation of United States manufacturing industry since 1960,' *Economic Geography, 59*, 112-43

Pounce, R.J. (1981) *Industrial Movement in the United Kingdom, 1966-75*, HMSO, London

Regional Studies Association (1983) *Report of an Inquiry into Regional Problems in the United Kingdom*, Geo Books, Norwich

Sant, M. (1975) *Industrial Movement and Regional Development*, Pergamon, Oxford

Secretary of State for Trade and Industry (1983) *Regional Industrial Development*, Cmnd 9111, HMSO, London

Singh, A. (1977) 'UK industry and world economy: a case of de-industrialization,' *Cambridge Journal of Economics, 1*, 113-36

Taylor, M. and Thrift, N. (1981) 'British capital overseas: direct investment and corporate development in Australia,' *Regional Studies, 15*, 183-212

Taylor, M. and Thrift, N. (1982) (eds.) *The Geography of Multinationals*, Croom Helm, London

Thirlwall, A.P. (1982) 'De-industrialisation in the United Kingdom,' *Lloyds Bank Review*, No. 144, 22-37

Townsend, A.R. (1982) 'Recession and the regions in Great Britain, 1976-81: analyses of redundancy data,' *Environment and Planning A, 14*, 1389-404

Townsend, A.R. (1983a) *The Impact of Recession*, Croom Helm, London

Townsend, A.R. (1983b) 'The use of redundancy data in industrial geography' in M.J. Healey (ed.), *The Data Base for Urban and Regional Industrial Research in Britain*, Geo Books, Norwich, pp. 51-64

Townsend, A.R. and Peck, F.W. (1985) 'An approach to the analysis of redundancies in the UK (post 1976): some methodological problems and policy implications' in D. Massey, and R. Meegan, (eds.), *The Politics of Method: Contrasting Studies in Industrial Geography*, Methuen, London

Watts, H.D. (1980) *The Large Industrial Enterprise*, Croom Helm, London

Watts, H.D. (1981) *The Branch Plant Economy: A Study of External Control*, Longmans, London

Watts, H.D. (1982) 'The location of European direct investment in the United Kingdom,' *Tijdschrift voor Economische en Sociale Geografie, 71*, 3-14

Who-Owns-Whom (various editions) 2 vols., Dun and Bradstreet, London

Yemin, E. (1982) (ed.) *Workforce Reductions in Undertakings*, International Labour Office, Geneva

7 REGIONAL DEVELOPMENT POLICIES AND ECONOMIC CHANGE

C.M. LAW

The post-war period has witnessed the emergence of some form of regional development policy (RDP) in most countries of the world. It is not easy to generalise either about the reasons for such policies or on their objectives since to a certain extent each country is unique in terms of area, location, size of population and economic wealth, historical evolution and political ideology. The term 'regional development policy' is not itself always used unambiguously, but in this essay it will be taken to mean policies operated by the state or state agencies which seek to influence economic development as between the major regions of the country. Policies initiated by local authorities or state policies concerned with intra-urban change will be largely ignored, although quite clearly there may be some overlap and interaction between them. The subject matter has grown enormously during the last two decades and space will only permit a review of the main features of the topic. The first issue to be discussed concerns the reasons why governments choose to have RDPs and what objectives they seek to achieve when such policies are adopted. There are many types of policy and these are briefly described in the next section, together with the approach to the delimitation of regions. Finally, and perhaps most importantly, the impact of these policies is assessed to see how far the objectives have been achieved. Although RDP is widely found, in many countries it is often only weakly developed. Discussion will inevitably focus on those countries where policies are important and where most research has been produced.

The Reasons for and the Objectives of Regional Development Policies

Discussions on RDP usually assume that such policies have arisen in the past and continue to be adopted today because of regional

219

inequalities. These inequalities may involve significant differences between regions in terms of income, employment opportunities and other aspects of the quality of life. Whilst there is no doubt that these disparities have been a major consideration, and in many countries are the most important reason for RDP there are many other arguments which have been used. It is therefore useful to review briefly the varied reasons for the emergence of regional development policy.

Strategic considerations have been and still are important in some countries. There are many examples in the past and still some today where a country finds that part of its territory is claimed by a neighbouring state. Examples include: Chinese claims on the eastern areas of the USSR; Arab claims to Israeli-held territory; and disputes in Latin America about poorly developed areas involving Brazil, Venezuela, Paraguay, Bolivia and Argentina. In these circumstances a regional development policy may be initiated which aims to settle the area with people, to develop economic activities and to integrate the disputed territory into the rest of the country. Another strategic consideration has concerned the effect that war and possible enemy occupation would have on the running of a national economy. One response has been to encourage a dispersal of economic activities with greater regional self-sufficiency. The Soviet Union attempted this policy after the Second World War. Another response has been to restrict the growth of large cities since during a war they would be easy targets for bombing. This argument was a major reason why in Britain the Royal Commission on the Geographical Distribution of the Industrial Population (the Barlow Report) in 1940 advocated limiting the growth of conurbations and encouraging the economic regeneration of depressed regions. Whilst such arguments are bound to be very powerful during a war, it would be wrong to limit their influence to such periods. Once adopted, policies have a considerable momentum. The advent of nuclear weapons has greatly reduced the strength of these arguments but not entirely eliminated them.

In recent years aesthetic and environmental considerations have been advanced for RDP. The continued growth of large cities may threaten to create urban sprawl which is regarded as aesthetically undesirable. Urban growth may also threaten environmentally attractive areas. To prevent these outcomes, policies to disperse growth to other parts of the country may be advocated. Such arguments have been important in the Netherlands and Switzerland, and in Britain in the late 1960s, when it was thought that the population might increase by 20 million by the end of the century, they lay behind the feasibility studies for expansion in estuarine areas.

Finally, there are cultural considerations. In many countries uneven development threatens to weaken the economic basis of regions occupied by cultural minority groups. In order to maintain the sub-culture RDPs may be directed towards these areas. The Gaeltecht areas in Western Ireland are a notable example of this consideration. However, often economic development can only be fostered by bringing in outsiders who then contribute to the weakening of the culture. Another example is found in South Africa where apartheid policies have resulted in the establishment of Bantustans where economic development is to be encouraged in order to keep the black population in these areas.

In many countries the principal reasons advanced for RDP are based on social and economic considerations arising from uneven development. The growth of population and economic activity frequently occurs unevenly across national space. Some regions attract growth whilst others are bypassed. The latter include predominantly rural regions as well as older industrial regions. In itself this may not create problems but when this is allied to differences in income, unemployment, net migration rates, and living standards it may provide the basis for social and economic arguments.

There are no theories which adequately explain regional development. The neo-classical spatial equilibrium theory suggests that regional inequalities will be self-eliminating via the interregional movement of either labour and/or capital. However, Myrdal (1957) in his principle of circular and cumulative causation suggests that as a result of multiplier effects regional inequalities may be self-perpetuating with the rich regions getting richer and the poor getting poorer. However, Myrdal admits that there may be some spread effects from the prosperous regions either in the form of demands for goods and services, the filtering down of industry or the redistribution of wealth by governments to the poorer regions. Physical factors, whether of the traditional type of land, climate and minerals or simply of attractive environments for living cannot be ruled out as factors in regional development. Also the growing concentration of power in governments and large corporations is having an increasing influence on spatial patterns of economic development. Thus in each country there is a unique combination of factors influencing development which must be placed in its historical context. In most countries there are regional inequalities and they appear to be reducing slowly if at all. They thus create problems for governments and provide the basis of arguments for RDP.

At its simplest level the argument for RDP is based on grounds of social equity. Modern societies are expected to reduce inequalities between individuals, or at the very least help the poorest, and if these inequalities appear to be related to place, then one way to help the poor is by area-based policies. Some would argue that when there are high levels of unemployment in an area, social justice demands that jobs be provided in that area or nearby. The state already accepts that inequalities should be removed. Thus if an area is poor and as a consequence, schools and hospitals are below nationally accepted standards, the state accepts the demand that resources should be redirected there to raise the standards. In the same way, many would argue that the state, by stimulating a growth of jobs in an area, can help to reduce unemployment to nationally accepted levels.

The demands of social justice already mean that poor regions receive subsidies to support their provision of welfare services. If they remain poor, these subsidies will go on for ever. However, if regional development policies can create self-sustaining growth in these regions, then the need for subsidies could be reduced and possibly eliminated. In this way regional policy could pay for itself. In the early 1960s Needleman and Scott (1964) argued that providing a job lasted for five years in an assisted area, the cost of creating that job would be more than recompensed by the savings the government made in unemployment benefit. However, since then the cost per job created has increased, and with high unemployment in all regions, creating a job in one place is more likely to be at the cost of a job elsewhere, so eliminating the savings.

Whilst it is probable that the social arguments have always been the most important, there have been attempts to justify RDP on economic grounds. One economic argument suggests that the continued growth of large cities places a burden on the economy. Whilst private firms may continue to be attracted to the city because of the advantage to them, it may be at the price of rising public costs, in infrastructure and transport subsidies, for example. Many of our present large cities grew to their present size in a past age with different technologies. The cost of either adapting them or running them under less than optimal conditions falls on the public sector. Thus it may be in the interest of government to stop the growth of cities and divert it elsewhere, including to the lagging regions. Some have taken this argument further, suggesting that there is an optimum size for cities, beyond which diseconomies of scale emerge. This would suggest that when cities reach this optimum size, their growth should be diverted elsewhere. However, it is unlikely that there is a general optimum size for cities, since they are all different, with unique histories and physical layouts (Richardson, 1973). At the very least, it would be necessary to look at each large city individually to examine whether it had passed the optimum size. It has also been argued that allowing large cities to continue growing is an inflationary element in the economy as their rising costs are passed on via prices and taxes to the rest of the economy. As with the other arguments, such problems might be answered by better management of the metropolitan economy. Even if the arguments are accepted, they are only a case for diversion of growth, and not necessarily for inter-regional policies.

Perhaps the most relevant economic arguments for RDP concern the underutilisation of resources in the poor regions. It is argued that by using these resources the national economy will have faster growth and greater wealth. These resources are of various types. First there is social capital. By allowing regions to decline, money invested in schools, hospitals, roads, houses, etc., will be wasted. This argument appears strong when social capital is in very short supply. In post-war Britain, when bombing had destroyed houses and factories in many cities, it was sensible to provide work for people in regions where social capital was available rather than encouraging them to move to areas where there was a shortage. However, this was an exceptional period and generally social capital is not so scarce. Often the population of poor regions is not declining so there would be no wastage of resources. Further much social capital is obsolete and needs replacing so that some decline can take place without underutilisation. Cameron (1974) has argued that only when decline was greater than 2 per cent per year would there need to be a concern about social capital wastage.

More important for advanced countries is the underutilisation of labour resources. Poor regions usually have higher unemployment, shown directly in unemployment rates, indirectly by lower activity rates and perhaps also by underemployment. When production in the prosperous regions is hindered by labour shortages there is an argument for either encouraging labour migration or industrial movement. However, it is unlikely that labour is perfectly mobile, and more likely that some labour reserves will be left in the lagging regions. These can only be tapped by moving jobs there. In theory, industry should move there of its own accord to find labour, but in practice, continuing economies of scale at existing plants, local linkages and a lack of perception of the labour availability may prevent this from happening, so that some form of RDP is necessary. This argument appeared relevant for much of the post-war period, but now that unemployment levels have risen in most regions it appears weak.

Finally, the underutilised resources may be physical, consisting of land, water and minerals. This argument may be particularly relevant to developing countries (Friedmann, 1966). When these resources lie unused the economy is missing a potential for increased growth. Such resources may remain unused because infrastructure is undeveloped and the exploitation of any one resource would not justify the operator providing it. However, if the government were to provide the basic infrastructure this would encourage entrepreneurs and firms to develop the resources. Thus for developing countries, regional development policies should not be considered as a luxury as they once were, but as a tool for achieving faster economic growth.

It would be naive to think that the arguments for RDP in any one country are advanced, analysed, accepted and then RDP is introduced. Clearly the political and governmental structure may influence the appreciation and acceptance of the arguments. In most democratic countries representatives are elected on a geographical basis. Each representative must, to a certain extent, speak for the interests of an area, and in this way the needs of regions will be brought to the government's notice. For a party to gain a majority in the government system it must usually attempt to win votes and representatives from all parts of the country. Where there are regional problems, parties must respond with policies for these regions. In practice parties vie with each other to win votes in the poor regions and in this way RDP becomes a permanent feature in democratic countries. Certainly it has been noted that democratic states are more likely to have RDP than totalitarian ones, as can be witnessed in Latin America.

These arguments may become more urgent when the population of a lagging region has a national identity and seeks greater independence. Should the differences in living standards between such a region and the rest of the country become significant, then demands for independence may increase, putting strains on the unity of the country. In order to maintain the territorial integrity of the state or of a supra-national entity like the European Community, it is likely that some form of RDP will be devised giving the lagging region some incentive for staying within the state.

Marxist commentators have suggested that RDPs arise when there is a crisis in capitalism. When capital accumulation, profitability to the non-marxist layman, declines the state will attempt to assist firms to create further wealth. By giving incentives to firms locating in certain areas, these firms are able to make greater profits than would otherwise be possible. It is also argued that in advanced capitalist countries, profitability may be reduced by labour militancy. In order to increase profits firms need to move to areas where labour is less militant. Regional development policies assist firms to make such moves. Like many conspiracy theories, these arguments are easy to suggest but difficult to prove. It is by no means obvious that large corporations are pushing hard for regional policies or that all of them are using them as marxist theory would suggest. Indeed, there are numerous complaints about the pressure from government to locate in the assisted regions.

It will be clear from the above that there are various motives for regional policy, and that the emphasis may vary from one country to another. A summary of objectives may be as follows:

1. To prevent the excessive concentration on centralisation of the spatial economy and with it the corollary of encouraging decentralisation.
2. To ensure better opportunities for living in all regions in terms of employment, incomes and services which to a certain extent will be measured in terms of national standards.
3. To establish a balance between regions, such that the need for government intervention is reduced and possibly eliminated. In other words, that the economic and social life of the regions becomes viable.
4. To achieve these goals without reducing the rate of growth in

the national economy, and to do so in the most efficient manner.

Policies for Regional Development

The evolution of regional development policies over the last 60 years has seen the formulation of a varied array of instruments and in this section there is only space to catalogue briefly the principal types of action that have been used (for fuller details see Allen, 1978; Emanuel, 1973; OECD, 1976; Yuill and Allen, 1982). Sometimes policies have been divided into those which involve 'directly productive investment' and those which concern 'non-productive investment'. The latter can be further divided into 'economic overhead capital' (i.e. roads) and 'social overhead capital' (i.e. housing).

The provision of infrastructure is probably the most widely used policy instrument. Lack of economic development may be hindered by poor infrastructure which if improved will encourage private investment. Infrastructure covers all forms of communication and public utilities, and may include the provision of commercial facilities like banks, educational facilities for vocational training and even housing for workers. For most governments the provision of infrastructure is a matter of normal administration allocated on some criterion of existing need. However, when used as RDP it must be provided in advance of need in order to encourage new activities. Improved infrastructure is usually perceived as a prerequisite for attracting investment, particularly in rural areas where it may be of a low standard. However, often on their own, infrastructure policies are not sufficient to generate economic growth, at least in the short term, and so governments must consider other policies. These may include the provision of industrial estates, the building of standard factories and even environmental improvements like derelict land clearance. The subsequent leasing of land and letting of factories frequently involves a subsidy.

Many lagging regions are peripheral to the main centres of the country so that merely improving transport facilities may not be sufficient to generate investment in economic activities. To achieve this, some form of transport subsidy may be necessary. In the case of islands, shipping costs may be subsidised and elsewhere railway charges may be cut to reduce the cost of distance.

Most governments find that to encourage economic development some form of financial incentive is required of which there are various forms (Allen, Hull and Yuill, 1978). One method is offer loans to expanding firms either to cover all their costs or only a proportion. Finance can be offered at normal rates of interest, subsidised rates or even at zero interest, the latter usually being only for a short period. The loan may be made via the government itself, via a state agency such as a regional development bank, or via a commercial bank with guarantees and subsidy payments. More generous forms of assistance involve direct grants or payments towards the cost of development. Often the grant is a fixed proportion of total costs such as 10, 15 or 20 per cent. Sometimes the percentage may vary with the scale of the development, so that large works receive a lower percentage. These grants may cover buildings and/or equipment. There is much discussion as to whether grants should be given automatically to all firms expanding in given areas or whether grants should be given on a selective basis only to those companies who would not make the investment without such a grant. In American terms the grant is then said to cause 'leverage' of private investment. Further discussion concerns whether the grant should be related to the number of jobs created. In the past, large grants have been made to capital intensive firms like chemical companies who only provide a small number of new jobs. To curb this possibility loans and grants may have an upper limit related to the number of new jobs created. The revised British regional policy introduced in November 1984 placed an upper limit for grants of £10,000 per job created in firms employing more than 200. For small labour intensive firms a grant of £3,000 per new job created was available as an alternative to the 15 per cent rate of assistance for capital expansion.

Most lagging regions are seeking extra jobs and therefore one way of encouraging this is to subsidise labour. At first sight this may appear unnecessary since these regions should have lower wages in view of their higher unemployment. However, often the strength of unions in large firms ensures parity across regions so that companies cannot benefit from lower labour costs. To make a labour cost saving, a subsidy is introduced, which should make the regions attractive for investment. In the United Kingdom the Regional Employment Premium from 1967 to 1976 offered a fixed sum for every person employed in manufacturing industry in an assisted area. In Italy a variant of this scheme is found with manufacturing firms being exempt from social security contributions. In both cases this method has been criticised for being non-selective, applying to all firms, old or new, and to those who would be in the region anyway. In Sweden the grant is only given for additional labour employed, whilst in other countries the subsidy is paid to new jobs for a limited period. This is sometimes referred to as an operational grant. Other labour subsidies involve grants for training sometimes in the form of a weekly sum for six months, and grants for the relocation of key workers to assist the establishment of new activities.

Another method of encouraging regional development is to give tax concessions to new activities in assisted areas. There may be a tax holiday (exemption) or a reduction of national or local taxes for a limited period or a modification such as accelerated depreciation. Clearly these incentives are more useful to the highly profitable company, and are not related to the number of new jobs provided or to the long term prospects of the firm. They may be difficult to apply when companies have many factories in different regions with the possibility that profits will be transferred to the plant in the tax free zone. Another tax modification is the tariff-free zone allowing the customs-free entry of goods for manufacture, with payments only for the final goods if they are not exported.

The above policies are well known and have been used often. They have had some successes, a topic which will be discussed in a later section, but there has been some frustration that they have not achieved sufficient results, and a feeling that some further efforts are required. Some left wing politicians have suggested powers to compel firms to build factories in assisted areas, but such draconian measures are unlikely to be adopted in democratic countries, except in war-time. In France and Sweden, attempts have been made to influence the location decisions of large firms through consultations at an early stage in the planning process. A similar idea, planning agreements between companies and governments, was unsuccessfully tried in Britain in the mid-1970s. Another way of gaining influence is via nationalisation. In Italy large state-owned firms are compelled to invest 40 per cent in the Mezzogiorno.

More recently governments have taken powers so that they can invest in the equity of firms which can be used to persuade firms to expand in assisted areas. This may be particularly important for new companies, a group of firms that most goverments are anxious to assist. In addition, technical and management centres may be established to help new and small companies in assisted regions. Governments may also make special provision for industrial sectors in trouble, as with steel, shipbuilding and textiles. Since these industries are often concentrated in lagging regions, programmes for these sectors may be regarded as a form of regional policy. This may also apply to support for agriculture and coal mining.

For most of the post-war period RDPs have been directed at manufacturing industry, a sector that was considered basic in contrast to the service sector that was regarded as dependent. However, in recent years manufacturing employment has either been stagnant or declining, while service employment has been growing. Moreover, whilst some service activities are closely related to population, some are relatively footloose and might be appropriate for encouragement in regional development. Accordingly, policies have been re-examined and where possible extended to cover the service sector. Two types of activity in particular have been singled out. First, tourism has been encouraged in areas with potential but underdevelopment. Secondly, office activity has been considered suitable for dispersal to lagging regions. For the private sector there are financial incentives as with industry. In Britain there are grants per job created, removal grants and awards for feasibility studies. For the government office sector, policies of dispersal have been implemented.

These policies may be implemented in various ways, directly by government departments, by devolved regional government, as in Northern Ireland, or by specially created regional development agencies (Yuill, 1983). Government departments usually have a limited sectoral coverage for the whole country and they are often poor at co-ordinating their programmes for an agreed regional strategy. To overcome this problem either regional governments or regional agencies may be established. The latter sometimes have limited fields of operation, such as simply industrial promotion, or wide powers to build, invest and assist industry as with the Scottish and Welsh Development Agencies (Eirug, 1983; Rich, 1983). Occasionally there is a central government department for regional development.

These positive policies for regional development may be complemented by negative ones seeking to limit and discourage growth in particular regions of the country (Nicol, 1979; Nicol and Wettman, 1978). Such regions may be regarded as 'congested' and therefore suitable for disincentive policies. In other cases, like Britain and France, the growth of large cities may be perceived as being causally linked to the problems of the lagging regions. Therefore, by limiting growth in these cities, other regions will have a better chance of attracting growth since firms will be forced to consider other locations. Also disincentive policies may be cheap to operate and reduce the need for large incentives in the lagging regions.

The simplest method of control is to require approval for all developments over a minimum size, whether new, expansion or change of use in the restricted areas, and to withhold consent when development there is not considered essential. Such a system can be used flexibly at the discretion of civil servants. In Britain, Industrial Development Certificates were used from 1945 to 1980 and Office Development Permits from 1965 to 1979. In France an occupation permit, the 'agrement' was introduced in 1955 for all large units in the Paris area. In the 1970s attempts were made to introduce similar controls in Italy and the Netherlands. These policies can be operated successfully when unemployment is low in the area where the controls are applied, but they are difficult to use when unemployment rises, since it is unacceptable to deny an area jobs when they are required. The abandonment of these policies in Britain in 1979/80 probably owes as much to rising unemployment in southern England as to any desire for policy changes.

Another disincentive measure is to tax new developments in congested areas. In parts of the Netherlands and Japan new industrial activities must pay a levy, equivalent to a percentage of the proposed cost. In France since 1960 there has been a tax, the 'redevance', on new industrial and office space in the Paris area. It is hoped that these taxes will raise costs and so dissuade investors from locating there. Also in the Paris area, businesses pay a transport tax, equivalent to 2 per cent of the payroll. It is argued that this contributes to the extra costs they cause by locating here. A final disincentive is to withhold tax benefits in congested areas, such as depreciation allowances, which are available elsewhere.

Policies of constraint have been used sparingly by governments. Some may feel that they are too interventionist for democratic countries, whilst others are worried by the possible consequences of these policies. Firms denied the possibility of expansion may not expand at all, with a loss to the economy. Other firms may move to another country, a clear possibility in continental Europe, and only a few may move as desired to the assisted regions.

The strategy behind regional policy instruments is to affect the operating costs in different regions of the country so as to affect the location decisions of firms. Infrastructure improvements such as better roads should make it cheaper to operate in a peripheral area. (Figure 7.1). In terms of Smith's (1971) framework of industrial location, the spatial margins of profitability will be widened. The effect of subsidies in assisted areas is to reduce costs and hopefully bring them within the spatial margins of profitability (Figure 7.2). Even if these areas are already within the spatial margins, the effect will be to make them more profitable. Likewise taxes in congested areas will make them less profitable and perhaps unprofitable. (Figure 7.2). Using accounting techniques, it is possible to calculate the benefits of incentives to firms, which will obviously vary from one industry to another, depending on the cost structure (Thomas, 1971). It is also possible to compare the level of benefits from one country to another.

Area Definition

Regional development policies are aimed at assisting poor and lagging regions, but on what basis should these regions be chosen, and how should they be delimited? Should there be one set of regions for all policies or a different set of regions for each policy? Should the regions be narrowly or broadly defined? These are the questions we shall consider in this section. The answers that each country gives to these questions will depend on the objectives of regional policy and how the regional problem is perceived.

Where the regional problem is seen as simply a lack of development or a lack of demand for labour, then the answer may be to delimit a series of regions to which all RDPs apply. However, in some countries the regional problem may be seen as different regions suffering from different problems; rural regions, old industrial regions and regions suffering from peripherality. In this case separate bundles of policies may be produced for each type of region with areas delimited for each type of problem. Thus policies

Figure 7.1: Transport Improvements and Regional Development

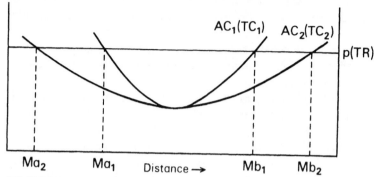

AC₁(TC₁) Cost curve before transport improvements
AC₂(TC₂) Cost curve after transport improvements
p(TR) Revenue

Figure 7.2: Regional Policies and the Spatial Margins of Profitability

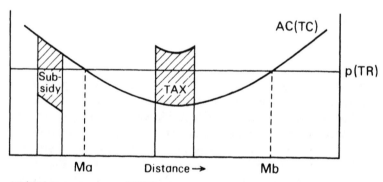

AC(TC) Cost curve,   p(TR) Revenue

for industrial conversion and adaptation and derelict land clearance may only be available in the older industrial regions. Whichever answer is given to this question some method must be chosen to define the regions.

In some countries assisted regions are chosen predominantly on one criterion. In the United Kingdom this criterion is unemployment, whilst in West Germany one type of assisted region is the border zone defined in terms of its distance from the boundary with communist countries. However, lagging regions have many characteristics and although they may be inter-related, any one criterion may not adequately reflect all others. It may therefore be useful and desirable to examine several criteria. In addition to unemployment these might include income, net migration loss, changes in population and employment, economic structure including dependence on declining industries, quality of social facilities and journey-to-work patterns. Such criteria could be used to produce scores of backwardness either giving each characteristic equal weight, or having some weighting system. Such a method is used in West Germany to define assisted areas. More sophisticated methods may be used such as principal components analysis to define the assisted areas (Smith, 1968). Intuitivity methods which use more than one criterion would appear more valid than those that use only one. However, once a few obvious characteristics have been used, other criteria may be of debatable value. For instance, is relatively slow population growth or even small population loss necessarily a sign that a region needs assistance? Many governments are loth to commit themselves to a precise system, whether using one or several characteristics, arguing that such delimitation cannot be a science. This leaves the door open for political considerations to be added to the list of criteria.

Using either one measure or several it is possible to grade regions according to their level of need. Some countries simply have one cut-off with regions either being assisted or not assisted. In other cases there are grades of assistance. Thus in Great Britain until November 1984 the worst or most needy areas were termed Special Development Areas. The next level was described as a Development Area, and the type of region receiving the lowest level of assistance was called an Intermediate Area. Where controls or negative policies are in force some grading of the non-assisted areas is possible. Congested areas, however defined, could be subject to the greatest restraint. In other areas where there is neither congestion nor a tight labour market the government may have a neutral attitude to development. In this way a country may be divided into five or six types of zones, although not all categories, particularly in the non-assisted areas, may be precisely mapped.

Another important question concerns the scale at which these regions should be defined. Should they be large macro regions of the country or small districts such as local labour market areas? Large regions will clearly contain within them areas of varying degrees of prosperity, including both prosperous and poor areas. Even poor lagging regions may have some prosperous sub-regions which do not appear to need assistance. So it can be argued that assistance should be confined to small areas, defined on the basis of their need. However, blackspots of high unemployment are often small, isolated and perhaps having little land suitable for development. Sometimes they are relics of a past industrial age with different technologies. They may be narrow valleys where either water power or minerals were once exploited. It can be argued that such areas should not continue to be propped up but instead the population should be encouraged to look for work in nearby areas. Within lagging regions there are often locations, not too far removed from the blackspots, which have some potential for development and are more likely to attract new economic activities. Perhaps because of a good location near main routes such districts will not fulfil the criteria to be designated for assistance if the boundaries are drawn too narrowly. It can therefore be argued that larger regions should be delimited for assistance, embracing both very needy districts and some with the ability to attract new activities. In Britain this debate has extended over 25 years with changes to small areas in 1958 and 1979. In the latter year macro regions of assistance were abolished in favour of small travel-to-work areas with high unemployment (Figures 7.3 and 7.4). Further changes in November 1984 reduced assisted areas to two tiers and rescheduled districts according to the new geography of unemployment (Figure 7.5).

The designation of assisted regions may be supplemented by the addition of growth points within them. This is a fairly common practice which is found, for example, in the Netherlands and West Germany. Although the incentives for industrial development may not vary throughout the assisted region, encouragement of the growth point is given through improvements to the infrastructure, whether in the form of transport or industrial estates: one argument for such a policy is that public expenditure can be most efficiently used if there is some concentration of growth. This idea has been taken further in France and Italy with the concept of growth poles. In France the regional problem has been seen as arising from the dominance of Paris. To counteract this influence rival cities or counter metropolises (metropole d'equilibre) need to be

Figure 7.3: British Assisted Areas in 1978

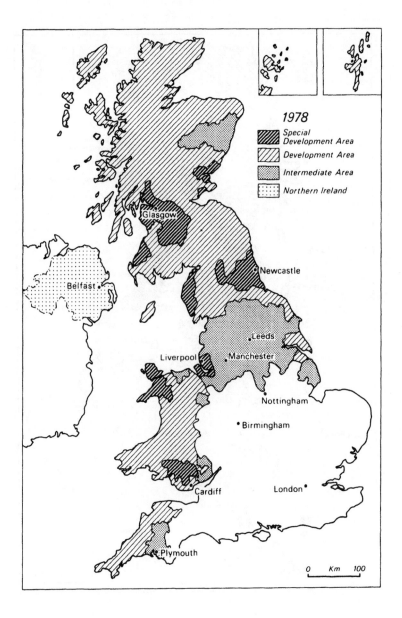

Figure 7.4: British Assisted Areas in 1982

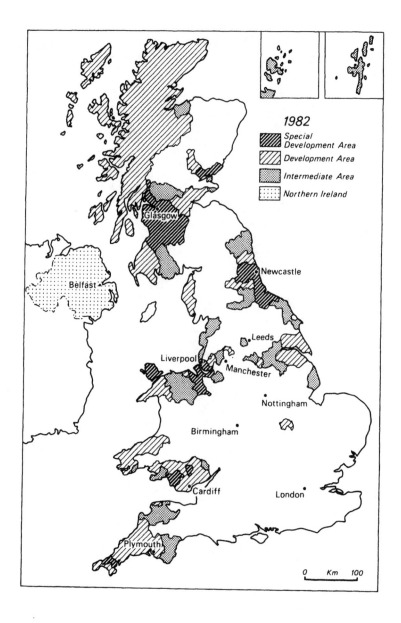

Figure 7.5: British Assisted Areas in 1984

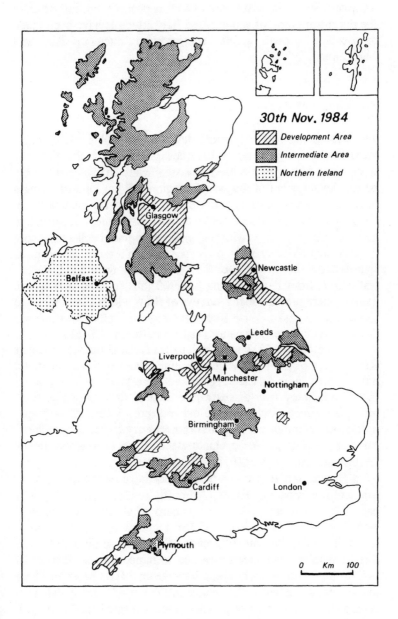

developed which are large and support a wide range of activities. In 1962 eight such centres were designated, receiving extra money for investment in infrastructure as well as positive discrimination in the decentralisation of activities. In Italy attempts have been made to develop growth poles, centres and nuclei (Allen and MacLennan, 1970).

The Impact of Regional Development Policies

The widespread use of regional development policies over many years has naturally prompted the question as to how effective they have been. Have they caused any significant change in the economic development of the assisted regions? What kind of changes have they caused, and to what extent has the regional problem been solved? At an elementary level most government departments and agencies concerned with regional development collect statistics of jobs created in assisted projects. Thus in France government figures show that in the period 1955-75 there were 3,200 decentralisations from Paris creating 462,000 jobs (quoted in Tuppen, 1980). There are also many surveys of firms which have moved to assisted areas, asking how important regional policy was in their decision to move (e.g. Expenditure Committee, 1973). However, in spite of this information it is difficult to be precise about the impact of RDP. Some of the firms which benefited from policies might still have located in an assisted region had there been no policy at all. In addition there may be extra jobs created as a consequence of multiplier effects, including the expenditure of employees' wages in the local economy. It is therefore necessary to develop sophisticated methodologies for evaluating the effects of regional policy (Armstrong and Taylor, 1978; Ashcroft, 1978).

In Britain and Europe methodologies have been developed to evaluate the impact of RDPs (Ashcroft, 1982; Nicol, 1982). The basis of such techniques is to compare what actually happened with what would have happened had there been no policy and to credit the policy with the difference. It is of course difficult to predict what might have been expected to happen in the absence of policy, but various techniques have been used. Most of these involve using the pattern of change in the period immediately preceding the introduction of policies. This is termed the 'policy off' period in contrast to the 'policy on' period. At its simplest level the methodology involves projecting the trends in the policy off period into the policy on period and observing the difference. The assumption that the difference between the expected and the observed pattern is due to policy has been criticised. The relationship between the performance of a regional economy and the national one is unlikely to remain static. New factors come along which may either help or hinder regional development. The discovery and exploitation of North Sea Oil has clearly been a new positive factor for the Scottish economy, which must upset any simple projection of past trends. The methodologies that have been developed involve the use of trend projection, standardisation techniques and explicit modelling. The first is usually perceived as being too simple, whilst the last, although technically the most sophisticated, suffers from practical problems in use (Nicol, 1982). Therefore standardisation techniques are the most widely used and will be the subject of discussion below.

In Britain the use of the shift-share standardisation technique has been pioneered by Moore and Rhodes (1973; 1976). The basis of this method is that regional economies are composed of a number of different sectors, each with its own rate of growth. It is assumed, at least initially, that each sector changes at the same rate as the national rate for that sector. By multiplying each sector of a regional economy by the national rate of change for a given period, it is possible to obtain an expected rate of change, which can then be subtracted from the actual change to give the residual policy effect. To check the assumption made, the policy off period is used to see whether each region was performing as could have been expected using national rates of change. If there was an under-performance this can be taken into account when crediting the policy effect during the policy on period.

There has been some technical discussion about the use of this method. A first issue concerns how to define a sector, whether at the SIC order level or at the MLH level. Each order combines several MLHs, each of which may be a separate industry. Thus the vehicles order includes motor vehicles, aircraft and railway equipment. Most research workers are agreed that at least some disaggregation from the order level is necessary for the technique to be effective. A second issue concerns the linkages between sectors. The shift-share technique assumes that each sector is autonomous, but in fact some are dependent on others. Thus, changes in the textile industry could have repercussions on chemical dyes and textile engineering. More importantly a growing manufacturing sector will cause an increase in population which in turn will demand more services and so create jobs in this sector. It is clear then that whilst shift-share is a useful technique it is unlikely either to accurately interpret past changes or precisely predict future trends. It can, however, provide some indication of likely changes, with which to estimate the policy effect.

The majority of the research on RDP evaluation has taken place in Britain and it is therefore useful to review the results for this country (Ashcroft, 1982; Marquand, 1980). The most prominent workers in this area have been Moore and Rhodes but work has also been done by Brown (1972) and Mackay (1978). The starting point for analysis in Britain is the comparison between the 1950s and 1960s. The 1950s are regarded as the policy off period as RDP was weak, although not only was there still some policy-encouraged development but the results of a strong policy in the 1940s were still having their effect. In contrast the 1960s and early 1970s are regarded as a policy on period when RDP was strong. Using shift-share analysis Moore and Rhodes' latest revised figures suggest that in the period 1960-76 294,000 manufacturing jobs were created in SDAs, DAs and in Northern Ireland, and a further 38,000 jobs in the Intermediate areas, giving a total of 332,000. Using a multiplier of 1.4 to estimate the induced effect on the service sector, a grand total of 480,000 jobs was derived for the impact of RDP. Work for the post-1976 period has had to take account of the rapid decline in manufacturing employment and the effect of North Sea oil on job creation in Scotland. Using a revised methodology Moore, Rhodes and Tyler have been able to estimate that for the period 1960-81 630,000 jobs in the assisted areas can be attributed to RDP (quoted in DTI, 1983b).

Attempts have also been made to disaggregate this total as between moves and indigenous growth. Using the data on the number of industrial moves to the assisted areas it is possible to estimate the increase in the number of moves caused by strengthened policies, and from this the number of jobs resulting from industrial movement policies. Some researchers have simply projected the trends from the policy off period in the 1960s, whilst others have attempted to relate the number of moves to either pressures of demand or investment demand (Ashcroft and Taylor, 1979). By comparing the effects of policy from one year to another, it has also been possible to estimate the effect of policy additions, such as the introduction of the Regional Employment Premium in 1967 (Moore and Rhodes, 1976). Finally, efforts have been made to estimate the effects of both positive and negative policies. Moore and Rhodes consider that control policies have been a significant factor in the success which British policies have had. Whilst most of the work quoted above has been concerned with evaluating the effects on employment, there has been similar work evaluating the effect of policy on the location of investment (see Marquand, 1980, for a review).

These statistics provide some estimate of the effects of RDP but not of the extent to which it has solved the regional problem. Once again it is possible to examine this question simply by comparing reality with objectives. A convergence of unemployment rates and income levels between regions might suggest that some success had been achieved. However, in the absence of this in Britain it is necessary to attempt a more detailed estimate of what has been achieved. For the 1960s an estimate was made of the number of jobs needed to be provided if the regional problem was to be solved. This included jobs to reduce the number unemployed, jobs to raise activity rates and jobs to prevent net outward migration from the assisted regions. This produced a total of 800,000 to one million jobs (Moore and Rhodes, 1974). Since Moore and Rhodes suggested that for the 1960s, RDP had only produced 250,000 to 300,000 jobs, then policies could only be said to be 30 per cent successful. However, another objective of RDP is to create self-sustaining growth which might be defined as the ability of a region to evolve new activities to replace declining ones without more than average support from central government. Whilst this could be measured in a quantitative way by the number of new jobs created, it may also require particular qualitative changes in the economy, and it is to that subject that we now turn.

Much of the analysis in this area has evolved over many years, originating in studies of industrial movement. These began in the late 1940s and early 1950s and were initially concerned with the cost of industrial movement. The basic question asked was whether firms that were persuaded to move to the assisted areas by RDP incurred higher costs which made them and the economy less efficient. The methodology for answering this question involved comparing costs in the original and new locations. Luttrell (1962) found that on average, and after allowing for a settling-in period of up to three years, there were no extra costs. He also found that large branch plants were more successful in moving long distances than smaller ones since they had the management structure to cope with distance from head office. Hague and Dunning (1959) had similar results, although they added to the methodology by comparing costs in the original location had expansion occurred, and not just those of the original plant. There have been many surveys of industrial movement since this period (see Marquand, 1980).

The availability of data on industrial movement for the post-war period from 1968 encouraged further studies on this topic. A dual hypothesis model was developed by Keeble (1972) suggesting that larger plants were moving longer distances and smaller plants short distances. He also suggested that for the period 1945-65 the number of moves from London and South East England, the main source area for industrial movement, to the assisted regions, was inversely related to distance and correlated to unemployment numbers. Thus, South Wales and Merseyside were the two most successful assisted areas in attracting mobile industry. This distance decay factor has also been found in other countries. In France it has been found that most movement from Paris was short distance (Tuppen, 1980).

These results encouraged further research into the consequences of industrial movement both for the firms and the destination areas. The majority of moves to assisted areas were found to be branch plants, often engaged in routine manufacturing operations and employing a workforce of relatively low skill level. Frequently the most important decisions were made by the head office elsewhere in the country and covered new investment, new product lines, purchasing of materials, marketing of products and the purchase of business services. Usually, research and development was carried out in another part of the country, so that the branch plant had no separate possibility of innovation. Further surveys using local data banks revealed that a high proportion of manufacturing plants in the assisted regions were indeed branch plants and that this proportion was increasing (Firn, 1975; Smith, 1978). This increase in external control was thus partly a consequence of RDP encouraging industrial movement, and also partly a result of mergers and acquisitions which created more centralisation in the economy.

The development of the branch plant economy in the assisted regions had many other consequences for the future development of the regions and the attainment of self-sustaining growth (Watts,

1981). First, the plants of the region were seen to be very dependent on decisions made elsewhere as to their future. It was felt that
remote branch plants would be the first to be closed in a recession,
and particularly so if either investment in machinery or the product
was nearing the end of its life. However, against this could be set
the advantages of RDP, which might encourage continued investment in these plants. Whilst there was some evidence to suggest a
higher rate of closure, it was by no means as simple as first suggested (Atkins, 1973). Secondly, there was the lack of multiplier
effects whether in terms of manufactured goods or business services. Head offices controlled the purchase of these goods and
services and they would be looking very widely, well beyond the
local region. Thus there were less likely to be local contracts for
components from branch plants, business services would most
likely be purchased from suppliers near the head office (Marshall,
1978). This would be to the detriment of business services in the
local provincial centre. Thirdly, there was the generally lower level
of skills to be found in branch plants, a consequence of the fact
that often routine and mechanised activities were relocated to the
assisted regions. This low level of skills applied both to white and
blue collar jobs. Lower skills would also result in lower incomes,
and a permanent differential compared to the more prosperous
regions in the country. Lower incomes could also have consequences for the demand for locally produced goods and services.

A fourth consequence of the branch plant economy was that
there would probably be a lower rate of new firm formation. Many
branch plants would be industries where the barriers to entry were
high. There would be little scope for new firms to contract to
supply components. Also the employees in these large branch
plants would probably have only had a limited managerial experience and therefore a lack of confidence to establish new firms.
Again, the general absence of research and development in these
regions would mean that few firms would be established to manufacture new products. These characteristics would suggest that the
branch plant economy has little innovative capacity and that it
comes to rely on attracting more branch plants from elsewhere,
either because of the supply of labour and/or because of RDP
incentives. Surveys of firms attracted here have suggested that
these are the two main advantages as perceived by the firms
(Expenditure Committe, 1973). It is thus a long way from achieving
self-sustaining growth.

Other surveys in assisted areas have examined in detail the multiplier effects of new plants. One question concerns the extent to which new factories employ the unemployed (Grime and Starkie, 1968; Jones, 1968; Salt, 1967). In practice only a small proportion of workers in new factories were previously unemployed, with the majority being attracted from existing firms. This is because a new firm may offer higher wages, or be closer to the residences of workers who are prepared to change work in order to shorten journey to work times. However, the transfer of these workers leaves gaps in other plants who will recruit from the unemployed. In this way there will be a cascade effect from new activities. Other surveys have tried to monitor local impacts, tracing local purchases and the jobs created to produce a multiplier of effect (Yeates and Lloyd, 1971).

Most research has focused on the effects of RDP in the assisted areas. Very little work has attempted to monitor the effects in non-assisted areas, and particularly on the congested areas where controls are applied. There are many unintended effects of RDPs. Controls in congested areas were intended to divert industry to the lagging regions, but many firms have only migrated short distances. Consequently, many regions adjacent to congested regions have benefited from regional policy; thus, in Britain, benefits have accrued to East Anglia, South West England and the East Midlands and in France to the outer Paris Basin. Concern has been expressed that controls limit the industrial evolution of the congested areas, keeping a narrow economic structure and hazarding the future should there be any decline in basic activities. The experience of the English West Midlands region might be a confirmation of such fears.

There is no doubt that RDP has had considerable impact on the assisted regions and elsewhere. Many new activities have been introduced and the industrial structure of these regions widened. However, it may be that differences in occupational structure between the regions are now more significant. (Massey, 1979). Also the problems of these regions have not been solved and they appear no nearer achieving self-sustaining growth than before.

Discussion and Conclusion

In retrospect the heyday of RDP was in the 1960s and early 1970s.

Since then several problems have arisen which have made RDP less effective. First, the world recession has stopped the continuing rise in government expenditures and forced governments to make cut-backs and re-evaluate their priorities. In some countries, like Britain, regional policy has suffered with reduced expenditure and attempts to make policies more cost effective. There is discussion over topics such as selectivity versus automaticity in regional incentives, limits to cost per job, and efforts to encourage community self help and vocational training schemes (DTI, 1983). Secondly, the rise in unemployment which has affected most regions has made it difficult to rely on policies which involve the diversion of jobs from one area to another. For many years industrial movement was the basis of success in RDP, but this is of little use when manufacturing employment is declining and the source regions have many unemployed. Thirdly, because of the decline in manufacturing employment, RDP must look to other sources of possible employment growth such as indigenous activity, including new firms, and the service sector. Policy in these areas in the past has been weak and it is difficult to see how these areas can provide jobs on a sufficient scale. Fourthly, the emergence of the inner city problem with its intra-regional contrast has complicated the simple inter-regional picture of inequalities. There is a need to relate inner city policies to regional development policies. Fifthly, the growth of unemployment has caused local authorities to intensify their promotional efforts. In Britain most local authorities have either an economic development department or an industrial development officer. Many of their efforts at promotion are counter-productive and they appear unco-ordinated with national regional development policy. Sixthly, the recession and unemployment have forced governments to consider how the long term economic future of their country is to be secured. This has encouraged them to propose policies for the development of high technology sectors such as electronics, biotechnology and health care. Frequently these non-spatial policies cut across or are not related to RDP. Seventhly, the growth of the European Community regional policy has still to be integrated with national policies to produce the most effective system for helping poor regions. Policies at the EEC and national levels should be complementary rather than independent.

In the early 1980s RDP appears to be suffering from a lower level of effectiveness compared to earlier periods, and conflicts of purpose as between different levels of government and different objectives. Since there appears to be no sign of a permanent return to high rates of economic growth, or greatly reduced levels of unemployment, the resolution of these problems seems improbable. Most probably governments will continue to down-grade the regional problem in favour of other problems. Only when economies appear to be growing successfully again will there be a chance of RDP being of greater prominence. However, the experience of the post-war period reveals that regional development policies can cause significant shifts in the spatial distribution of economic activitiy, but that they still fall short of creating self-sustaining growth in the problem regions.

References

Allen, K. (ed.) (1978) *Balanced National Growth*, Lexington Books, Lexington, Mass.
Allen, K., Hull, C. and Yuill, D. (1978) 'Options in regional incentive policy' in K. Allen (1978) *Balanced National Growth*, Lexington Books, Lexington, Mass.
Allen, K. and MacLennan, M.C. (1970) *Regional Problems and Policies in Italy and France*, George Allen and Unwin, London
Armstrong, H. and Taylor, J. (1978) *Regional Economic Policy and Its Analysis*, Philip Allan, Oxford
Ashcroft, B. (1978) 'The evaluation of regional economic policy,' in K. Allen (1978) *Balanced National Growth*, Lexington Books, Lexington, Mass.
Ashcroft, B.K. (1982) 'The measurement of the impact of regional policies in Europe: A survey and critique,' *Regional Studies 16*, 287-305
Ashcroft, B.K. and Taylor J. (1979) 'The effect of regional policy on the movement of industry' in D. McLennan and J.B. Parr (1979), *Regional Policy*, Martin Robinson, Oxford
Brown, A.J. (1972) *The Framework of Regional Economics in the United Kingdom*, Cambridge University Press, Cambridge
Cameron, G. (1974) 'Regional economic policy in the United Kingdom' in M. Sant (ed.) *Regional Policy and Planning for Europe*, Saxon House, Farnborough
DTI (1983a) *Regional Industrial Development* HMSO, Cmnd 9111, London
DTI (1983b) (Department of Trade and Industry) *Regional Industrial Policy*, London
Eirug A. (1983) 'The Welsh Development Agency,' *Geoforum, 14*, 375-88
Expenditure Committee (1973) Trade and Industry Sub-Committee Minutes of Evidence, 4 July 1973
Emanuel, A. (1973) *Issues in Regional Policy*, UECD, Paris
Firn, J.R. (1975) 'External control and regional development: the case of Scotland,' *Environment and Planning A*, 7, 393-414
Friedmann, J.R.P. (1966) *Regional Development Policy*, MIT Press, Cambridge, Mass.
Grime, E.K. and Starkie, D.N.M. (1968) 'New jobs for old: an impact study of a new factory in Furness,' *Regional Studies 2*, 57-67
Hague, D.C. and Dunning, J.H. (1959) 'Cost in alternative locations: the radio industry.' *Review of Economic Studies 22*, 203-12

Jones, R.M. (1968) 'The direction of industrial movement and its impact upon recipient regions,' *Manchester School, 36*, 149-72

Keeble, D.E. (1972) 'Industrial movement and regional development in the United Kingdom,' *Town Planning Review, 43*, 3-25

Luttrell, W.F. (1962) *Factory Location and Industrial Movement*, 2 vols., Cambridge University Press, Cambridge

Mackay, R.R. (1978) *Planning for Balance: Regional Policy and Regional Employment*, University of Newcastle, CURDS

McLennan, D. and Parr, J.B. (1979) *Regional Policy: Past Experiences and New Directions*, Martin Robinson, Oxford

Marquand, J. (1980) *Measuring the Effects and Costs of Regional Policy*, Government Economic Service Working Paper No. 32

Marshall, J.N. (1978) *Ownership, Organisation and Industrial Linkage*, University of Newcastle, CURDS

Massey, D. (1979) 'In what sense a regional problem,' *Regional Studies, 13*, 233-43

Moore, B.C. and Rhodes, J. (1973) 'Evaluating the effects of British regional economic policy,' *Economic Journal, 83*, 87-110

Moore, B.C. and Rhodes, J. (1974) 'The effects of regional economic policy in the United Kingdom' in M. Sant (ed.), *Regional Policy and Planning for Europe*, Saxon House, Farnborough

Moore, B.C. and Rhodes, J. (1976) 'A quantitative analysis of the effects of the regional employment premium and other regional policy instruments' in A. Whiting (ed.), *The Economies of Industrial Subsidies*, HMSO, London

Myrdal, G. (1957) *Economic Theory and Underdeveloped Regions*, Duckworth, London

Needleman, L. and Scott, B. (1964) 'Regional problems and location of industrial policy in Britain,' *Urban Studies, 2*, 153-73

Nicol, W.R. (1979) 'Relaxation and reorientation: parallel trends in regional disincentive policy,' *Urban Studies, 16*, 333-9

Nicol, W.R. and Wettman, R. (1978) 'Background notes to restrictive regional policy measures in the European Community' in K. Allen (ed.) Balanced National Growth, Lexington Books, Lexington, Mass

Nicol, W.R. (1982) 'Estimating the effects of regional policy: critique of European Experience,' *Regional Studies, 16*, 199-243

OECD (1976) (Organisation for Economic Cooperation and Development) *Regional Problems and Policies in OECD Countries*, 2 Vols., Paris

Richardson, H.W. (1973) *The Economics of Urban Size*, Gower, Aldershot

Salt, J. (1967) 'The impact of Ford and Vauxhall plants on the employment situation in Merseyside,' *Tijdschrift voor Economische en Sociale Geografie 58*, 255-64

Sant, M. (1974) (ed.) *Regional Policy and Planning for Europe*, Saxon House, Farnborough

Smith, D.M. (1968) 'Identifying the "Grey Areas", a multivariate approach,' *Regional Studies, 2*, 183-93

Smith, D.M. (1971) *Industrial Location: An Economic Geographical Analysis*, Wiley, New York

Smith, I.J. (1975) *Ownership Status and Employment Changes in Northern Regional Manufacturing Industry 1963-73*, University of Newcastle, CURDS

Thomas, R. (1971) 'The New Investment Incentives,' *Bulletin of Oxford University Institute of Statistics, 33*, 93-105

Tuppen, J.T. (1980) *Studies in Industrial Geography: France*, Dawson, Folkestone

Tyler, P. (1980) 'The impact of regional policy on a prosperous region: the experience of the West Midlands,' *Oxford Economic Papers, 32*, 151-62

Watts, H.D. (1981) *The Branch Plant Economy: A Study in External Control,* Longman, London

Whiting, A. (1976) (ed.) *The Economics of Industrial Subsidies,* HMSO, London

Yeates, M.H. and Lloyd, P.E. (1971) *Impact of Industrial Incentives,* Policy and Planning Branch, Dept. of Energy, Mines and Resources, Ottawa

Yuill, D. and Allen, K. (1982) (eds.) *European Regional Incentives,* University of Strathclyde, Glasgow

Yuill, D. (1983) (ed.)*Regional Development Agencies in Europe: An International Comparison of Selected Agencies,* Gower, Aldershot

8 THE INDUSTRIAL GEOGRAPHY OF THE THIRD WORLD

G.B. NORCLIFFE

There are two main grounds for arguing that the industrial geography of the Third World is a topic of current importance. First, standard measures of employment show that the Third World now accounts for a major slice of world industry. And second, the growth of world systems of production, of marketing, and of corporate ownership have created a whole series of dependencies and interdependencies, particularly between the North and the South, so that a full understanding of industry in any area requires an appreciation of the global organisation of industrial production.

Within a hierarchical system of production, the highest level is occupied by multinational corporations which have become the global connection of greatest importance to Third World industry. Beneath this in the hierarchy are locally-owned industrial corporations, some of which are quite large. At the bottom of the hierarchy are small-scale enterprises, often of an informal character. These three main elements in the industrial geography of the South will here be labelled *international production, national production*, and *small-scale production*.

The industrial geography of the Third World acquires special significance in the context of development. Lefeber (1974) argues that western-style urban-industrial development (Kuznets, 1971) cannot possibly be replicated by underdeveloped countries. Circumstances today are crucially different. First, the massive nineteenth century out-migration from Western European states to their colonies that contributed to rising labour productivity in Western agriculture, as well as providing colonial markets for Western manufactured goods is not an option today in the Third World. Second, possibilities do not exist for underdeveloped countries to establish a favourable trading environment comparable to those established by colonial powers in the past, indeed the failure of a series of UNCTAD conferences suggests that their position remains an unfavourable one. And third, developing countries are finding it most difficult to accumulate capital. Colonial powers, in

249

contrast, were able to use profit transfers, debt repayment, and repatriation of savings on retirement to maintain a net inflow of capital. Thus, Dunford and Perrons (1983, chs. 10 and 11) find that, as British industry became progressively less competitive in the late nineteenth century, the economy was increasingly supported by an inflow of payments from the colonies. In consequence, Lefeber argues, urban-industrial development is not an option in most of the Third World today. What, then, is the role of industry in development in these countries? Industry must obviously play an important role for the simple reason that many Third World countries are overpopulated in relation to their agricultural resources, often to the extent that diminishing returns have set in. But this leaves open the possibility for several kinds of industrial policy including rural development based on both agriculture and industry.

These introductory comments set the stage for some of the themes that are to be explored. The essay is structured as follows. First, some gross estimates of world employment in various kinds of industry will be presented. The three sections that follow will examine, in turn, the international, the national, and the local small-scale systems of production. The concluding section will examine broader issues concerning the role of industry in Third World development.

Global Patterns of Industrial Employment

An unreliable and incomplete data base and inconsistent definitions make it difficult to estimate global patterns of industrial employment. However, since it would be extremely useful to have estimates at least of the employment magnitudes, data have been compiled, and estimates made using the sources and procedures described in Appendix 1. The results are presented in Tables 8.1 and 8.2. Economic participation rates are highest in the Eastern Bloc (about 50 per cent) with most Western countries averaging closer to 45 per cent. Participation rates in Latin America are far lower — usually around 35 per cent — partly because children constitute a larger fraction of the population, but also because there are very few employment opportunities for women outside agriculture. Rates in Africa and Asia vary. In the Islamic bloc, cultural taboos on female employment outside the household reduce participation rates to around 30 per cent. However in non-Islamic countries, participation rates are mostly in the 35 per cent to 45 per cent range. Employment in formal manufacturing ranges from 0.5 per cent of the economically active in Ethiopia to 35.5 per cent in Czechoslovakia and the German Democratic Republic. This range reflects enormous differences in the activity structure of these countries, with agriculture and informal activities being of major importance in most of the Third World.

Table 8.1: Activity Participation Rates and Employment in Formal Manufacturing in Large Countries, 1980

Country	Population (millions)	Economically Active %	Economically Active No. (millions)	Employment in Formal Manufacturing % of E.A.	Employment in Formal Manufacturing No. ('000s)
Africa	*469.0*	*42.2*	5.6* *197.7*	*2.5*	*4,943**
Algeria	18.6	30.0*	5.6[	5.7*	320*
Egypt	42.0	28.6	12.0	6.7*	800*
Ethiopia	32.6	47.2	15.4	0.5	80
Ghana	11.5	44.0*	5.1*	1.8	90
Kenya	16.4	45.0*	7.4*	1.7	129
Morocco	20.2	30.0*	6.1*	6.6*	400*
Mozambique	10.5	40.0*	4.2*	1.2*	50*
Nigeria	77.1	44.0*	33.9*	1.9*	650*
South Africa	29.3	45.0*	13.2*	10.3	1,355
Sudan	18.7	30.0*	5.6*	0.9*	50*
Tanzania	18.0	45.0*	8.1*	1.2*	100*
Uganda	13.2	40.0*	5.3*	0.6*	30*
Zaire	28.3	40.0*	11.3*	0.9*	100*
Rest of Africa	150.6	42.8*	64.5*	1.2*	789*
Asia	*2,558.0*	*41.1*	*1,050.9*	*5.3*	*56,020*
Afghanistan	15.5	24.6	3.8	1.0	39
Bangladesh	88.7	28.7	25.5	1.6	405
Burma	35.3	45.0*	15.9*	1.3*	200*
China	956.8	45.0*	430.6*	6.0	25,644
India	663.6	40.0*	265.4*	2.4	6,432
Indonesia	151.9	43.2	65.6	1.3	864
Iran	37.5	28.9	10.8	4.6*	500*
Iraq	13.1	26.1	3.4	5.9*	200*
Japan	116.8	48.2	56.3	18.3	10,328
Korea	38.2	38.5	14.7	14.4	2,117
Malaysia	13.4	36.8*	4.9	8.3	407
Nepal	14.0	35.0*	4.9*	2.0*	100*
N. Korea	17.9	40.0*	7.2*	8.3*	600*
Pakistan	82.4	29.5	24.3	3.1*	750*
Philippines	48.4	31.9	15.4	5.1	778
Sri Lanka	14.7	35.0*	5.1*	3.2	161

Table 8.1: continued

Country	Population (millions)	Economically active		Employment in formal manufacturing	
		%	No. (millions)	% of E.A.	No. ('000s)
Thailand	46.5	48.4	22.5	4.4*	1,000*
Turkey	45.4	30.0*	13.6*	5.8	792
Vietnam	52.3	50.0*	26.2*	6.1*	1,600*
Rest of Asia	105.6	33.0*	34.8	8.9*	3,03*
Latin America	*368.0*	*34.3*	*126.1*	*6.1*	*7,703*
Argentina	27.1	38.7	10.5	2.1	220
Brazil	123.0	38.0*	46.7*	8.6	4,000
Chile	11.1	33.4	3.7	6.1	225
Colombia	27.5	32.0*	8.8*	5.9	520
Mexico	71.9	28.3	20.3	3.4	693
Peru	17.8	31.6	5.6	1.3	70
Venezuela	13.9	34.0*	4.7*	9.2	433
Rest of Latin America	75.7	34.1	25.8	6.0*	1,542*
North America	*251.5*	*47.6*	*119.8*	*18.0*	*21,567*
Canada	23.9	46.7	11.2	17.0	1,900
USA	227.6	47.7	108.6	18.1	19,667
Europe	*484.0*	*44.5*	*215.3*	*23.0*	*49,518*
Czechoslovakia	15.3	48.0*	7.3*	34.5	2,518
France	53.7	43.1	23.1	22.7	5,250
German DR	16.7	50.0*	8.4*	34.5	2,902
German FR	61.6	44.4	27.4	26.4	7,229
Hungary	10.7	47.5	5.1	27.1	1,384
Italy	57.0	39.4	22.5	15.2	3,423
Netherlands	14.1	37.4	5.3	18.0	954
Poland	35.6	51.2	18.2	23.4	4,259
Rumania	22.3	45.0*	10.0*	31.3	3,127
Spain	37.4	35.7	13.4	16.9	2,260
UK	55.9	47.1	26.3	26.3	6,923
Yugoslavia	22.3	42.4	9.5	22.2	2,106
Rest of Europe	81.4	47.7	38.8	18.5*	7,183*
Australasia	*22.8*	*43.4*	*9.9*	*15.1*	*1,494*
Australia	14.6	44.7	6.5	17.8	1,154
Rest of Oceania	8.2	41.0*	3.4*	10.0*	340*
USSR	265.5	51.4	136.5	23.1	31,464

Sources: See Appendix 1.
* Estimated.

Table 8.2: Gross Estimates of Employment for Formal Manufacturing, the Informal Sector, and Small-scale Manufacturing (millions)

	Formal manufacturing[a]	Informal sector[b]	Small-scale manufacturing[c]
North America	21.6	—	—
Western Europe	32.0	—	—
Japan and South Korea	12.4	—	—
Australasia	1.5	—	—
Total, First World	67.5	—	—
USSR	31.5	—	—
Eastern Europe	17.6	—	—
China	25.6	—	—
Vietnam and North Korea	2.2	—	—
Total, Second World	76.9	—	—
Latin America	7.7	53.0	13.2
Africa	4.9	65.0	16.2
East, South, West Asia	15.7	180.7	45.2
Total, Third World	28.3	298.7	74.6

Notes: — No estimate.
   a. From Table 8.1.
   b. Individual estimates for each Third World country were made using data drawn from Anderson and Leiserson (1978), Table 1, p. 17. Estimates for Latin American countries ranged from 40 to 45 per cent and averaged 42. Estimates for African countries ranged from 30 to 35 per cent, and averaged 32.9. Estimates for Asian countries ranged from 30 to 40 per cent, and averaged 35.
   c. Using figures from Anderson and Leiserson (1980), p. 232, and Mazumdar (1976), pp. 11-13.

Table 8.2 records total employment in formal manufacturing for the main blocs, and gives estimates for the informal sector and for small-scale (informal) manufacturing only for the Third World. It is evident that the Communist bloc accounts for the largest portion of employment in formal manufacturing, followed by Western Europe which outranks the whole of the Third World (indeed France, alone, outranks Africa). Within the Third World, the biggest concentration of formal manufacturing is found amongst the Newly Industrialised Countries (NICs) of South Asia.

Because no reliable data are available, no estimates were made of employment in informal activities outside the Third World. Nevertheless, they are important with all sorts of moonlighting and basement operations taking place, including unregistered sweat shops exploiting illegal immigrant labour and paying well below minimum wage levels (Peet, 1983). In the Third World, the informal sector has been extensively studied so that a range of estimates is available (Anderson and Leiserson, 1978; Mazumdar, 1976). These estimates suggest that the informal sector as a whole accounts for up to 45 per cent of all economically active persons in some Latin American countries, down to 25 per cent in some Asian countries. Within the informal sector, the largest group is engaged in services (around 30 per cent), followed by manufacturing (25 per cent) which is, therefore, a major source of employment. To put it in perspective, employment in small-scale manufacturing in the Third World (est. 74.6 m) exceeds employment in formal manufacturing in the First World (67.5 m) and is nearly treble employment in formal manufacturing in the Third World (est. 28.3 m).

To sum up the evidence, employment in formal industry in the Third World amounts to some 28 million jobs. Of this, only a small part is directly accounted for by transnational corporations; the remainder, amounting to some 25 million jobs, is employed in locally owned formal enterprises. Small-scale production is by far the largest component as far as employment is concerned, totalling 75 million jobs.

International Production

Transnational Corporations

The geography of multinational corporations is the subject of another essay in this book (see ch 5), so they will be discussed only briefly here (see also Taylor and Thrift, 1982; UN, 1979). But they cannot be ignored because they are so important to contemporary Third World development. The most important point is that these corporations can be classified into four main types, as follows:

Control of Inputs. This type of transnational corporation seeks to control its input supply lines, particularly of agricultural, energy and mineral resources. For example, Brooke Bond-Liebig owns large tea estates in Kenya (Kaplinsky, 1978), the major oil companies have huge investments in OPEC countries, and ALCAN has investments in bauxite mines in several Caribbean countries (Auty, 1982).

Control of Markets. Many newly-independent states embarked on promoting domestic industries that had been discouraged during the colonial era. Not wishing to be excluded from these expanding markets, transnational companies became active participants in these industrialisation programmes. Firms pursuing this strategy have one or more of the following specific motives. The product may be fairly bulky and expensive to transport so that transport cost savings are gained from production or assembly in a Third World country. The national market for a product may be protected by high tariffs which can be avoided if the plant is located inside the tariff barrier. In addition, many newly independent countries have embarked on policies of import substitution in manufacturing. Lacking sufficient local capital, they have offered favourable terms to foreign companies that are prepared to invest in local production.

Cheap Inputs. The reason most commonly given by transnational corporations for investing in the Third World is to take advantage of cheap factor inputs. Of these inputs, low wage labour is the major attraction, and will be discussed presently in the section on the *new international division of labour.* However, other low cost factors, notably abundant mineral, energy and biotic resources, have also attracted foreign capital. For instance, with the widespread exploitation and depletion of the best timber in temperate forests, a number of forest product and pulp companies have begun to exploit high-yielding tropical forests (see Myers, 1979, ch. 13). Similarly Japan, which has limited and costly energy and mineral resources, has invested capital in developing low-cost foreign resource industries including oil in Brunei, steel in Brazil, and coal in western Canada.

Portfolio Investment. Firms making this kind of investment in the Third World are seeking lucrative investment opportunities. Commonly, investment takes the form of an acquisition of a company which is permitted to operate under its existing management provided it remains profitable. Asset stripping of such firms is not uncommon.

The Old International Division of Labour (OIDL)

Much has been written on the new international division of labour (NIDL), ignoring the fact that for several centuries there has existed a rather different division of labour which lay at the heart of the mercantalist empires. The colonial powers extracted various resources from their foreign enclaves, in return trading manufactured goods. Thus plantation agriculture, mining, forestry and, sometimes, indigenous agriculture were promoted in the colonies. Hut, poll and other taxes were often imposed on native peoples to force them to become wage earners in plantations, in resource industries, in building transport infrastructure, and in domestic service. Where the indigenous population was too small for the needs of the colonists, as in the Americas, the iniquitous system of slavery was established. And when slavery was abolished, it was replaced by a system of indentured labour that was scarcely more humane. Elsewhere, local people were dragooned into the workforce, and became part of the old international division of labour. Manufacturing was kept largely as the preserve of the mother country (Hobsbawm, 1969). Thus the cotton textile industry that began to develop in India early in the nineteenth century was suppressed in response to political pressures from vested interests in the Lancashire cotton industry (Bagchi, 1972). Mabogunje (1980, pp. 154-9) records a similar impact on long-established Nigerian metal working and blacksmithing industries.

Much of this old international division of labour still survives despite the growth of labour-intensive industries in many Third World Countries. From rubber plantations in Malaya, to tea gardens in Kerala, and from copper mines in Katanga to tourism in Barbados, there survives a huge network of export-oriented agriculture and resource industries supplying developed countries. Ownership is still largely in the hands of foreign corporations, although various forms of joint ventures and partnerships have appeared in recent years as former colonies have sought to assert their independence. Even colonial patterns of employment are frequently to be found in these resource industries, with expatriates occupying key management positions. The old international division of labour requires the export of manufactured goods from the North to the South; this, too, persists, although in a modified form. The manufactured exports are no longer the products of labour-intensive industries; competition from newly industrialised countries (NICs) in these activities is too intense. Increasingly, products with high technical inputs such as military hardware, cars, electrical and precision goods, plus a variety of consumer luxuries are exported. During this century, several countries that did not formerly have colonies in the Third World, including the United States, the Scandinavian countries, and Japan, have joined in this trade.

In essence, the persistence of the old international division of labour is attributable to the prodigious consumption of resources by developed countries. The West, which uses a disproportionate amount of the world's non-renewable resources including metals, minerals and energy resources, has been able to sustain high levels of resource consumption by importing a large part of their requirements from Third World countries, and in return trading sophisticated manufactured goods and various services. This is nothing more than an up-dated version of the old international division of labour.

The New International Division of Labour (NIDL)

With the progressive breakdown of Empire, colonial powers were no longer in a position to monopolise manufacturing, and suppress its development in former colonies. Third World countries that achieved independence through the 1950s and 1960s were, therefore, able to establish their own economic priorities, usually by adopting five-year development plans. Almost invariably, the first of these plans pursued import substitution programmes which began to reclaim from colonial powers some of the more obvious forms of industry. However, for a variety of reasons, a substantial group of Third World countries — particularly in Africa — have not succeeded in taking industrialisation much further. Domestic markets are small. There is only a small workforce with industrial skills and experience. Local capital is limited in supply, and the local bourgeoisie may prefer to invest in land and urban real estate, or spend their income on conspicuous luxuries. And foreign investment may not be forthcoming if potential investors perceive the state to be unstable, or the workforce to be undisciplined or unproductive, with high real labour costs.

In a few countries, however, industrialisation has proceeded rapidly beyond the import substitution phase to the export phase. In crude terms, the Heckscher-Ohlin hypothesis describes the mechanism that is involved (Ohlin, 1967). It states that there are two key factors of production — labour and capital — which influence the international location of industry. Since capital is fairly mobile internationally in response to investment opportunities, and since there are quite a number of international aid agencies that make loans to Third World countries to promote development, real interest rates do not vary greatly amongst nations and are assumed to play a relatively minor role in the international development of industry. Labour, in contrast, is relatively immobile so that, as Table 8.3 shows, large differences arise in wage rates in accordance with labour productivity and local labour market conditions. As Frobel *et al.* (1980, p. 5) remark in the definitive study of NIDL: 'This vast industrial reserve army of extremely cheap labour feeds a process of industrialisation which can be observed in many contemporary developing countries.'

Matching these international differences in real labour costs are differences in labour input requirements which, Scott (1982) observes, arise because of the uneven application of modern technology. Some activities have become highly automated so that labour inputs have been drastically reduced. Other activities, of

Table 8.3: Hourly Wages in Manufacturing in Selected Countries (US$)

	Unskilled	Semi-skilled	Skilled	Year
Asia[a]				
Hong Kong	0.43	0.61	n.a.	1975
India	0.15	0.21	0.31	1974
Indonesia	0.23	0.34	0.56	1973
Malaysia	0.16–0.18	0.18–0.23	0.36–0.42	1974
Philippines	0.15	0.19–0.23	0.23–0.28	1975
Singapore	0.38	0.41	0.72	1974
Taiwan	F 0.23	0.25	0.72	1974
	M 0.25	0.34	n.a.	1974
Africa[a]				
Ivory Coast	0.41	0.44–0.53	0.57–0.77	1975
South Africa	F 0.34	0.38	0.75	1974
	M 0.46	0.60	1.05	1974
Latin America[a]				
Brazil	0.25–0.36	0.58–0.82	1.17–1.40	1975
Mexico	0.56–0.85	n.a.	n.a.	1975
Other[b]				
Canada	3.33	4.61	5.70	1975
UK	F 1.37	1.73	1.96	1975
	M 1.92	2.37	2.67	1975
USA	3.19	4.58	6.07	1975

Source: a. Froebel, Heinrichs and Kreye (1980), p. 351.
    b. International Labour Office (1976), *Yearbook of Labour Statistics*, ILO, Geneva, Table 19.

their nature, lend themselves less to automation and still require large inputs of semi-skilled labour. It is in these labour-intensive activities that low-cost labour economies in the Third World have a comparative advantage (see Table 8.4). Thus the Heckscher-Ohlin hypothesis provides an economic basis for NIDL whereby some Third World countries (the so-called Newly Industrialised Countries) have become major exporters of manufactured goods that require substantial labour inputs including electrical goods, footwear, clothing and fancy goods. Other 'intermediate' countries such as Ireland, in which labour costs are significantly lower than in the main western industrialised nations, have also gained some labour-intensive industries as part of NIDL (Perrons, 1981).

Having argued the basis of NIDL in terms of neoclassical trade theory, it must be stressed these economic processes need be set in their political and institutional context. NIDL has progressed furthest in countries that are politically receptive to western investment in labour-intensive industries, and which practise authoritarian corporatism.

Authoritarian Corporatism

The large labour surplus in most Third World countries has put unions in a weak bargaining position and made collective action risky. Unions also lack the financial resources to pursue broad labour withdrawal strategies. Faced with this situation, unions in newly-independent countries often adopted a more political strategy by asking government for protection from employers in return for their support. The unions had sufficient strength in a few key sectors such as the civil service and public utilities to exert some influence on wobbly new governments. Thus by giving up

Table 8.4: The Cost of Building a 30,000 Tonne Ore Carrier (US$)

	France $	South Korea $
Hourly cost of labour including social security charges, fringe benefits, etc.	23.40	3.54
Total cost of labour	25,500,000	3,855,000
Cost of materials	21,050,000	12,510,000
Total	46,550,000	16,365,000

Source: Grosrichard (1984).

their autonomy in return for assurance of government protection, both labour unions and governments strengthened their respective positions. Subsequently, as the governments' position became stronger, unions were often brought under greater government control.

Many newly independent nations were approached by transnational corporations seeking to invest in the Third World. These corporations prefer to work through a strong central government that will, if necessary, exert authority to protect their interests (Malloy, 1977). At this point, Deyo (1981) suggests, two types of authoritarian corporatism may emerge (see Table 8.5). Where labour has a weak influence on government as, for instance, in Malawi or Zaire, authoritarian corporatism is of a bureaucratic nature and may be quite repressive. But when labour has a strong voice in government (as in Nkrumah's Ghana, or Peron's Argentina), then the authoritarian regime may enjoy widespread popularity.

Authoritarian corporatism develops in stages (Deyo, 1981). Initially, local businessmen may have considerable influence on government, but as foreign firms become established, local influence wanes and the ruling elite becomes more dependent on foreign firms. At the same time there emerges a relatively well-paid labour aristocracy that is employed in the foreign sector. This group is highly dependent on the system for its position and allies itself with the authoritarian regime. Economic benefits accrue disproportionately to a few privileged groups which may press the regime to adopt an increasingly authoritarian and militarist position. Bellows' (1976) description of Taiwan is apposite. Between 1969 and 1976, two-thirds of the investment in manufacturing was foreign capital which was strongly attracted by the tight controls exerted by the Kuomintang government over wages and industrial

Table 8.5: Forms of State-Labour Relations

		State control of unions	
		Low	High
Labour penetration of Government	Low	collective bargaining	bureaucratic authoritarian corporatism
	High	populism	popular authoritarian corporatism

Source: Deyo (1981), p. 13.

conflict. Authoritarian corporatism is the prevailing orthodoxy in most NICs. Countries such as Tanzania and Burma that have not been willing to forge strong links with transnational corporations have not joined the ranks of NICs. Transnational corporations appear to have invested most heavily in countries with a regimented workforce.

Singapore has become a classic example of authoritarian corporatism. As early as 1964 the ruling People's Action Party (PAP) had co-opted the trade union movement and persuaded labour that the proposed industrialisation strategy, based on foreign capital, would be of mutual benefit. Thereafter, corporatism grew apace, while labour was increasingly subordinated, subjected to legislative controls, and governed by an institutionalised incomes policy. Massive foreign investment (totalling S$2.3 b in the five years 1973-77) in export-oriented industry was the result. The clean sweep made by PAP in subsequent elections suggests that this policy has broad popular support. Deyo (1981, p. 116) concludes:

> Given Singapore's growing economic crisis during the 1960s, there were probably few alternatives to the development strategy adopted ... the remaining questions relate to the ability of political elites to nurture those social and cultural commitments which will transform Singapore's modern economy into a more human one too.

Newly Industrialised Countries (NICs)

Perhaps the major outcome of the processes discussed above has been the appearance of a relatively small number of NICs which have the following characteristics:

(a) They are densely populated, but may vary greatly in size.
(b) Their governments practise authoritarian corporatism with varying degrees of local support: the local workforce is disciplined, and foreign capital is welcomed.
(c) Foreign capital is invested mainly in labour-intensive industries, and in processing local primary products.
(d) Much of the output is exported to developed countries.
(e) Economic links with the West are usually matched by political links of various kinds.

The majority of NICs, including South Korea, Taiwan, Hong Kong, the Philippines, Thailand, India, Singapore, and Malaya, are in South East Asia. There are no obvious candidates in Africa. In Latin America, Brazil and Mexico have joined the ranks of NICs.

South Korea illustrates the spectacular industrial growth that can be achieved if the required sacrifices are made (Hasan, 1976). Between 1960 and 1972, agriculture shrank from 41 to 25 per cent of GNP, while manufacturing grew from 11 per cent to 26 per cent (and over 35 per cent by 1980). The growth rate of real GNP was a remarkable 10 per cent for the decade beginning in 1963, and was financed mostly by foreign capital, initially in the form of loans to South Korea's financial business empires, but increasingly (in the 1970s) in the form of direct foreign investment which usually involved a joint venture with local enterprise (Cohen, 1975). These investments were mainly in export-oriented manufacturing, so that exports rose from 2.4 per cent of GNP in 1962 to 30.8 per cent in 1976, a 13-fold increase in 14 years (Kim, 1978). South Korea has concentrated on labour-intensive industries such as textiles, steel and shipbuilding which are protected. This policy now poses a problem for South Korea because, in attempting to diversify into new export industries, Korea is being increasingly rebuffed for its protectionist policies (Patterson, 1983). South Korea's giant corporations work very closely with the government, and exert pressure for protection. One of the counter-pressures forcing trade liberalisation is the emergence of export processing and free trade zones in many developing and developed countries.

Export Processing and Free Trade Zones

In the last decade, policies creating industrial zones of various kinds have been adopted by many countries seeking to capture a larger share of world industrial investment and employment. Industrial zone policies in the North, which include enterprise zones, free-trade zones and maritime industrial areas — MIDAS — (see Pollock (1981) and Goldsmith (1984)), are often in direct competition with Third World industry. MIDAS are designed to attract industries which process imported commodities and resources (often originating in the Third World). Enterprise zones, in one version, are supposed to create mini-Hong Kongs in declining western inner city areas (Norcliffe and Hoare, 1982). The response in developing countries has been the creation of export processing zones and free trade zones that are intended both to retain as much as possible of the value added to locally-produced commodities and resources before they are exported, and to attract light labour-intensive manufacturing. Private enterprise appears to have been the main beneficiary, as various countries have competed for the attention of investors by offering a growing list of incentives.

These incentives are broadly of three kinds (Takeo, 1978). First, there are labour incentives: these may include waiving of minimum wage legislation and limits to working hours, exemption from worker safety and health regulations, and prohibition of collective action. In practice, this opens the way for labour exploitation. The second set of incentives are capital subsidies: most commonly, public capital in the form of port infrastructure, a serviced industrial estate, and various producer services are provided. Direct capital subsidies and preferential credit are almost always offered (Frobel *et al.*, 1980, p. 320). Thirdly, tariffs and duties may be waived so that raw materials and semi-finished goods are imported duty free for processing, manufacture and assembly before being re-exported.

Some of the advantages and disadvantages of export processing zones are illustrated by the case of Singapore. In 1983, Singapore was rated as the world's third largest oil refining centre after Houston and Rotterdam, with oil refining and oil products accounting for 40 per cent of the country's industrial output (Sherwell, 1983a). These refineries and related downstream petrochemical plants are located in an EPZ. Most of the refining facilities are owned by major oil companies, but the petrochemical complex under construction on Pulau Ayer Merbau is a joint venture between the Singapore Government (50 per cent), the Japanese Government (10 per cent), and private Japanese companies (40 per cent). This industry is subject to short-term supply and demand fluctuations. Refining capacity in Singapore, for instance, will be cut back substantially over the next three years (1984-87) while grave doubts have been expressed whether the petrochemical complex on Pulau will ever operate profitably (Sherwell, 1983b). Meanwhile, these activities are typically capital-intensive, they create a lot of jobs only during the construction phase, and the import content of capital equipment is high. Thus they hardly match the factor endowments of Third World economies.

The free-trade zone version is normally aimed at creating jobs in labour-intensive industries. The first was created at Shannon Airport in Ireland in 1958, but it was in East Asia that the next several were created, including major ones in Korea (at Masan in 1970), Taiwan (at Kaohsiung in 1965 and at Nantze in 1970), the Philippines (at Marivales in 1972) and Indonesia (at Asahan) (Takeo, 1978). Frobel *et al.* (1980, ch. 14) report that in 1975, the number of 'free production zones' in operation was: Asia 11; Africa 5; and Latin America 9. A further 39 zones were reported to be under construction, mostly in India and South East Asia.

The major attraction of a free trade zone is its workforce which is, typically, in almost unlimited supply, is highly productive, is extremely cheap, and is very compliant (Frobel *et al.*, 1980, pp. 328-9). A wide spectrum of activities is attracted by these labour conditions including some that are quite capital intensive. A good example is Mexico's Border Industrialisation Program which operates as a free trade zone (Hansen, 1981). In the first ten years from its inception in 1965, it attracted 470 US plants seeking cheap labour inputs: mostly *maquiladore* (components for assembly) industries were present with electronics and engineering prominently represented.

International Capital and Third World Industrial Development

The most contentious current issue in development studies concerns the role of foreign capital: does foreign investment have a benevolent or a malevolent influence in developing countries? In academic circles, an enormous amount of ink has been spilled in defending the opposing viewpoints.

Broadly put, the argument in favour can be summarised as follows. Developing countries have a surplus of labour but, as Lewis (1954) argued in his classic paper, there is a shortage of capital. Equally important, some localities have good natural resource endowments. Resources are, by definition, immobile, and labour is fairly immobile internationally due to immigration controls. Thus full development of Third World labour and natural resources requires the importation of foreign capital and the export of agricultural and industrial products which embody the resource and labour endowments. Some of the needed capital is imported in the form of aid and government loans. However, the argument goes, since governments are notoriously inefficient managers of agriculture and industry, private sector investment must play a key role in making optimal use of underutilised natural resources and labour. Capital investment and international trade give rise to substantial increases in total production because countries specialise in activities in which they have a comparative or an absolute advantage. These advantages are split between the trading partners so that both countries benefit.

In a recent book, Isaiah Frank (1980) seeks to demonstrate the beneficial effects of foreign capital, and to refute the 'extensive literature [that] has been spawned on the role of transnational enterprises in the Third World, most of it highly critical' (p. 143). Interviews surveying the attitudes and perceptions of senior executives of transnational corporations toward host countries revealed a 'basic sympathy among the multinationals for the broadly stated national goals of the developing nations' (p. 144) which is manifested in the specific actions of the firms in many ways. The problem with Frank's approach is that it is intrinsically indeterminate; interviewees' responses are necessarily subjective. Much more convincing is the work of Auty (1980, 1981) who has developed detailed cost and benefit data to show that the high rate of revenue leakage from the Caribbean bauxite industry is attributable not to the LDC status of the region, but is an inherent characteristic of the capital-intensive production functions of the industry. Moreover, as the industry becomes less oligopolistic, there will be new opportunities for local ownership, thereby reducing capital leakages. He suggests (1982, p. 276):

> The multinational corporations are now far from being the scapegoat for the region's economic ills ... their capital and expertise are critical to the realisation of the bold new energy-based growth prospects in the Southern Caribbean, and the attendant spin-off throughout the broader Caribbean region.

In contrast to the above interpretations, the majority of the recent literature on development is far less sanguine about the role of multinationals. Broadly termed the 'theory of underdevelopment', it is argued that, although specialisation and trade yield benefits, these benefits are commandeered to an overwhelming degree by the rich countries in which the transnational corporations are based (Hymer, 1975). De Souza and Foust (1979, ch. 11) suggest three main reasons why this is so.

1. Manufactured goods still only account for approximately 20 per cent (by value) of the exports of LDCs, compared to 75 per cent of the exports of developed countries. For LDCs, this poses a difficult problem. Rigidities on the supply side make primary commodity prices subject to much greater fluctuations than are the prices of manufactured goods. The resulting large periodic income variations introduce considerable uncertainty into budgetary forecasting. Attempts by successive UNCTAD conferences to solve this problem have thus far failed.

2. Third World industry is typically labour-intensive; industries with high technical inputs are located mainly in developed countries. In the last 25 years, the terms of trade have shifted away both from non-OPEC primary commodity producers and from the labour-intensive industries in which NICs have specialised, and in favour of 'high-tech' industries producing goods with high income elasticities. In part, this is due to the bias of technical progress which has favoured the substitution of capital for labour, and has increased the efficiency with which primary inputs are used and recycled. This works against Third World industry which has concentrated on both resource processing and labour-intensive activities.

3. Foreign capital has deeply penetrated Third World industry, in some cases resulting in an impressive growth performance, especially in NICs. The West provides much-needed capital and technology, and LDCs provide cheap labour. Such a matching of interests could be to mutual advantage. But, the argument goes, despite the dynamism shown in the economies of most NICs, theirs is a dependent form of development with the following disadvantages. The transnational corporations capture a disproportionate share of the profits, either by direct repatriation, or through charging management and licensing fees, or by surreptitious transfer pricing. There is limited diffusion of the technologies and skills imported by the MNCs. Senior personnel are frequently expatriates, who perform their tasks and return home with their savings. The import content of capital equipment in these industries is very high, and once established, the plants tend to develop few local linkages so that spillover effects are quite limited. And finally, the incomes paid to most employees are relatively low, while those paid to a few senior personnel including expatriates and members of the national elite are high, with a significant portion spent on imported luxuries.

Not surprisingly, these lines of argument give rise to much debate. The empirical evidence, as it has accumulated, has mainly supported the underdevelopment interpretation (see Amin, 1973; Frobel *et al.*, 1980; Griffin, 1969; and Mabogunje, 1980 amongst others). There are exceptions, including the case of the Caribbean bauxite industry examined by Auty (1980, 1982) but it is fairly unusual for an industry to become less oligopolistic. More commonly, ownership of capital in large scale industry tends to become more concentrated.

At the heart of this debate is the issue: what, precisely, is development? Few nowadays would equate development with economic growth, though it is important to have rising aggregate income available for redistribution. Dudley Seers' (1969) three criteria for development have gained increasing acceptance. First, there is the need to *eliminate absolute poverty*. This is the goal of the *basic needs* (BN) approach to development (Streeten and Burki, 1978). The provision of specific minimum requirements of food, water, clothing, shelter, and health and education services will do far more to eliminate absolute poverty than will an approach aimed at raising incomes. With some exceptions, transnational corporations do not produce low cost goods and services needed by people in absolute poverty. Second, Seers argues that everyone should have *the right to a meaningful job*. In this respect, international capital has a mixed record. Where investment is in large-scale agriculture, in resource industries, and sophisticated industries with fixed technical coefficients, methods of production are capital-intensive and surprisingly few jobs have created. On the other hand where investment has been in labour-intensive industries (mostly in NICs), a large number of jobs have been created and unemployment levels have dropped. Seers' third criterion is the need for *equality of opportunity* to remove social and racial tensions. Here, international capital has a divisive effect. The workforce in multinational branch plants is often paid a wage which, although low by western standards, is significantly above the subsistence wage levels earned by the masses. Mabro (1967) attributes the wage premium paid by MNCs partly to political expediency, and partly to a desire for a co-operative workforce that will accept capital-intensive methods of production. Even more glaring is the inequality between the low wages earned by the urban proletariat and the 'world salaries' paid to senior personnel in branch plants.

In 1977, Seers made a further contribution to the definition of development. He argued that *self-reliance* should be added to the three original criteria. Once again, multinational industry scores poorly. Resource-oriented and labour-intensive industries mainly serve foreign markets. And even when a branch plant serves a domestic market, the aim is to use mass production methods to take advantage of economies of scale and serve as large a market as is economically possible from a single manufacturing plant. There are, of course, enlightened entrepreneurs who are anxious to promote development as well as economic growth through their investments in Third World manufacturing. But taking Kenya as an example, the weight of evidence from the many case studies presented in Kaplinsky (1978) and Langdon (1981) indicates that transnational investment in Third World industry has contributed little to local development.

National Production

In most Third World countries, direct foreign investment accounts for a substantial proportion of formal sector industrial production; the remainder is domestically owned. The degree of foreign penetration of industry depends on two major factors. First, there are political factors including the level of foreign investment during the colonial era, and the degree to which economic nationalism has been pursued since. For instance, in comparison with Kenya, Tanzania received less British investment in the colonial era, and since independence has adopted more nationalistic and socialistic policies towards industry so that today there is less foreign investment and a higher level of domestic ownership. The second factor is the size of the domestic market. In large countries such as India and Brazil, the market can support a broad range of industries including basic industries such as heavy chemicals, iron and steel, and assorted consumer industries. Commonly, there has been some reluctance to permit large scale foreign investment in industries that serve domestic markets, whereas direct foreign investment in export industries is welcomed. There are two corollaries to this. As Deyo (1981, p. 67) observes, foreign ownership is usually higher amongst exporting firms than amongst firms serving the domestic market. And second, countries with a large domestic market tend to have higher levels of domestic ownership of industry than do small countries and, especially, NICs. An appropriate example is provided by Singapore where there is a high level of foreign investment in exporting activities. Gross investment in Singapore has varied a lot from year to year, but for the five years 1973-77, local investment accounted for only 21.7 per cent of the S$2692 m invested in formal manufacturing (Deyo, 1981, Table 4.6). Thus almost 80 per cent of the capital invested came from foreign sources, notably Japan and Hong Kong.

From a geographical viewpoint, there are two interesting aspects of national production: its structure, and its location. Structurally, national production is concentrated in activities in which foreign producers are at a competitive disadvantage because of transportation costs. The goods may be perishable, fragile, or simply bulky and costly to transport. Such industries include meat, fruit and fish packing, various types of milling, baking, creameries and assorted other food industries, saw milling, furniture making, brewing, and the manufacture of bricks, cement and concrete products. Transportation advantages are such that these sorts of industries do not normally need protection from foreign competition. Where a country has promoted industrial development beyond this first group of market-oriented industries, it is usually into activities with low technical inputs such as the textile, clothing and leather industries. In NICs, economies of scale are achieved in such industries either by serving a large domestic market and/or by exporting to foreign markets. Where such economies of scale cannot be achieved, unit production costs are higher and manufacturers commonly seek protection.

From a geographical perspective, both national and international investment in manufacturing tends to be located in major cities or, where Weberian principles apply, at locations close to resources or agricultural inputs, often in a development enclave. National capitals such as Manila, Saigon, Colombo, Dakar, Cairo, Dar es Salaam and Santiago dominate (see Wescott and Norcliffe, 1981, p. 90). To some extent this concentration of formal industry can be accounted for by market orientation. Urban systems in most Third World countries show considerable primacy (Berry, 1961) so that major cities account for a substantial fraction of the national market. They are also the foci for distribution networks serving the rest of the country. These tendencies have been reinforced by policy decisions, two of which are of widespread importance. First, as Lee (1971) notes for Taiwan, Fossung (1983) for

Cameroon, and Okhawa and Rosovsky (1960) for Japan, agricultural pricing policies and taxation have been used to achieve a major transfer of capital from rural areas to major cities which as a result have enjoyed a greater share of disposable income. Secondly, government expenditures tend to be disproportionately concentrated in major cities, which again favours industrial primacy. If Bigsten's (1978) data for Kenya are representative, then this imbalance is serious: in 1973/74 total Kenyan government recurrent expenditures in Nairobi were KShs 71 *per capita*, or more than ten times as high as in the rest of the country.

Small-Scale Production

The estimates presented in Table 8.2 suggest that employment in small-scale manufacturing in Third World countries approaches 75 million, or more than double Third World employment in formal manufacturing, and equal to employment in formal manufacturing in either the First World, or the Eastern Bloc (including China). Thus in terms of Seers' second criterion for development — the right to a meaningful job — small-scale production has enormous significance.

Until around 1970, most writers on development viewed the Third World as having a dual economy with a modern (formal) sector representing the forces of progress, and a traditional (small-scale) sector that was inefficient and was a residual from bygone days. The two sectors were seen to exist side by side with minimal connections. As waves of modernisation swept through the space economy, so the traditional sector would be slowly submerged, to be replaced by western-like and modern systems of production. This modernisation paradigm sees small-scale production as an old fashioned way of doing things that will be supplanted by modern methods as producers become aware of them, as consumers demand their superior products, and as the capital needed to produce the modern way becomes available. This switchover is spurred on by healthy competition between the two methods of production.

More recently the dependency paradigm has largely superseded these ideas of modernisation within a dual economy. According to the new paradigm small-scale production plays a role that differs from that assigned to it in the modernisation paradigm in three important respects. Firstly, the two sectors are seen to be closely related, both in a positive and in a negative way. The formal sector subcontracts to the informal sector (Bienefield, 1975) and assigns to it a variety of mostly labour-intensive tasks that can be performed at lower cost by petty producers. There are also links between large-scale agriculture and rural manufacturers in making and repairing tools, providing farm supplies, and processing farm products (Freeman and Norcliffe, 1984). Thus the formal sector makes purchases from small-scale producers and, since this involves a large purchaser dealing with atomistic suppliers (in effect, a monopsony), informal sector producers find themselves in a weak bargaining position. Secondly, the formal and informal sectors compete over almost the complete product range. This may seem unlikely: in activities like oil-refining, for example, there would appear to be no way of producing on a small scale. But the informal sector collects used oil from repair shops, filters large particles and wax out of it, and re-sells it as a low-cost alternative to premium refined oil. Likewise from furniture to tools, and from footwear to bricks, informal producers use intermediate technologies to compete with large-scale producers. Moreover what they cannot produce, they will often repair. In many cases, however, the competition is unequal. Large-scale producers frequently obtain duty remissions on imported capital equipment, which amounts to an implicit capital subsidy (Cook and Von Hobenbalken, 1981, p. 149). Government purchasers favour formal producers. The informal sector is often harassed, and sometimes subject to bribes. And small-scale producers are usually excluded from government credit and loan schemes, and have difficulty in obtaining loans from banks and similar institutions (Norcliffe *et al.*, 1984). Thirdly, many now argue that small-scale production is the most appropriate route for Third World development. Its production characteristics match local factor endowments: it is labour-intensive, it uses simple to intermediate technologies, and it does not require large inputs of capital. Thus modernisation is not seen to be inevitable, nor even desirable, though in a few activities with rigid technical requirements, it may be appropriate.

These introductory remarks are intended to emphasise two key points. That small-scale production accounts for a very large number of jobs in the Third World. And that, far from being a relic from the days of traditional society, it is now seen as a viable alternative to large-scale production. Indeed if handicaps suffered by small-scale producers were removed, the informal sector would grow to occupy a position of even greater importance. Having thus set the scene, in the sections that follow the workings of the small-scale sector will be described and interpreted in greater detail.

Rural Industry

It is useful to draw a distinction between the urban and rural components of small-scale industry, even though it does raise some definitional problems. Freeman and Norcliffe (1983) define the rural component to include activities located in the bush (such as gravel crushing and charcoal making), those practised in rural homesteads (essentially cottage industries), and those located in rural market towns. Many would classify the last of these as urban, but they are so intimately bound up in the rural economy on both the input and the sales side that it seems appropriate to conform with the World Bank (see Anderson and Leiserson, 1978) and the International Labour Office (see Chuta and Sethuraman, 1984) by treating market towns as rural. It follows from this definition that urban informal industry is found only in larger towns.

Rural industry is one component of the huge rural nonfarm sector which also includes hunting and gathering, construction, retailing, and a wide range of personal and community services. According to Anderson and Leiserson (1980) about 30 per cent of rural employment is in non-agricultural activities. In turn, between 25 and 30 per cent of non-agricultural employment is in industry. However, these figures understate the importance of rural industry. Thus, a sample survey in Kenya found that rural industries were practised in almost 50 per cent of all rural households, although often on a part-time basis, and quite commonly for consumption within the household (Freeman and Norcliffe, 1984b).

Rural industry can be classified into five main groups: resource extraction and processing; plant, fibre and animal products (including clothing); wood and metal products; repairing; and transportation. The mix of industries differs substantially between rural households (which specialise in resource extraction, processing farm products, reed and basket work, and wood industries), and market centres (which specialise in clothing, metal working, furniture and repairing). The incidence of rural industry also varies from region to region. The major influences on the regional mix of industry are the local resource base, local culture, and proximity to major cities which have both a positive and a negative impact on their surrounding areas. These three relationships are illustrated by a study of the provincial distribution of rural nonfarm activities in Kenya (Freeman and Norcliffe, 1984b). Localised resources such as fish, wood, and clay and reeds, as well as the local climate are crucial to many activities. The specialisation of the Kamba tribe in woodcarving, of the Borana in metalworking, and of certain coastal tribes in making *mnazi* (a beverage based on coconuts) are examples of how local culture is a factor. And in Central Province, close to Nairobi, activities such as wood and metal working use perceptibly more advanced technologies than are used in other less accessible regions.

Urban Informal Industry

During the 1970s the urban informal sector was the subject of numerous investigations. The results, some of which are summarised by Mazumdar (1976) and Peattie (1980), reveal a sector of enormous significance. For instance, over half the total employment in cities such as Bombay, Djakarta, Lima and Belo Horizonte was reported to be in the informal sector. Within the urban informal sector, industry (including transport and construction) generally accounts for around 20 per cent of employment which, although lower than in the rural nonfarm sector, is still of major importance. Resource and processing industries are almost totally absent, whereas metal workers, carpenters, tailors, cobblers and repairers are well represented.

Data presented by House (1981) permit the comparison of factor inputs to certain industries in Kenya's formal sector; Nairobi's informal sector; and the rural nonfarm sector of Central Province (Norcliffe, 1983, Table 2). Not surprisingly, both the amount of fixed capital and output per worker are much higher in the formal sector. Perhaps less obvious is the discovery that for these samples, capital inputs and output per worker in rural industry are roughly double those of urban informal industry, partly as a result of a higher savings ratio leading to high levels of capital reinvestment in rural industry. Also, several of the capital-output ratios of informal industries in Nairobi are higher than those of rural industries. If these ratios apply at the margin so that incremental capital-output ratios (ICORs) are also higher in Nairobi, then the Harrod-Domar growth model would lead us to the following conclusion: since this model, in its simplest form, sees growth as a direct function of the savings ratio, and an inverse function of the ICOR, growth prospects for rural industry are higher than for urban informal industry. It is difficult to say how representative these samples are, but this is certainly an area deserving more extensive investigation.

The urban informal sector as a whole plays an important role in the rural-urban migration process. In most large Third World cities, the rate of population increase has far exceeded the rate of job growth in the formal sector. The remainder are absorbed by the informal sector, or join the pool of unemployed. House (1981) reports that from 1964 to 1972, Nairobi's workforce grew in aggregate by 9.1 per cent annually, with the formal sector workforce growing by a lowly 3.2 per cent, and the informal sector by a remarkable 28 per cent annually. Harris and Todaro (1970) interpret this process as follows: although most migrants hope to find a secure and well-paying job in the formal sector, this is most unlikely, so they begin by spending a period unemployed, and then move to a lowly paying job in the informal sector, often beginning as an apprentice with minimal pay. From this base, most continue a prolonged search for a formal sector job. Others come to accept the informal sector as their destiny, and a few find profitable niches within it that are more rewarding than the formal sector. Thus migration is not simply a function of the rural-urban wage differential: the informal sector plays a complex intermediary role in the process.

Operating Characteristics

Small-scale industry operates in a way that matches both the resources and the requirements of the Third World. It is for this reason that small-scale producers have withstood competition from large-scale industry so well, despite the latter's advantages discussed earlier. The ILO (1972) has identified seven operating characteristics, to which an additional one is added here.

1. The vast majority of these small enterprises are operated by a family, indeed many are single-person operations. Even when the enterprise is larger, the family is still crucial to ownership and employment. A husband may farm while his wife runs a rice mill. A son may work for his father transporting water. In a larger workshop, an extended family is usually at work. And,

where sub-contracting of work takes place, again it is often within a network of family contacts.

2. The majority of these enterprises are very small indeed. In Central Province, Kenya, for example, two-thirds of the enterprises are single-person operations and the average workforce is 1.8 employees. The premises, inputs, sales, and inventory of these industrial enterprises are also, in most cases, equally small.

3. Most enterprises are labour-intensive and use intermediate technology, but there are very large variations. At one extreme, the depreciated assets of reed and wood cutters, charcoal makers, stone masons, herbalists and snuff makers are often under £5. On the other hand some wood and grain millers, car repairers and metal workers have assets in excess of £1,000. Likewise technologies vary from the simplest hand looms to electric welders (Bhalla, 1981).

4. Many of the skills required of small-scale industry are acquired within the system of small-scale production (King, 1977). The family orientation means that skills are normally passed from mother to daughter or father to son. Most craftsmen are surrounded by spectating youngsters who learn by watching. The next step is to become an apprentice, and then a poorly-paid assistant. In the Kenyan survey, over 90 per cent of industry operators were trained on the job (Norcliffe, 1983). However, most operators had gone further in the formal school system than had the average head of household, suggesting that general skills of literacy and numeracy gained within the formal school system may also be important to the successful operation of a small industrial enterprise.

5. Small-scale producers make better use of local resources than do large-scale producers. They are labour-intensive in surplus labour economies. They use local materials, process agricultural, forest and fish products, and substitute inputs that are locally abundant. Perhaps most important, they re-cycle goods by repairing them so that repairing is one of the most important activities within this sector.

6. Small-scale producers customise their work in a way that is not possible with mass production. For example, in many Third World countries, especially in Africa, altering second-hand clothing is a major activity for tailors. Likewise shoes, furniture and spare parts are made to order.

7. In activities requiring considerable skills and capital (and

often generating substantial profits), it is not easy to become established. But other activities have minimal entry requirements and therefore present an opportunity for families living in poverty either to provide use-value goods needed within the household, or to sell their products for a small amount of cash to supplement family income.

8. In comparison with the formal sector, small-scale producers operate in a highly competitive milieu, but the level of competition varies. Competition is probably more fierce amongst urban producers than in rural areas, mainly because the distance separating market centres in rural areas adds a form of spatial monopoly. And activities with minimal barriers to entry are certainly more competitive than are activities with substantial barriers. In general, competition amongst small-scale producers is intense, and there is a high birth- and death-rate amongst these enterprises.

Types of Small-Scale Enterprise

Several aspects of the diversity of small-scale industry have already been noted. An amazingly diverse range of activities is represented, there are considerable variations in the operating characteristics of the enterprises, and there are important differences in the mixture of industries both between rural and urban areas, and amongst regions. Two further aspects of diversity need stressing, namely: the various roles filled by enterprises in this sector; and the variety of economic types.

In examining the role of informal enterprises, Bienefield (1975) found that there were three types of activities:

1. Activities undertaken intermittently to supplement household income, often during slack phases in the farming year. These are usually done on a very small scale, mostly in rural areas, and the income derived from them is often minimal.

2. Activities that are neglected by the formal sector either because the activities do not lend themselves to mechanisation or because the local market is too small to interest the formal sector.

3. Small-scale industries that are supported either by the government (mainly through purchases) or by the formal sector (through subcontracting).

Five main types of small-scale enterprise have been identified by Miles and Norcliffe (1984). Three groups consisted of very small enterprises — a profitable group, an unprofitable group, and a third group whose main characteristic was the large cost of their labour inputs. Two groups consisted of larger enterprises. One group was *successful*, indeed a few enterprises showed signs of achieving formal status; the second group was *static*, showing no sign of recent growth despite their larger size.

Small-Scale Industry and Development

The variability and diversity of small-scale industry make it difficult to categorise the sector's role in the development process. Statements by Leys (1973), such as 'the informal sector ... denotes primarily a system of very intense exploitation of labour, with very low wages and often very long hours', assign to small-scale industry a uniformity of purpose which, in practice, is difficult to discern. It is also difficult to generalise about the role of this sector in the process of economic development. The central issue is whether the informal sector exists as a dualistic entity beside formal industry, with both sectors independently pursuing their goals, or whether it is composed of 'penny capitalists' (to use Sol Tax's (1953) memorable phrase) who are highly dependent upon the formal sector. Moser (1978) suggests that we recognise the diversity of the sector, and conceptualise the urban economy as consisting of a continuum of activities from very large and formal to small and informal. Thus the relationship is not simply dualistic; there are a whole host of dependencies and interdependencies both within and between the two sectors. At the apex of the pyramid of economic organisations are transnational corporations: these alone are relatively free of dependencies. Beneath them in the economic pile are quite large companies which nevertheless are highly dependent on transnational corporations. Conversely, there are small informal industries occupying protected niches that are largely independent of the formal sector, although the niches themselves are defined by the latter. Peattie (1980, p. 24) concludes that we should recognise the diversity and complexity of structure of the informal sector, and that seems wise advice. Thus we concur with Tokman's (1978) argument that although, *in toto*, informal industry is subordinate to large-scale industry, the relationship is a heterogeneous one that defies simple categorisation.

The diversity of small-scale industry presents a multitude of opportunities for development. It is labour-intensive and creates many jobs although they are usually poorly paid. It presents some opportunities even for the poorest stratum in society either to generate cash income, or to produce goods with use value, and therefore helps to reduce absolute poverty. Its effect on income equality is open to debate since a petty bourgeoisie appears to be emerging amongst the operators of the more remunerative and capital-intensive small enterprises. Finally, small-scale production promotes self-reliance and sets the stage for the recovery of territorial life (see Friedmann and Weaver, 1979). Thus there is potential for promoting development, but its realisation would require major policy shifts in favour of rural development including: the sub-division of large holdings; higher prices for agricultural products; a large shift of government expenditures and programmes from urban to rural areas; and the removal of a wide range of implicit and explicit biases in favour of large-scale production.

Conclusion

The point is often made that the revenues of the world's largest transnational corporations exceed the GNP of many Third World states. Moreover, these corporations are highly adaptable: they can shift their production and trading patterns, their assets and interests, and their subcontractors and markets quite rapidly in response to changing economic and political circumstances. It is for this reason that transnational corporations are identified here as having a central role in the industrial geography of the Third World. They are few in number, they are comparatively minor employers in the whole picture, yet they are the point of reference for virtually all industrial activity in the Third World. Beneath transnational corporations in the hierarchy of organisations are nationally-based companies. Sometimes they are protected by nationalistic governments, sometimes by distance and transporation costs, and sometimes they are innovative and productive so that they can compete successfully with TNCs. In the long run, the most successful of these companies will grow into TNCs themselves, but most will play out their role on a small national stage. The remainder of Third World industry is accounted for by the myriad small-scale enterprises employing far more people than the other two sectors combined. The majority of enterprises have one operator, or are run by partners. And another large part of the sector never sells its products: they are used within the household or are bartered around the extended family.

Each of these three types of Third World industry, if developed to its fullest, offers a distinctive pattern of development. If a country wishes to promote foreign investment by transnational corporations, its workforce should be disciplined, and a favourable political climate needs to be created. The results are to be seen in NICs. Hours of work are long, wages are low, and the workforce is closely supervised by the government. The results in terms of growth of GDP, and jobs, are often impressive. However, Sachs (1979) would class this as *maldevelopment*: there is precious little time left to the workforce for living.

Economic nationalism is the motive for promoting locally-owned industry, and few countries have followed this route as successfully as Japan. This strategy is intended to minimise the outflow of capital, but is it difficult to pursue without creating a system of inefficient monopolies. It is far from clear why one country finds itself endlessly protecting domestic producers from foreign competition, while another country sees its protected industries progessively transform into export-oriented companies. Either way, although the repatriation of profits by foreign capital may be halted, they are distributed unequally at home so that for purposes of development, the end result is not very different.

A number of individuals and agencies have advocated small-scale production as the best strategy for Third World development. Recognising that these countries lack the army of economic planners needed to manage a state-controlled economy, they argue that small-scale production is the best alternative: its operating characteristics most closely match what is needed to achieve development, while the opportunities for exploitation are limited by the fragmentation of production, by competition, and by close ties with the local community. Small-scale production also provides the best answer to Sachs' question: 'Industrialisation for what?' He continues (1979, p.644)

The problem is, then, how to plan concretely the contents of the industrialization process in the context of 'another development' — self-reliant, need-oriented, ecologically sound, and striking an entirely new balance between town and countryside, industry and agriculture, rather than by hopelessly trying to exhaust the rural population by absorbing it into the 'modern sector'.

Currently, an extended definition of this 'another development' is the most important task facing industrial planners of the Third World.

Appendix 1

Data Sources and Methods of Estimation used in Table 8.1

Countries

Data are presented for every country with a population exceeding 10 million in 1980. Smaller countries are grouped by continent. Sub-totals are given for each continent, and for the USSR which is separated from Europe and Asia. Turkey is included in Asia.

Population (Column 1)

Source: United Nations (1982) *Demographic Yearbook, 1980,* (UN, New York), Table 3.

Economically Active

Estimates were based on data for neighbouring countries, or on countries with similar employment characteristics. Note that data were available for many smaller countries that do not appear individually in the table. Source: International Labour Office (1982) *Yearbook of Labour Statistics,* 1982 (ILO: Geneva). Tables 1 and 3.

Employment in Manufacturing

Source: United Nations (1982) *Yearbook of Industrial Statistics, 1980 Edition: Volume 1. General Industrial Statistics* (UN, New York) Part One, National Tables, pp. 1-583. The standard definition is the number of persons 'engaged' in industry, which includes proprietors, partners and unpaid family helpers, but excludes homeworkers. The definition excluded mining and utilities. Data for smaller countries were invaluable in making estimates for larger neighbouring countries.

References

Anderson, D. and Leiserson, M.W. (1978) *Rural Enterprise and Nonfarm Employment*, World Bank, Washington D.C.

Anderson, D. and Leiserson, M.W. (1980) 'Rural and nonfarm employment in developing countries,' *Economic Development and Cultural Change, 28,* 227-48

Amin, S. (1973) *Accumulation on a World Scale*, Monthly Review Press, New York

Auty, R.M. (1980) 'Transforming mineral enclaves: Caribbean bauxite in the nineteen-seventies,' *Tijdschrift voor Economische en Sociale Geografie, 71,* 161-71

Auty, R.M. (1981) 'MNC strategy, spatial diversification and nationalization,' *Geoforum, 12,* 349-57

Auty, R.M. (1982) 'The regional growth stimulus of Caribbean bauxite, 1960-1980' in L. Collins (ed.), *Industrial Decline and Regeneration*, University of Edinburgh, Edinburgh, pp. 249-78

Bagchi, A.K. (1972) 'Some international foundations of capitalist growth and underdevelopment,' *Economic and Political Weekly*(Bombay), 7, August Issue, 1559-70

Bellows, T. (1976) 'Taiwan's foreign policy in the 1970s: a case study of adaptation and viability,' *Asian Survey, 16,* 593-611

Berry, B.J.L. (1961) 'City size distributions and economic development,' *Economic Development and Cultural Change, 9,* 573-87

Bhalla, A.S. (1981) (ed.) *Technology and Employment in Industry: A Case Study Approach*, International Labour Office, Geneva

Bienefield M. (1975) 'The informal sector and peripheral capitalism: the case of Tanzania,' *Bulletin of the Institute of Development Studies, 6,* no. 3, 53-73

Bigsten, A. (1978) *Regional Inequality and Development: A Case Study of Kenya*, Department of Economics, University of Gothenburg

Chuta, E. and Sethuraman, S.V. (1984) (eds.) *Rural Small-Scale Industries and Employment in Africa and Asia*, International Labour Office, Geneva

Cohen, B. (1975) *Multinational Firms and Asian Exports*, Yale University Press, New Haven, Conn.

Cook, P. and von Hohenbalken, B. (1981) 'Accounting prices for project appraisal in Kenya' in G.B. Norcliffe and T. Pinfold (eds.), *Planning African Development*, Croom Helm, London, 148-68

de Souza, A.R. and Foust, B. (1979) *World Space Economy*, Charles Merrill, Columbus, Ohio

Deyo, F.C. (1981) *Dependent Development and Industrial Order: An Asian Case Study*, Praeger, New York

Dunford, M. and Perrons, D. (1982) *The Arena of Capital*, Macmillan, London

Frank, I. (1980) *Foreign Enterprise in Developing Countries*, Johns Hopkins University Press, Baltimore

Freeman, D.B. and Norcliffe, G.B. (1983) 'The rural nonfarm sector: development opportunity or employer of last resort?' *Ceres, 16,* 28-34

Freeman, D.B. and Norcliffe, G.B. (1984a) 'Relations between the rural nonfarm and small farm sectors in Central Province, Kenya,' *Tijdschrift voor Economische en Sociale Geografie, 75,* 61-73

Freeman, D.B. and Norcliffe, G.B. (1984b) 'National and regional patterns of rural nonfarm employment in Kenya,' *Geography, 69,* 221-33

Friedmann, J. and Weaver, C. (1979) *Territory and Function: The Evolution of Regional Planning*, University of California Press, Berkeley, Calif.

Frobel, F., Heinrichs, J. and Kreye, O. (1980) *The New International Division of Labour* (translated by P. Burgess), Cambridge University Press, Cambridge

Fossung, E.Y.W. (1983) *Rural Urban Linkages: the Case of the Southwest Province of Cameroon*, Unpublished doctoral dissertation, Department of Geography, University of Waterloo, Ontario

Goldsmith, W.W. (1984) 'Bringing the Third World home: enterprise zones for America' in L. Sawers and W. Tabb (eds'), *Sunbelt/Snowbelt: Urban Development and Regional Restructuring*, Oxford University Press, Oxford, pp. 339-53

Griffin, K. (1969) *Underdevelopment in Spanish America*, Allen and Unwin, London

Grosrichard, F. (1984) 'How the South Koreans sank Europe's shipbuilding industry,' *Manchester Guardian Weekly*, February 26, p. 12

Hansen, N. (1980) 'Mexico's border industry and the international division of labour,' *Annals of Regional Science, 15*, no. 3, 1-11

Harris, J.R. and Todaro, M.P. (1970) 'Migration, unemployment and development: a two-sector analysis,' *American Economic Review, 60*, 126-42

Hasan, P. (1976) *Korea: Problems and Issues in a Rapidly Growing Economy*, Johns Hopkins University Press, Baltimore

Hobsbawn, E.J. (1969) *Industry and Empire*, Penguin, Harmondsworth

House, W.J. (1981) 'Nairobi's informal sector: an exploratory study' in T. Killick (ed.), *Papers on the Kenyan Economy*, Heinemann, Nairobi, 357-68

Hymer, S. (1975) 'The multinational corporation and the law of uneven development' in H. Radice (ed.), *International Firms and Modern Imperialism*, Penguin, Harmondsworth

International Labour Office (1972) *Employment Incomes and Equality: A Strategy for Increasing Productive Employment in Kenya*, International Labour Office, Geneva

Kaplinsky, R. (1978) (ed.) *Readings on the Multinational Corporation in Kenya*, Oxford University Press, Nairobi

Kim, C.I.E. (1978) 'Emergency, development and human rights: South Korea,' *Asian Survey, 18*, 363-78

King, K. (1977) *The African Artisan*, Heinemann, London

Kuznets, S. (1971) *Economic Growth of Nations*, Harvard University Press, Cambridge, Mass.

Langdon, S.W. (1981) *Multinational Corporations in the Political Economy of Kenya*, St. Martin's Press, New York

Lee, T.H. (1971) *Intersectoral Capital Flows in the Economic Development of Taiwan, 1895-1960*, Cornell University Press, Ithaca

Lefeber, L. (1974) 'On the paradigm for economic development,' *World Development, 2*, 1-8

Lewis, W.A. (1954) 'Economic development with unlimited supplies of labour,' *The Manchester School, 22*, 131-91

Leys, C. (1973) 'Interpreting African underdevelopment: reflection on the ILO report on Employment, Incomes and Equality in Kenya,' *African Affairs, 73*, 419-29

Mabogunje, A.L. (1980) *The Development Process: A Spatial Perspective*, Hutchinson, London

Mabro, R. (1967) 'Industrial growth, agricultural unemployment, and the Lewis model: the Egyptian case study, 1937-1965,' *Journal of Development Studies, 3*, 322-51

Malloy, J.M. (1977) 'Authoritarianism and corporatism in Latin America: the modal pattern' in *Authoritarianism and Corporatism in Latin America*, J.M. Malloy (ed.), University of Pittsburgh Press

Mazumdar, D. (1976) 'The urban informal sector,' *World Development, 4*, 655-79

Miles, N. and Norcliffe, G.B. (1984) 'An economic typology of small-scale rural enterprises in Central Province, Kenya,' *Transactions, Institute of British Geographers*, N.S., *9*, 150-70

Myers, N. (1979) *The Sinking Ark*, Pergamon, Oxford, ch. 13

Norcliffe, G.B. (1983) 'Operating characteristics of rural non-farm enterprises in Central Province, Kenya,' *World Development, 11*, 981-94

Norcliffe, G.B. and Hoare, A.G. (1982) 'Enterprise zone policy for the inner city: a review and preliminary assessment,' *Area, 14*, 265-74

Norcliffe, G.B., Freeman, D.B. and Miles, N.J.O (1984) 'Rural industrialisation in Kenya' in E. Chuta and S.V. Sethuraman (eds.), *Rural Small-Scale Industry and Employment in Africa and Asia*, International Labour Office, Geneva, 9-24

Ohlin, B.G. (1967) *Inter-regional and International Trade*, Harvard University Press, Cambridge, Mass.

Okhawa, K. and Rosovsky, H. (1960) 'The role of agriculture in modern Japanese economic development,' *Economic Development and Cultural Change, 9*, 43-67

Patterson, D.S. (1983) 'South Korea will find it harder to grow,' *Globe and Mail* (Toronto), 5 Dec. 1983

Peattie, L.R. (1980) 'Anthropological perspectives on the concepts of dualism, the informal sector, and marginality in developing urban economies,' *International Regional Science Review, 5*, 1-31

Peet, R. (1983) 'Relations of production and the relocation of United States manufacturing industry since 1960,' *Economic Geography, 59*, 112-43

Perrons, D.C. (1981) 'The role of Ireland in the new international division of labour: a proposed framework for regional analysis,' *Regional Studies, 15*, 81-100

Pollock, E.E. (1981) 'Free ports, free trade zones, export processing zones and economic development' in B.S. Hoyle and D.A. Pinder (eds.), *Cityport Industrialisation and Regional Development*, Pergamon, Oxford, 37-46

Sachs, I. (1979) 'Development, maldevelopment and industrialisation of Third World countries,' *Development and Change, 10*, 635-46

Scott, A.J. (1982) 'Location patterns and dynamics of industrial activity in the modern metropolis: a review essay,' *Urban Studies, 19*, 111-41

Seers, D. (1969) 'The meaning of development,' *International Development Review, 11*, no. 4, 2-6

Seers, D. (1977) 'The new meaning of development,' *International Development Review, 19*, no. 3, 2-7

Sherwell C. (1983a) 'Singapore uses public works plan to sustain growth,' *Globe and Mail* (Toronto), 21 Nov. 1983

Sherwell, C. (1983b) 'Sunset plant will operate,' *Globe and Mail* (Toronto), 17 Dec. 1983

Streeten, P. and Burki, S.J. (1978) 'Basic needs: some issues,' *World Development, 6*, 411-21

Takeo T. (1978) 'Free trade zones in Southeast Asia,' *Monthly Review, 29*, no. 9, 29-39

Tax, S. (1953) *Penny Capitalism-A Guatemalan Indian Economy*, Smithsonian Institute, Washington, D.C.

Taylor, M. and Thrift, N. (1982) (eds.) *The Geography of Multinationals*, Croom Helm, London

Tokman, V. (1978) 'An exploration into the nature of informal-formal sector relationships,' *World Development, 6*, 1065-75

United Nations (1979) *Bibliography on Transnational Corporations*, UN Centre for Transnational Corporations, New York

Wescott, C. and Norcliffe, G.B. (1981) 'Towards a locational policy for manufacturing industry in Kenya' in G.B. Norcliffe and T.A. Pinfold (eds.), *Planning African Development*, Croom Helm, London, 79-109

Notes on Contributors

Dr P J Bull	Department of Geography, Queens University, Belfast, N Ireland
Dr P W Daniels	Department of Geography, University of Liverpool, England
Dr A G Hoare	Department of Geography, University of Bristol, England
Mr C M Law	Department of Geography, University of Salford, England
Professor W F Lever	Department of Social and Economic Research, University of Glasgow, Scotland
Professor G B Norcliffe	Department of Geography, York University, Ontario, Canada
Dr M Pacione	Department of Geography, University of Strathclyde, Glasgow, Scotland
Dr F J Peck	School of Geography and Environmental Studies, Newcastle-upon-Tyne Polytechnic, England
Dr I J Smith	Centre for Urban and Regional Studies, University of Newcastle-upon-Tyne, England
Mr A R Townsend	Department of Geography, University of Durham, England

INDEX